CLASH OF THE FINANCIAL PUNDITS

HOW THE MEDIA INFLUENCES
YOUR INVESTMENT DECISIONS
FOR BETTER OR WORSE

JOSHUA M. BROWN
JEFF MACKE

New York   Chicago   San Francisco   Athens   London   Madrid
Mexico City   Milan   New Delhi   Singapore   Sydney   Toronto

1 2 3 4 5 6 7 8 9 0 /DOC/DOC 1 2 0 9 8 7 6 5 4

ISBN   978-0-07-181792-9
MHID   0-07-181792-1

e-ISBN   978-0-07-181790-5
e-MHID   0-07-181790-5

This publication is designed to provide accurate and authoritative information in regard to the subject matter covered. It is sold with the understanding that neither the author nor the publisher is engaged in rendering legal, accounting, securities trading, or other professional services. If legal advice or other expert assistance is required, the services of a competent professional person should be sought.
> —*From a Declaration of Principles Jointly Adopted by a Committee of the American Bar Association and a Committee of Publishers and Associations*

Library of Congress Cataloging-in-Publication Data

Brown, Joshua M. (Joshua Morgan)
    Clash of the financial pundits : how the media influences your investment decisions for better or worse / by Joshua M. Brown and Jeff Macke.
        pages cm
        ISBN 978-0-07-181790-5 (alk. paper) — ISBN 0-07-181790-5 (alk. paper) 1. Investment advisors—United States. 2. Investments—Forecasting. 3. Investments—Decision making. 4. Finance, Personal—Psychological aspects. I. Macke, Jeff. II. Title.
HG4928.5.B773 2014
332.601'9—dc23

                                                                        2014006539

McGraw-Hill Education books are available at special quantity discounts to use as premiums and sales promotions or for use in corporate training programs. To contact a representative, please visit the Contact Us pages at www.mhprofessional.com.

JEFF:
For Anne, John, and Helena

JOSH:
For my partners Barry, Michael, and Kris.
Possunt, quia posse videntur.

CONTENTS

Foreword by Dylan Ratigan vii

Acknowledgments ix

Introduction: Crash of 1929 1

1   The Myth of the Media Diet 7

2   The Birth of Financial TV: A Conversation with
Jim Rogers 11

3   The First Media-Blown Bubble 29

4   Being Right and Wrong: A Conversation with
Ben Stein 35

5   The Single Most Important Trait 47

6   Tough Gig: A Conversation with Karen Finerman 51

7   The Man Who Moved Markets 69

8   Redemption Song: A Conversation with
Henry Blodget 81

9   Dow 100,000! 101

10   Welcome to the Madhouse 111

11   Tales from the News Cycle: A Conversation
with Herb Greenberg 121

12   The Wanderer: A Conversation with James Altucher . . . 139

13   The Confidence Trick 155

14 The Bull Market for Opinions: A Conversation
with Barry Ritholtz 159

15 All Your Investment Rules Contradict Each Other 181

16 Martin Zweig and the Biggest Market Call
of All Time. 185

17 They Don't Get Cramer! 191

18 The King of Commentary: A Conversation
with Jim Cramer 201

19 Make a Prediction Without Making a Prediction 219

20 "Car People": The Live Blog 223

Conclusion: Clash of the Pundits! 235

Index 239

FOREWORD

In 2008 I was hosting the CNBC show *Fast Money* when the financial crisis hit. As the world unraveled, Jeff Macke was one of the first pundits to grasp the depths of the crisis and explain it to our audience. With a keen eye and lacerating wit, Macke helped expose the phonies and warned investors that many of the officials "rescuing" us from the crisis were just shifting the risk from the banks to ordinary Americans. When many financial journalists were cheering from the sidelines, Macke was one of a handful of people with the brains and guts to go on air and tell investors the truth night after night.

Now that stocks have come back, there's a whole new crop of false prophets and scammers getting rich off Main Street. In this book, Macke and Josh Brown take readers behind the scenes of financial media and into the minds of pundits who are really trying to help the audience. The result is a book that's funny, useful, and surprisingly moving.

The reality of finance is that the tables will always be tilted against the little guy. There's more information coming out of the financial media than ever, but most of the pundits you see today are going to disappear at the first sign of another bear market. Financial education is the only defense for Main Street investors. With this book, Jeff Macke and Josh Brown share firsthand insights that will help readers separate the sages from the shysters before the next crisis hits.

—DYLAN RATIGAN

ACKNOWLEDGMENTS

JOSH:

Right after I promised my wife that I wouldn't blow another summer writing a book again, I quickly went under contract and began work on this one. Thanks to Sprinkles, TJ, and the Nugget for understanding and tiptoeing around me while I banged my head against the desk.

Thanks to everyone at McGraw-Hill for a second go-round. Was I easier to deal with this time?

Thanks to my dad, who read me to sleep each night—even when I shoved books about Greek mythology into this lap, and to my mom, who encouraged my storytelling even when the teachers told her not to.

Thanks to John Melloy for bringing me into the mainstream media and to Lydia Thew for keeping me there. Thanks to Melissa, Scott, Jamie, Shannan, Lisa, Re-Essa, Patty, Katie, Courtney, and all of the talented producers I get to work with each week. It's a pleasure and an honor to be a part of the most exciting show on finanical television.

Thanks to Stephanie Link for all her help behind the scenes. Thanks to all of our interview subjects for being so enthusiastic about the project.

Lastly, thanks to all the readers of *The Reformed Broker* blog, viewers of CNBC's *Fast Money*, and my friends on the Twitter. Your encouragement continues to mean the world to me.

JEFF:

A special thanks to Guy Adami, Pete Najarian, and Karen Finerman, my fellow members in the Secret Society of the original *Fast Money*. Guy has made a wildly underrated contribution to the financial well-being of anyone who has ever watched the show. Pete and Karen are simply two of the kindest, most generous people I've ever met. It would take a whole book to properly describe either of them.

Diane Galligan and scores of Yahoos past and present deserve credit (or blame) for giving me the opportunity to come out of exile when I was damaged goods. Without that platform, I'd be just another guy talking to his television set.

Thanks to Knox Huston at McGraw-Hill and to Josh for putting up with months of my lousy drafts and endless tweaking. I wasn't at all sure I wanted to tell this story and it showed. Thank you to Janice Race at McGraw-Hill and to Rebecca Stropoli at Yahoo for cleaning up my horrid punctuation and love of vulgarity.

There are a lot of people who ignored me when I spent the better part of two years asking the world to please leave me alone. Chief among them is Dale Olsen, a friend since second grade. Dale called me every single Friday morning from the time my dad got sick until I started at Yahoo. That's 10 years and more than 500 phone calls. He is the Cal Ripken of friendship.

My daughter, Helena, got the best qualities of her mom and me. She protected her brother and stood tall through a divorce, reconciliation, and everything else in between. To me she is perfect and always will be. When he was four, my son, John, insisted on camping out with me at my divorced-dad house whenever he could, even though it meant being away from his sister, his friends, and his regular bedroom. One day, when I asked him why, he looked me in the eye and said, "I don't want you to be lonely." I can't tell the story without crying. Helena and John were the stars that kept me in orbit no matter how hard I tried to escape.

Finally, a special thank you to my ex-wife, current girlfriend, and love of my life, Anne. In 1998 we promised to lead an interesting life together. So far, so good.

CRASH OF 1929

Markets are never wrong, opinions are.
—JESSE LIVERMORE

On September 5, 1929, noted businessman, investor, and statistician Roger Babson took the podium at his name-sake Massachusetts college to discuss the state of the stock market. Speaking to the annual gathering of the National Business Conference during that late summer afternoon, Babson cut right to the chase:

> I repeat what I said at this time last year and the year before, that sooner or later a crash is coming which will take in the leading stocks and cause a decline of from 60 to 80 points in the Dow-Jones Barometer.
>
> Fair weather cannot always continue. The economic cycle is in progress today as it was in the past. The Federal Reserve System has put the banks in a strong position, but it has not changed human nature. More people are borrowing and spec-ulating today than ever in our history. Sooner or later a crash is coming and it may be terrific. Wise are those investors who now get out of debt and reef their sails. This does not mean selling all you have, but it does mean paying up your loans and avoiding margin speculation.
>
> Sooner or later the stock market boom will collapse like the Florida boom. Some day the time is coming when the market will begin to slide off, sellers will exceed buyers, and paper

1

profits will begin to disappear. Then there will immediately be a stampede to save what paper profits then exist.

Snippets of Mr. Babson's prediction began crossing the tape on the New York Stock Exchange at around two o'clock in the afternoon that day. Babson's warnings had been roundly ignored when he had made them in 1927 and again in 1928, but this time the market took notice.

The boundless optimism of the Roaring Twenties, which had been manifest virtually everywhere up until that morning, had turned to white-hot panic in just a moment's time. With no warning, it was as though someone had flipped a switch and limitless greed immediately turned into palpable fear. Over the next 50 minutes, stock traders would stage an epic bout of selling into the close, the Dow Jones dropping 3 percent with an astounding 2 million shares changing hands.

That afternoon rout would soon become known as "Babson's Break," after the man whose speech, given 176 miles away, had essentially nailed shut the greatest bull market up to that time. In just minutes, a rally that had taken U.S. stocks up fivefold over nine years had reached its zenith owing to the words of an obscure pundit somewhere in New England.

In hindsight we know that Babson's Break during that Labor Day–shortened week represented a high point that stocks would not revisit for another 25 years. We know that just 55 days later, the crash of 1929 would begin, causing the Dow Jones to lose 90 percent of its value in less than 3 years, along with the insolvency of some 400,000 banks and lenders and the loss of 13 million jobs.

Did Babson see it all coming? Did he bring it about with his opinions? A scan of the news and headlines that week shows that nothing else should have precipitated the selling or the end of the bull market, so Babson has gotten the credit for it, historically speaking.

The reality is that conditions were already ripe for an explosive sell-off; all it took was someone to strike the match. Speculators had been running rampant for years, driving stocks up thousands of percentage points to price-earnings ratios above 30. And as both novice investors and even celebrities like Groucho Marx joined the party, the gains had begun accelerating thanks to a record margin debt stockpile of over $7 billion. The overheated markets only needed an excuse at that point, and Babson's address had provided it.

It would become one of the most famous bits of market punditry in history and certainly among the most controversial. There were many who'd denied that Babson's speech had been the proximate cause of the selling that day. There was also no shortage of dissent as bullish pundits raced to take the other side.

A couple of days after the speech had shaken the markets, the *Chicago Tribune* published retorts from rival forecasters from around the nation. These responses ranged from haughty indifference to a questioning of Roger Babson's patriotism. The famous Yale economist Irving Fisher, he of the "permanent prosperity" theories that banks and brokerages were so thrilled to bask in, had issued a response to Babson's pessimism that night, and it was picked up nationally: "There may be a recession in stock prices, but not anything in the nature of a crash." The *New York Times* noted that "Roger Babson was derided up and down Wall Street" when the stock market had recovered some of the damage later that week.

As stock market speculation had become the national pastime during the course of the late 1920s, there was more attention being paid to financial pundits and their predictions than ever before— especially as stocks had ceased to continue making new highs and volatility had set in. This sudden jolt left millions of new investors in search of answers about why their easy money had stopped rolling in.

Economists, professors, politicians, traders, bankers, and captains of industry couldn't wait to fill this void with their guesses, speculations, predictions, and conspiracy theories. Most had quite a bit to lose, both financially and reputationally, by an ongoing stock market crisis, and this bias comes through in their pronouncements.

Professor Fisher had been spending his evenings soothing audiences of financial institutions and investment houses in the fall of 1929, and on October 17, just a week before the crash, he dropped this memorable line: "Stock prices have reached what looks like a permanently high plateau. I do not feel there will be soon, if ever, a 50 or 60 point break from present levels. . . . I expect to see the stock market a good deal higher within a few months."

Of course, as the market proceeded to drop by 38 percent on Monday, October 24, and then another 30 percent the next day, denials quickly turned to dismissals.

"This crash is not going to have much effect on business," opined Arthur Reynolds, chairman of the Continental Illinois Bank on Black Monday.

"There will be no repetition of the break of yesterday. . . . I have no fear of another comparable decline," Arthur W. Loasby, president of the Equitable Trust Company, told the *New York Times* the following day.

The Harvard Economic Society weighed in on November 2, saying "despite its severity, we believe that the slump in stock prices will prove an intermediate movement and not the precursor of a business depression such as would entail prolonged further liquidation." The *Times* of London's columnist had noted, "Hysteria has now disappeared from Wall Street," that same day.

On November 15, the legendary financier-turned-statesman Bernard Baruch fired off a cablegram to Winston Churchill across the Atlantic, which read "Financial storm definitely passed."

By February 1930, the crash had been digested, but the Great Depression triggered by it was really just getting under way. This did not stop Treasury Secretary Andrew Mellon from famously pronouncing that "there is nothing in the situation to be disturbed about."

All of a sudden, everyone had an opinion about the stock market and the economy. Even Al Capone, upon being asked why he wasn't investing on Wall Street, had told reporters from his Chicago headquarters: "It's a racket. Those stock market guys are crooked."

The rest, as they say, is history. But as we know, history is known to repeat or at least rhyme.

This is why the assessments and prognostications of the chattering classes from 80 years ago feel so modern and familiar to us. In fact, most of these historical statements could be retrofitted for the pundits of today as they try to explain and forecast the markets of the twenty-first century. You could probably recycle most of these quotes and fool pretty much everyone with just a few changed names and places.

What the old financial experts have in common with those from every other era (including our own) is that they are oftentimes doing their best with limited information and that their biases are almost always on full display. There's a phrase among traders that "everyone talks their book," by which we mean that if people are offering an opinion, it's most likely colored by the way they're currently invested in the market. This is human nature, and, of course, it has always ever been thus. I should point out that this phenomenon is not unique to finance. Political commentators are almost uniformly partisan during their media appearances, and the new breed of sports commentators have taken to wearing their team allegiances on their sleeves these days—literally—some even donning a jersey on game day while covering a match.

Warren Buffett once said that "forecasts may tell you a great deal about the forecaster; they tell you nothing about the future." Buffett claims to pay no attention to market predictions or the economic outlooks of others. He also tries his hardest to avoid making predictions of his own, despite the endless exhortations of the media. "We have long felt that the only value of stock forecasters is to make fortune-tellers look good. . . . I continue to believe that short-term market forecasts are poison and should be kept locked up in a safe place, away from children and also from grown-ups who behave in the market like children."

What comes easy for Buffett, however, is very difficult for a majority of investors, be they professional or amateur. Avoiding being pushed and pulled by news and opinion has never been harder. Each day, investors are barraged with more advice, regardless of the outcomes from the last batch delivered the day before. Each week the lights are flashing brighter and the volume is growing louder. Each passing year brings more confusion, not less—more opportunities to be led astray, to be prodded into the childish behavior in the markets that Buffett alludes to.

But we can fight back.

We can arm ourselves with wisdom and historical awareness. We can take control of our media diets and learn to contextualize the things we are reading and hearing. We can categorize the opinions we're inundated with and know when they matter and when they can be safely ignored. We can remind ourselves that much of the content being generated in the financial media each day is what some would call "news-flavored entertainment"—but that there's nothing wrong with people having biased opinions or participating in the creation of entertainment so long as we, as investors, know better than to reflexively act upon what we're hearing.

As in all aspects of life, there are legitimate commenters in the financial world, and there are charlatans. There are people who genuinely want to get things right, and there are those for whom deception is more profitable. In this book, we explain that it has always been thus. Throughout history, the names and situations have changed, but the conflicts have not. Everything that has already happened will happen again.

This book will make you a smarter market participant and will give you a heightened level of awareness as you survey the investment landscape. It will reveal the tricks and idiosyncrasies of your favorite talking heads, in some cases humanizing them enough so that you can extract the best of what they have to offer while side-stepping the rest.

It's gotten harder than ever to sort through the calamitous clutter, and yet it's never been more important to do so. Welcome to the first-ever book written to tackle this most daunting component of investing: our guide to help you become a more informed consumer of financial news and conjecture.

Welcome to the Clash of the Financial Pundits.

CHAPTER 1

THE MYTH OF THE MEDIA DIET

*Our job is to find a few intelligent things to do, not
to keep up with every damn thing in the world.*
—CHARLIE MUNGER

In a perfect world, you can put your money to work across stocks
and bonds, cash and commodities, REITs and real estate, and
be done with it. You can allow your invested assets to grow like
mushrooms in the dark, and go through life utterly unfazed by the
daily doings of others and the unfolding of economic and geopolit-
ical developments in real time.

Sounds great, until you realize that this is not a perfect world
and that news actually matters as it pertains to your portfolio.
Things happen. These things can have an impact on the investments you've made and sometimes do require a reaction from you
or at least a conscious decision about whether to react at all.

Paying no attention to "the media" allows you the luxury of
blissful ignorance, and if you plan to die young, we highly recommend it. If, on the other hand, you have some hope that your
portfolio will help you to maintain your purchasing power through
decades of retirement and complement whatever money will or
will not be there from Social Security, then you may want to set
your news and media consumption limits surgically as opposed to
absolutely.

This is not to say that being aware of the news will help you become a better investor. In fact, there is a strong case to be made that prolonged exposure to headlines and commentary has a better chance of becoming a hindrance to successful investing. But because time marches on and history is constantly unfolding—sometimes slowly and sometimes suddenly—the news becomes an inexorable part of the equation. It can no sooner be eliminated than can gravity or the tides.

It can be helpful, therefore, to keep in mind the following: awareness does not necessitate action. Being informed should not automatically mean you are goaded into actually doing something. Sometimes the added knowledge from an article is good enough—most times, in fact.

Most shock diets fail, and weight gain is the inevitable result. The same is true for media diets. "I'm going off the grid for a while" is what the frustrated market participant typically says after becoming frazzled by the day-to-day noise of the news. This is admirable. Only it never lasts, and the old habits of sloppy, unordered consumption return, just as the fasting fat man comes right back to the eating habits that got him there to begin with once the attempted starvation has failed.

Regular news consumption helps you develop the ability to sort out what matters from what doesn't. How many projections from "professionals" have you observed as being far from accurate in the final analysis? How many brilliant minds and eloquent speakers have themselves been fooled by their own inability to extrapolate their present beliefs into the future? It is partly amusing to witness this wrongness play out, but it is also partly frightening to watch as the smartest, most experienced people with unlimited resources and research capabilities at their fingertips come to such incorrect conclusions: "They've got analysts and Bloomberg terminals and inside contacts and analytics and a career spanning decades! If they can't get it right consistently, what hope is there for me or anyone else?" At a certain point, the folly of forecasting becomes obvious. It is at the dawning of this realization that we begin to grow as investors.

The catch is that we must ourselves be fooled by the forecasts of others in order for this larger wisdom to set in. We must believe and live through the shattering of these beliefs before a stronger, better set of beliefs can be rebuilt on the rubble. This is rarely an event—rather, it is a process. The path to investment enlightenment is bracketed by blaring flat-screen televisions on either side and a cobblestone of price targets underfoot. Our disenfranchisement with "the system" is the impetus that sets us on this road, and we are propelled for the first few miles by tears and the pangs of regret over letting ourselves be so gullible.

That which does not kill us makes us stronger, said the philosopher Friedrich Nietzsche, shortly before contracting syphilis, having a mental breakdown in the street, and then dying from some combination of manic-depressive illness with periodic psychosis, multiple strokes, and paralysis resulting in the loss of speech and mobility. Okay, so Nietzsche is maybe not a great example of this concept personally. But his aphorism does mostly ring true as it pertains to our ability to withstand that which we are regularly assaulted with.

Two weeks after getting a flu shot, your body begins to produce antibodies to fight off the "foreign invaders" you've introduced into your system. This willful triggering of a physiological response is a form of training. Should your body encounter an actual influenza virus later in the season, it will remember what its response must be, and a counteroffensive from the immune system is launched quickly until the hostile attack is neutralized. But immunity doesn't last forever, nor can it cover every new strain, which is why a new vaccination is required every fall.

In much the same way, investors who wish to maintain control over their responses to the bombardment of "breaking news" need to continually introduce it to their decision-making process. Isn't the weightlifter constantly tearing and stretching his muscle fibers so that they can more robustly reconstruct themselves?

A true media diet virtually assures an overreaction to market volatility and expert prognostication once the dieter returns to the flashing lights and headlines. And how well equipped can one be to cope with the stimuli—the blinding rays from a thousand Las Vegas billboards and the deafening roar of bells and whistles—after too much time spent in solitude?

And so if haphazard digestion of financial media is disruptive to our composure and total ignorance of it dangerously lowers our resistance to the worst aspects of it, what can we do? How can we reconcile our concurrent need and revulsion?

There are several tools at our disposal. These include setting of boundaries, intelligent curation, methodical and scheduled intake, awareness of one's own investing time frame, a healthy skepticism, the ability to contextualize and order information, some grounding in market and economic history, and, last, a good sense of humor.

CHAPTER 2

THE *BIRTH* OF FINANCIAL TV

A CONVERSATION WITH JIM ROGERS

I t's not uncommon for men who have made their fortunes to go into teaching. Punditry itself is, of course, just another form of teaching. What makes Jim Rogers unique is his almost complete immersion in the teaching and learning process. He's a proactive subject willing, able, and palpably hungry to take a conversation as deep or shallow as he thinks you can handle.

Raised in Demopolis, Alabama (population 7,500), Rogers started working at five years old, collecting bottles for change. Thirty-two years later he stopped working when he stepped down from the Quantum Fund after racking up a 4,200 percent return in less than a decade.

Early on, Jim's primary goal, like that of many people on Wall Street who accumulate enormous wealth at a young age, was financial independence. By his own account in the following interview, Rogers worked obsessively toward that goal, true to a certain type on Wall Street.

Where Rogers differs from the norm is that he didn't really retire into a specific niche. Instead he seems to have done everything he wanted. He rode a motorcycle around the world between 1990 and 1992, including through China, which was hardly receptive to the idea at the time.

He took a similar journey at the end of the millennium, book-ending the 1990s with trips identified by the *Guinness World Records* book more or less just for being a spectacular trip.

He's a man of rigid propriety seemingly incapable of seeing boundaries, physical or intellectual. He lives in Singapore because he believes China is the future and the air in Singapore is cleaner than that in Hong Kong. He's tremendously modest but delighted by those who know of his achievements.

He claims not to be a market timer or a trader, which is demonstrably, hilariously false. He called the crash of 1987, bought a mansion in the 1970s and then sold it in 2007, and has generally been on the right side of every major trend for the past 45 years. It's an absurdly strong track record that is widely known, but he'll politely deny it unless prodded.

I spoke to him from his home in Singapore in early May 2013. As has been the case in every conversation I've had with him, he was slyly evasive at first, skimming along the surface of the conversation, probing to see just how serious I was about the discussion.

At first he was exercising as we spoke, his day starting as mine was ending owing to the 12-hour time difference. About 10 minutes in, he scoffed when I asked him if it was possible to help people understand that the world is a fluid, constantly evolving place, one in which mobility such as his was a practical necessity yet far from the norm.

"Well, my gosh, Jeff, if you can solve that question, you'll be the greatest person in world history."

I reminded him that he had a philosophy degree from Oxford and had spent much of his life trying to solve that exact problem.

I'd passed some sort of test with him. There was a change in the tone of the conversation from interviewer and subject to two men having a more serious discussion. The real interview had started.

MACKE: You're best known for your books and success as an investor, but what they don't know is, you had one of the original financial TV shows. You were on FNM, which became CNBC. How did that come about?

ROGERS: I hosted a show for Dreyfus on WCBS in the '80s, the late '80s, and then when FNM started, I guess they had seen the show or they knew about the show, and they called me and asked me if I would do it, and I said, "Sure, why not?"

The next thing you know, there I am on FNM. I had to stop the FNM show, because I took off around the world on my motorcycle. When I came back, CNBC was up and running, and I went over there and did a few guest appearances. Then they said, "Hey, why don't you do a show for us, too?" I guess I was one of the first investors on financial TV, because I didn't have a job, so I had the time. Every serious person had a job, so they didn't have time to do things like that.

MACKE: Every serious person was working for a living. You had the means and you had the ability to do whatever you wanted, and obviously the interest and motivation to travel around the world for the rest of your life. What drove you to talk to people about stocks on television?

ROGERS: Well, at the beginning I guess it was more or less the novelty of it all. I did not and still do not have a TV, so I don't watch anything on TV, unless I'm in a hotel room or something. But when I started doing it, it was fun. It was an adrenaline rush I guess, partly because it was new and different. One thing led to another, and I guess I'm still doing it. Producers know I have a little time since I don't have a job. So that's the whole story. I mean, a not very interesting story. It's pretty simple, but that's how it all happened.

MACKE: You're underplaying a little bit; there are reasons for calling you beyond your availability. You've also been a professor at Columbia, written books, and dedicated a fairly large portion of your life to helping people from your experiences. Is there a void you're trying to fill?

ROGERS: Well, yes; in that regard, yes. Some of the people that I see on TV, even some of the people I've seen in academia, do not have what I consider a sound approach. Now they obviously do consider it sound, or they wouldn't be doing it. So, yes, I do like to have the opportunity to give a different view. You know, I hear a lot of really strange stuff in the press, on TV, in academia. I sit and say to myself, "How can people really believe that stuff?

How could people say stuff like that, much less how could they believe it?" So, yes, I don't mind at all giving a different view.

MACKE: When it comes to finance, do you think people really do believe everything they say, or are they selling something? As often as not, the strangest opinions in finance are provided by people with a newsletter or some other product to sell.

ROGERS: Well, I hope they believe what they say. I hope that that's their view. I don't know. Some things I've heard; you know, I've heard people in Washington. Let's use that, because it's more neutral. They stand up and say what we need to do is increase government spending and debt. My reaction to that is I cannot believe that grown-ups really believe that the solution to the problems with too much spending and too much debt is more debt. Now, they're politicians or bureaucrats, so they may not really mean what they say, but there are people who favor these things, which I consider really very strange.

On Wall Street, well, not just on Wall Street, it's most aspects of life, many people have things to sell, so it's obviously to their benefit, even if they don't quite believe it, to give a view which helps them sell. I don't have anything to sell, so I don't know any better than just to give my own view.

MACKE: The best way to be a certain kind of pundit is to have one single take and to repeat it over and over and over again. You're more of a trader by nature. Your message over the years has changed and evolved. You've called bubbles and bought subsequent crashes. The disconnect for viewers is that the pundits with the strongest voices are the ones who never change their minds.

ROGERS: Well, I concur with that. My only sort of nuance is I don't consider myself a trader. But from what you mean, I consider traders to be very short term. I'm not very short term in my views, but I do change them. My goodness, if you don't change, you're going to certainly go bankrupt, because the world is always changing. I wrote a new book recently called *Street Smarts*, and in there I talk about how the world is constantly changing. You can pick any year you want, Jeff. Any year in the past, well, history, and you know 10 or 15 years later the world has changed dramatically. Look at 1900 or 1950 or 1980. You pick the year and 10–15 years later it's not even the same world anymore, although at the time most people say, "Well, this is the way the world is, and this is the way it's going to continue to be." So, yes, I do try to change because the world does change, and the way to be successful at anything is to figure out the change, anticipate the change, and then change with the world.

MACKE: Why is that so hard for people? I hear all the time where people just keep going back to the same well over and over again, long after it's dry and they run out of ideas, money, and time. Why do you think it's so hard for people to know this world is constantly evolving?

ROGERS: Well, that's a very good question. If you can solve that question, Jeff, my, gosh, you're going to be the most extraordinary person in world history.

MACKE: You're the one who studied philosophy at Oxford, my friend, not me. I figured you learned a lot in that big fancy school. That's why I came to you.

ROGERS: Okay. I suspect the reason is that it's easier not to have to change your view once you get into a groove. I won't call it a rut. I'll call it a groove. Once a person gets into a groove, it's fairly difficult to get outside that groove. I'm sure I make the mistake at times, too. Sometimes it takes me a while to change my view of what's going on. When everybody else is saying, "My gosh, the sky is blue," it's pretty hard to say, "Listen, I just went to open the window. It's not blue." Nobody wants to hear that, because it's different from what everybody else in the room is saying. So I guess it's partly how easy it is to go along with everybody else. It's difficult to form a view in the first place. Certainly an independent view. Once you have it, I guess it's hard for the brain cells to keep moving.

MACKE: You're critical of the manipulation, I guess. Basically you understand that the game's a little bit skewed. That the central banks are manipulating markets to make up for the politicians and keep the economy afloat. That makes us pretty far removed from a free market. How do you feel like you're supposed to navigate that? Whenever I talk to people, I'm afraid—I'm telling them how to position themselves to avoid getting hurt because the game's fixed. Do you ever just get so cynical that you want to chuck it?

ROGERS: Well, it is certainly manipulated by the politicians and by bureaucrats, yes. They're trying to do whatever they can to keep their jobs. You and I try to keep our jobs, too.

MACKE: The politicians and the bureaucrats are trying to keep their jobs—there's no question about that—so they do whatever's necessary to keep their jobs. So they boost the markets in the easiest, fastest way, squashing interest rates. That doesn't mean it's not going to work. The FOMC obviously thinks it's going to work.

ROGERS: I know that, throughout history, printing money has ended up badly, for example. But unfortunately, Jeff, as you know, very few politicians know any history at all. They know even less economics, and unfortunately most economists know very little history, and most of them know very little economics it turns out. I mean, Dr. Bernanke knows very little economics. He knows nothing about demand. He knows nothing about currencies. All he basically knows is printing money, so he prints money. That's an example of someone who cannot change his views.

He's been studying the printing of money for decades, so he sees the world through the eyes of a money printer. I happen to think, from my reading of history and previous economic situations, that this is going to end very badly. But I don't see how he could ever change his mind because it would discredit everything he's ever done in life. Now there is some hope. Yes, he's resigning, apparently after the end of this term. So even he realizes it's going to end badly, too, finally. It may be good news, but unfortunately, he'll probably be replaced by another money printer, a "manipulator," to use your term. [Note: Janet Yellen replaced Bernanke as Fed Chair in February 2014, extending the policies Bernanke put in place.]

MACKE: And you traded during the '70s, which was rampant with manipulation. When Nixon went off the gold standard, we had just crazy inflation and lines for oil. How would you trade it today? You say you're not a trader and the market's always been manipulated, and yet you're a market animal and manage to do quite well.

ROGERS: The only way to survive a recession in the investment world is to see what's going on. Somebody once said, "Don't fight the Fed." Or there are people who've said, "Don't fight the tape." You cannot fight reality, because the market is going to go straight ahead and bowl you over if you just stick with your views and fight what's happening in the world, the changes of the world. One cannot do that. I mean, if I gain 10 pounds, I can't fight. I can't try to make my suit smaller to fit me. I've got to somehow accept the reality that I've gained 10 pounds.

MACKE: But you've moved to a longer-term stance. In the '70s how were you able to grind out returns as well as you did at Quantum? Did you have a two-year focus or were you thinking in longer terms?

ROGERS: Well, no. In those days we used enormous leverage, and we were constantly on top of things. You know, for me, I was consumed by the market. There was nothing else I wanted to do. I wished the market had been open seven days a week. The person I worked with was also very consumed with the whole thing. So we were very much on top of it, and we moved as we had to. It didn't mean we didn't make mistakes, but we did change with the markets, when it told us to change or when we realized that things had changed.

MACKE: You were able to kind of ride out some of the bumps along the way. Did your returns vary a lot during the Quantum years? And did your investors understand, or was it a whole different age then?

ROGERS: Well, the '70s, that was a long time ago for me, Jeff. You might as well ask about my first wife. Yes, well, we were up 4,200 percent in those 10 years. The market was up 47 percent. Of course, things varied; there were some pretty hard bumps along the way, but basically things were going up.

I don't work nearly as hard at it as I used to in those days. I've got other things I'm doing. I've got a couple of little girls, and now I'm consumed by these little girls. There are other things on my mind.

MACKE: Those kids will do that to you. Do you think market people are like chess prodigies or something? That once you get older and have enough to live the way you want to, you can't be consumed enough to win anymore or it's just not worth your time?

ROGERS: That's an extremely good question. I do know that there are people who don't quit—at least I read about cases of people who don't quit and who keep at it—and sometimes they lose everything, or they lose a lot. Now you don't read that many cases of them, because they usually disappear, as you know, and hide under a rock or something. But there are many people who keep at it. I don't keep at it. As I say, I try to do other things in life now.

I worked for Roy Neuberger at one time. He was the man who founded Neuberger Berman. I mean, Roy, until he was in his late nineties, I think even until he was 100, was going down to the office every day and trading. Now, he was a great trader, a great short-term trader, and he was certainly consumed by watching the tape, if you will, and he never lost everything, as you know. He continued to be successful until he died. There are stories like that. I'm not one of them. I think the thing is, Jeff, the ones who keep doing it and fail we don't hear about, unless it's a spectacular failure. The others like Roy just keep going and keep doing it. I don't know why. I mean, if that's what they want to do, that's fine with me. It's not what I want to do.

MACKE: Do you think they lose it all because there's a regression to the mean? Do you think that there is just a tiny fraction of people who can actually beat the market but that for most big traders if they hang out long enough, they're due to give it all back?

ROGERS: I know of very few people who can beat the market over time. I mean, I'm not the only one who's observed that.

Academic studies have shown repeatedly that most people do not beat the market over any long period of time, for whatever reason. They may be like me; they get lazy, you know? Or just quit or turn over their money to somebody else. But in fact, I don't know any who have beaten the market consistently for any long periods of time. There may be some; I just don't know about them.

MACKE: But with it being the case that people can't beat the market over time, wouldn't that make punditry a little bit of a racket? What do you think of financial media? You've got this constant reporting, this buy on the short term; what are they going to earn this quarter? Is it just a mugs game from top to bottom?

ROGERS: I don't begrudge anybody finding a way to make a living and to do it. I mean, you do a brilliant job.

MACKE: I'm not criticizing them. I don't want you to misinterpret that. I'm not criticizing anything about the networks. I'm talking about the end consumer of financial media. So as people are trying to drink out of this fire hose of information they suddenly have, it's hard for them to know what any of it means. There's endless information coming at readers and viewers, but do you think it's presented to folks in a way that's going to help them invest?

ROGERS: As you point out, much of this stuff that's there is not very useful, and some of it's downright wrong. The novices, the first 70 times they watch it, I'm sure they think everybody on there knows what they're talking about, because they sound plausible and they wear nice suits. But you and I know that much that's presented is not true.

Now, it's a danger for novices not to understand that. I guess they learn the hard way eventually that, my goodness, you know a lot of this stuff I see on the TV or the Internet is not accurate. And I don't know how you teach people that. That's even something you read in the *New York Times*, even the *Wall Street Journal*; a lot of that stuff that you're going to read is not going to be accurate in the end.

MACKE: Do you think there's an understanding of just how much work it is to actually be good at this game? Do you think the flood of information and opinions gives the impression this is so much easier than it actually is?

ROGERS: Mankind and human beings have not changed; most of us still make the wrong judgments. So the fact that we get a lot more information faster, I don't think that's going to help us or hurt us. What we have to develop is good judgment. Now, back to being on TV, you asked me about being on TV. If nothing else, what I try to do, and one reason I do it, is so that I can present different views.

I mean, I try to spread this message all the time, Jeff. It doesn't work. Everybody wants a hot tip. Everybody wants to be rich this afternoon. You can sit there all day long and say, "The emperor has no clothes." Nobody wants to hear it. They all want a hot tip.

MACKE: And then suddenly the emperor's naked, and everyone claims they saw it all along.

ROGERS: Right.

MACKE: Do you think your comments are just twisted in the headlines to be more salacious?

ROGERS: Yes, some journalists are different from others, as you well know. But I have seen complete fabrications—I mean, I've seen headlines about something I supposedly said, and even I'll read the article and I didn't say it. But there are certainly plenty of times when they garbled or confused what I said. Part of the problem is that many journalists aren't experienced, especially the young ones, experienced in the actual markets themselves.

People repeat stories; stories turn into rumors. Stories turn into garbled stories. The stories turn into things where somebody is trying to promote something. But now we can all see it instantly from five or six different sources. A lot of years ago, we could talk to five or six different guys down at the coffee bar or coffee shop and get different stories.

I used to tell students, people would ask about inside information, and I would say, "Gosh, I used to get inside information all the time, but then I realized most of it was wrong." Most of it was something where somebody had totally garbled a story, or somebody was trying to promote a position, or who knows what? I would explain to them, you've got inside information from the president of a company, you're going to lose half your money. You get it from the chairman, you're going to lose all your money.

MACKE: Do you think laws on insider trading are actually being enforced fairly? It seems like the SEC is just kind of dragging people down to make the splashiest headline.

ROGERS: I don't have much confidence in the SEC. I hope you don't either. You know the SEC went to visit Bernie Madoff six times in 12 years and came out every time saying everything is okay. You know, the SEC has cracked very few cases, big cases. They find some minor guys all the time.

MACKE: And they make a huge deal out of it. I mean, they make an enormous, enormous deal out of it, as though they've put an end to Wall Street fraud.

ROGERS: The SEC's like everybody else. They're trying to promote themselves, trying to keep their jobs, trying to get bigger budgets, etc. I haven't seen many cases where one would stand up and say, "Oh my gosh, look what the SEC did to save us all." I see very few like that.

MACKE: I don't know precisely how they're going to go about deciding what they enforce. It's not just a question of whether or not it's useful. The question is whether or not there's any such thing as insider information anymore in the information age.

ROGERS: That's an extremely good question. No, I'm conceivably somebody who's sat down and did a lot of research and spoke to a lot of people. It could be what I see in the press these days; they could be accused of having inside information.

MACKE: That's the whole point. Why do you have a team of analysts if you're not looking for material, nonpublished information, but the information's not hollow; you paid someone $2 million to get it for you. So you're out to put the pieces together. Well, if you hire an analyst, his job is to figure something out in a way that other people haven't, so you can profit from it. That would be material information. You would have accumulated that from a lot of insiders, and for it to be strung that way, it could be you've broken the law.

ROGERS: That's my point, that some of this stuff I read about in the press these days, I would wonder if I would consider that inside information, because that's what these guys are paid to do. That's what all investors are supposed to do: figure out what's going on, what's really going on, analyze it, and then make a judgment. It's what we're paid to do.

These days, I mean, I don't know how they define inside information. I guess everybody needs to announce it on your show, before they do anything so everybody can say, "Ah, it's not inside information. He made it public." But that destroys the market.

MACKE: They can do it on Twitter now. They can do it on Twitter and Facebook. You can announce material things. Does that really level the playing field? I mean, you're not on Twitter all day. Does it make it fair if you're setting up these social networks on which you can distribute things?

ROGERS: That's a good point. I guess if somebody were going to buy XYZ, he could say I'm buying XYZ for these reasons on Twitter, and it wouldn't be inside information anymore.

MACKE: Well, the CEO of Netflix, he said that he'd got over a billion streams or something, and he said it on his Facebook page. And the SEC ruled that you can go ahead and say things like that on social media, but it counts as disseminating information.

ROGERS: No, that's what I mean. I guess next time Joe buys a stock, he says, "Guys, I'm buying stock X for these reasons," then he goes and buys it. Then his defense would be, "Wait a minute; it's not inside information. I publicly announced it before I acted, and therefore it's not inside information." The point is, it's difficult. It's always been difficult to define inside information. I mean, for us it's pretty clear; if you and I are working on a takeover and we know the takeover's coming and we go and do something, that's wrong. That's acting on inside information. That's pretty clear, but a lot of the stuff that now seems to be blamed on inside information, I find extremely marginal. Because I don't know why anybody has to research the problems, because they can all be blamed on having inside information.

MACKE: So what do you look at? How do you keep up to date? What are the media outlets that you use?

ROGERS: I maybe use, like I explained to you before, I don't have a TV. I maybe use the Internet. You've done a very good thing by going to Yahoo. I will tell you that when I'm on your show or other—well, it's mainly your show, and I've been on Yahoo, I'm always amazed at how many e-mails I get. It used to be that way with the TV media, but now if I'm on your network or maybe one other, I get floods of e-mails. When I'm on the TV, I don't get nearly as many. I also notice that when I get e-mails from the TV viewers, most of them don't have much understanding. A lot of e-mails lack the understanding of how markets work. For whatever reason, the people on the Internet seem to be better qualified.

MACKE: Sometimes. They're also the biggest crackpots on earth.

ROGERS: It doesn't mean there are not plenty of fools watching the Internet, Jeff. Don't get me wrong, and probably there are even one or two fools watching your show.

MACKE: I'm sure. There might even be one or two hosting my show.

ROGERS: I've been on your show two or three times, so I had fun.

MACKE: It was magic. You do great. You did great. So besides watching my show, how do you think if you're 20, you're 21, not old guys like me and you, but kids who are that young and they're trying to figure it out. If you had one thing to give them as a piece of advice, would it just be do your homework, after you hear from these guys? Would you tell them not to have a television set? How should they go about building knowledge?

ROGERS: I would say start with what you know. Every 20-year-old has got a lot of knowledge about something, whether it's sports or fashion or cars or hairdressing, something. And he or she should start there and say, "Okay, I know a whole lot about fashion." So then she should check out the company when she sees something new happening, whether it's a new store, a new designer, a new manufacturer, whatever it is, and learn as much as she can about that company and the other companies in the industry. Then from that, she can build on enough knowledge to perhaps make an investment.

But just watching somebody on TV or on the Internet who says, "Oh my gosh, I own X," and rush you to go out and buy X and put a good story in buying it, it's going to lead to disaster, repeated disaster. So what everybody needs to do is stay with what they know, do a lot of homework. You know, Jeff, if you only have 25 investments in your life, you would be very careful about those investments. You would be sure that you knew what you were doing before you made an investment. That's not the way people approach all this. They jump in and out. People spend more time doing research on which car to buy than they do on which stock to buy. Yeah, you should check the car you buy, but you should spend a lot more time when putting your money into markets, because that can be much more dangerous, or much more lucrative if you do it right.

MACKE: If you were running Quantum today, would you go on TV?

ROGERS: I probably wouldn't have time, Jeff. I was working 14-hour days, or whatever. I was traveling a lot. I don't think I would have time to be on TV now, because I was too consumed, too busy doing other things.

MACKE: Have you seen the guys, though? It's become a trend for hedge fund managers to have come out of the dark and pop up on TV. You've got guys who are respectable, guys that have done tremendously well; they're sitting there yelling at each other on the television set. It's kind of unseemly. Have you seen it? I mean, what do you think of it?

ROGERS: Well, I haven't seen it, because I don't have a TV, so I don't know. And I commented maybe there comes a time when you've got enough money, and like I said before, many people get lazy and too many people get sloppy. How many people get overconfident, including me? I just haven't seen it, so I don't know.

MACKE: Are you continuing to learn, in terms of are you teaching more? Where's your mindset? You're one of the more intellectually curious people I've ever met, and yet you're having time to convey it as well. You're trying to teach as well. Is there a balance between the two? Should people just shut up until they're kind of 45 and they know what they're talking about? How do you learn and teach?

ROGERS: First, I want to make a point because you brought up a good thing. I run into people all the time who are two or three or five years into the business who people say are very smart, and they probably are. And they think that they're very smart, and they probably are. I mean, it takes a while to understand how all this works. You know, this is the whole world. You may think you're buying a stock in X, but no, no, X is influenced by everything that's going on in the world. It all fits together, and I don't see how it's humanly possible to pull all that together after two or three, or four or five, years of experience.

So people do need a lot of experience, a lot of knowledge, a lot of foundation before they can make decisions. At least in my case that was true. It still is true. It's the danger of instant TV, instant Internet, and instant newspapers now; once we get all this information, we think we know what we're doing, and we don't.

MACKE: Do you think being really smart or really accomplished in one field leads to investment traps? It seems like people assume that intelligence is more fungible than it is. Meaning if I'm a heart surgeon, I think I can pick stocks whereas you and I are okay at picking stocks, and we would never dare to perform heart surgery. The thing about it, it's money. I don't know why folks think that it's that easy just because they come into it with a little mental horsepower.

ROGERS: Well, that's very true. Many doctors, lawyers think, "Thank gosh, I got into medical school. I got into the Ivy League. I must be a smart person, and so this must be easy, too." No, it's a mistake that we've talked about before, and of course, if the heart surgeon is sticking with what he knows, then fine. But if the farmer is sticking with what he knows, if everybody is sticking with what they know, they're going to make a lot of money as investors.

But unfortunately, what happens is often a heart surgeon thinks he's a pretty smart guy, "Why don't I make an investment in a dot-com. I'm a smart guy. I know what I'm doing." And they really don't know much about the dot-com, yet they go out and buy dot-com stocks.

MACKE: They have the power to give life. They're a doctor. What would stop them?

ROGERS: And they went to medical school. It's hard to get into medical school, so they must be smart.

MACKE: Do you think people should go to business school? Information's so much easier to get now. You can learn online, offline. Fifteen years ago I had to pay Mr. Bloomberg $2,000 a month to get a terminal, and now I can key all of that online. I went to business school, and everything I paid to learn is now free online. Are we just outmoded in terms of the way we teach people?

ROGERS: Well, yes. In my new book I explain why many schools now are going to go bankrupt—why American education is going to see some starving, some shocking bankruptcies coming out of American tertiary education—and business school is certainly not much use. I was once a full professor in an Ivy League business school, and I will tell you, Jeff, most of what goes on is not very useful at all, except to the professors. They charge huge amounts of money. They teach a lot of conventional wisdom, so the kids who come out, come out in the hole financially but also knowledge-wise; their peers who went to work are way ahead of them financially after two years, but secondly knowledge-wise, too, because a lot of what they teach in business school is flat-out wrong.

These poor kids have to unlearn it and start over. In my view, if you do your own work and teach yourself or start with what you know, you will come out way, way, way ahead of going to business school. I consider business school a complete waste of time, money, energy, and everything else. I'll tell you what, Jeff, you go down and short soybeans one day, you'll learn more in the first six weeks than you'll learn in 10 years at any business school. The Internet and real life is a fast way to learn, if you're really interested.

MACKE: Who's out there in the pantheon with you that you think is conveying the message? Guys like Buffett who are out there talking it, but your friend George Soros is talking to the world about markets constantly. Is there someone along those lines that you listen to? Do you listen to all of them and then make your own decisions? Who's doing a good job of helping the whole lot, in a sense?

ROGERS: Buffett is good at it, but after that I don't really know, Jeff. As I say, I don't have a TV. I don't watch people. I rarely—I just don't know. I'm sure there are always spectacular guys in any business, and I know there's got to be really smart, insightful guys in the world of finance right now; I just don't know them.

MACKE: And I'll let you go. You've been very generous with your time. Where do you think we are in five years in terms of the way the financial media's going? Do you think the noise just gets louder and louder, or do you think that it kind of blows itself up, and we end up with a little bit of sanity?

ROGERS: From my own limited experience, I said to you before about the reaction I get when I'm on TV versus when I'm on the Internet. I mean, I'm not the first to realize that the world is moving from established media, whether it's newspapers, magazines, and TV to the Internet, but that's going to continue. There is certainly going to be a glut of Internet financial pundits. Anybody can do it. I mean, it doesn't take any money. It doesn't take any brains. You just sit down and start doing it.

CHAPTER 3

THE *FIRST MEDIA-BLOWN BUBBLE*

> *Stock market bubbles don't grow out of thin air. They have a solid basis in reality, but reality as distorted by a misconception.*
> —GEORGE SOROS

We like to think that the modern media machinery is behind the boom-bust-boom investment cycle that has characterized the last couple of decades. We're fond of pointing out the ways in which the television or the Internet is somehow responsible for each mania that arises—as though basic human emotions like fear or greed have only come into existence at around the time of the transistor or the microchip.

As foolish as it would be to blame the media for speculative excess, however, it would be equally foolish to completely dismiss its role entirely. While the press rarely creates an investable bubble, its involvement is certainly essential for the proliferation of it, its care and feeding so to speak. Where else can the crowd draw the sustenance necessary to persist in its madness? How else can the distorted reality become the *actual* reality for so many players in such concurrent synchronicity?

The important thing to recognize is that this role of the media's is a very old one. It did not originate with traders wearing Zuckerberg hoodies on the eve of the Facebook IPO. Nor was its genesis during the era of sock-puppet dot-com mascots. No, the origins of the media-assisted financial frenzy predate these examples by a good three centuries or so.

England in the early 1700s was a nation awash with debt, largely as a result of its involvement in the Wars of Spanish Succession. The endless costs of financing what should be known as the first true world war left virtually all the major powers of Europe financially exhausted and without means to even begin to pay back their creditors—England's Parliament had amassed more than £9 million by 1711.

But as we so often find throughout history, when catastrophe meets avaricious ingenuity, a problem for the many very quickly becomes a tool of enrichment for the creative few. Into this balance sheet breach stepped Robert Harley, a Tory politician and the man who would soon be Lord Treasurer. Harley cleverly came up with a scheme to create the first joint-stock offering in England, the South Sea Company. Created by an act of Parliament, the South Sea Company was granted the exclusive rights to begin trading with Spain and its colonies as opposed to warring with them. English citizens and other creditors who had lent the government money over the preceding years had their claims converted from debt to equity—they became the "shareholders" in this new, adventurous trading enterprise and were entitled to a share of its profits.

This creation of a company where only a pile of IOUs had existed prior served the dual purpose of both ending the war and relieving the nation of its public debt. But creating the entity and whipping up enough public support for its existence were two separate endeavors. In order for the South Sea Company to function in its role as recapitalizer of the nation's finances, the investing public had to truly buy in.

That's where the media comes in.

Trading with the colonies and conquistadors of the New World held all the sex appeal to speculators that the dot-com bubble would a few hundred years later. There were astronomical projections of potential profits, and the South Sea Company's shareholders were in line to collect them exclusively by writ of law. How could the shares possibly lose? This was the message presented by South Sea, its management, and its many agents in the press.

As Jim Harrison wrote in *Harvard Magazine* (as fate would have it, in the spring of 1999 during a stock market free-for-all every bit as overheated), "It was an optimistic age. People had a passion for business and followed developments avidly through a newly burgeoning medium, the newspaper. In 1702 London had one daily newspaper; by 1709 there were 18. Harley had able propagandists, Jonathan Swift and Daniel Defoe among them. The managers of the South Sea Company understood the value of publicity (as well as fine print) in the advancement of their affairs and once issued a press release, surely an early example of that genre."

Swift and Defoe, working directly for Robert Harley and spearheading the public relations campaign for South Sea, wasted no time in capturing the public's imagination. They accomplished this through pamphlets and newspaper accounts of the New World's vast wealth and opportunity for investment. The two writers published fantastical lists of English items for export and invented stories of fabulous riches across the sea. This early form of media blitz had primed the pump for stock sales to investors from all over England and financiers from around the continent.

Had investors been paying attention to more than just the publicity efforts of the board, they'd have recognized the fact that apart from a small agreement on slave shipments, South Sea had been entirely unsuccessful in generating any kind of heat to match all the light surrounding it. No agreements of any substance had ever materialized between the company and Spain's interests in the New World. And when war had broken out between the two powers once again in 1718, England found itself once more drowning in debt.

South Sea's directors went double or nothing on the scheme and converted another whopping amount of government liability to corporate equity, diluting the holdings of preexisting shareholders still further while making even more outrageous claims to keep the investors playing along. Bribes and payoffs proliferated in broad daylight to keep the politicians on the right side while the company created shares out of thin air and sold them at virtually whatever price it wished, so great was the clamor for participation.

In the meantime, the London Stock Exchange was in full swing, producing almost 200 new issues for sale in what we would call today initial public offerings. Across the Channel, the French were going wild for a speculative bubble of their own—the Mississippi Company, another American adventure, this one perpetrated by a Scotsman named John Law.

These things, of course, never end well. As Harrison explains it, "On January 1, 1720, the price of a share of South Sea stock stood at £128. On June 24 it hit £1,050. In September came the crash. By December the stock had returned to £128. Thousands declared themselves ruined. Banks could not collect loans on inflated stock and failed. Specie was in short supply. Work stopped on half-built homes. Investigations and revenge ensued, and a long struggle to restore stability."

At once, the proponents of the scheme during its rise denounced the greed and recklessness as though they had been warning of it all along. The very newspapers whose breathless accounts of wealth creation had enabled the bubble just months earlier were now filled with accounts of despair and suicide as a result of the collapse.

The "celebrity" spokespeople and literati, whose help had been enlisted during the early stages, were now using the disaster as fodder for new material. The sharp-witted poet and humorist Alexander Pope had weighed in on "the damn'd South Sea" in verse. Meanwhile, Jonathan Swift, an early supporter and later satirist of the business, compared desperate traders in Exchange Alley with drowning victims whose souls depart as their bodies wash up on a South Sea shore:

> Subscribers here by thousands float,
> And jostle one another down,
> Each paddling in his leaky boat,
> And here they fish for gold, and drown.
> Now buried in the depths below,
> Now mounted up to heaven again,
> They reel and stagger to and fro,
> At their wits' end, like drunken men.
> Meantime, secure on Garraway cliffs,
> A savage race, by shipwrecks fed,
> Lie waiting for the foundered skiffs,
> And strip the bodies of the dead.

In one widely distributed print, *South Sea Scheme*, illustrator William Hogarth showed oblivious investors being led around in circles on a carousel, and the artist delighted in depicting stockjobbers and company officials as bound for an audience with the devil himself.

In the aftermath of manias, we frequently—with the benefit of hindsight—ask rhetorically, "How could people have been so foolish? What were they thinking?" This is easy to say in the aftermath, of course, but while the bubble is in its early stages, it is always based on some kernel of truth, some undercurrent of realism that will later be used to justify more and more excess. And with the siren song of riches being accumulated by others at every turn, staying above the fray becomes very difficult, even for the wisest among us.

In February 1720, Sir Isaac Newton bought into the South Sea bubble and was able to sell out his shares worth £7,000 a month later, with a tidy return of 100 percent on his original investment. He is said to have been very pleased—until hearing about more investors, including his friends, with subsequent returns on South Sea shares that were even better.

It is important to understand that at this time, Newton was perhaps the most brilliant man in all England and quite possibly the world. His scientific achievements were unrivaled during his day, and his influence on all future innovation and progress since cannot be overstated. It should also be understood that he was well versed in finance at this time, serving as England's Master of the Mint and one of the nation's foremost authorities on foreign coinage. In other words, he was what we would call today an "accredited investor" and certainly no dummy.

And yet despite this unparalleled combination of wisdom and experience, Sir Isaac Newton came to believe that his profit taking had been in error. So great was the public uproar over South Sea shares that he ended up buying back in. It was June 1720, and Newton's second lot of stock was purchased just weeks before the top at prices nearing £1,000 per share. Sure enough, the price began to collapse, and by the fall of that year, Newton had lost nearly his whole fortune of £20,000—millions in today's money.

We are all susceptible to some degree, and the media's role as exacerbator has been a constant, ever-present one since the dawn of the exchanges. Watching one of the great geniuses of human history succumb to the South Sea calamity reminds us that intellect and worldliness are not impregnable defenses against a mass delusion in full blossom.

Posterity records just a solitary quotation from Sir Isaac Newton pertaining to his losses in the affair, but it's a great one: "I can calculate the motion of heavenly bodies but not the madness of people."

CHAPTER 4

BEING RIGHT AND WRONG

A CONVERSATION WITH BEN STEIN

B en Stein wrote speeches for Nixon, prosecuted Wall Street fraud, worked as an economist, and has been a financial pundit. He's written for the *American Spectator,* Yahoo Finance, and the *New York Times,* and he is the author or coauthor of 30-odd books. He is at once arrogant, humble, and brilliant and also maddeningly unwilling to cede ground on certain points.

For all his teaching and experience, Stein's status as the closest thing in this book to being a pure pundit (as in "person paid specifically to offer his or her opinion") opens him up to criticism that's vicious even by the gladiatorial standards of pundit-on-pundit abuse.

The most frequently used cudgel for attacking Stein is his views of 2007 and 2008, when he underestimated the size and extent of the looming financial meltdown. He did so in print and on television in arguments that lacked either subtlety or, as it turned out, prescience. Plenty of people shared his views at the time. When stocks fall 50 percent, it's safe to say the majority of investors will be caught by surprise.

Personally, I think Ben Stein is brilliant. Better than that, he's got an opinion on everything and seems emotionally if not physically incapable of suppressing it regardless of the venue. For everything he's done, he's probably still most famous for playing Ferris Bueller's economics teacher in 1986. "Bueller . . . Bueller?" is still something people say to him on the street.

What most people don't know is that Stein ad-libbed a genuine economics lecture during the film when he took down the Hawley-Smoot Tariff of 1930. "Did it work? Anyone? Anyone? It did not work and the United States sank deeper into the Great Depression."

Anyone able to slip a lesson on free markets into a Hollywood teen comedy classic is good by me.

I spoke to Stein by phone on April 11, 2013.

MACKE: You've been in the spotlight, speaking, teaching, writing, and being a pundit for years. It's an unusual path. How did you get into punditry?

STEIN: I like the attention, so it's a certain amount of narcissism. I like the fact that it occasionally leads to paying gigs giving speeches. I like that. I have an awful lot to say. My little brain is running all the time, and I'm trying to analyze things and draw some conclusions all the time. That is the training that I got from my father, and also from being in law school.

At law school, you are presented with a set of facts, and you are told to try to analyze them, to try to fit them into some general intellectual framework, so they're compared and contrasted with other sets of facts. That is what I try to do, and I have a certain set of biases and prejudices, and I try to analyze what's going on in the world with reference to whether those things conform to my prejudices and biases, and if not, to try to change my prejudices and biases.

MACKE: You've taken a decent amount of heat for some of the things you've written, particularly during the financial crisis. Do you beat yourself up over mistakes?

STEIN: I don't do that; I really don't do that. I'm sorry—what I meant is I've made many mistakes. I told people that I didn't think the recession would last very long, and it lasted a long time, so I feel very bad about that. I think the general point I made that it wouldn't go on forever was true. In terms of financial punditry,

I didn't think the bank stocks would stay down anywhere near as long as they did, so I feel bad about that. I especially flagellate myself over when I told people that they needn't be as attentive to their savings or retirement as some told them. Because that was wrong, and probably they should be even more attentive than the strictest tell them. But otherwise, on public policy matters, I've been pretty good, and I don't flagellate myself on that.

If I feel I've caused people to lose money, I feel bad about that, but in terms of public policy issues, I almost never feel bad about that.

MACKE: But they don't pay us to go out there and pontificate, or do you get paid by making calls?

STEIN: Well, no, they don't pay us—first of all, I don't get paid when I'm on *The View*, and I don't get paid when I'm on any of these shows. I can't think of a single show I'm on except *CBS Sunday Morning* where I get paid.

MACKE: I meant "get paid" in the sense of winning. No money straight out, but you get invited back as a guest.

STEIN: I think I am paid to pontificate. I think I'm paid to give general moral preachment. I think, in a way, a pundit is a preacher, and a pundit is telling people not only what is politically right but what is morally right. I do think I'm paid to pontificate. I think that's part of the job of a pundit to say, "This course of action is not just wise but is morally correct."

MACKE: If we're preachers, we're preaching in a lousy part of town. On the finance side it's more financial than moral standards, but, wow, it's ugly!

STEIN: There are some moral issues involved. For example, a great deal of my work in my life has been management buyouts, and those are morally wrong. So when I write about that, that's not just a call about whether or not the stock price offered in the management buyout is a good price. It is a cry against a moral injustice, which is management trading on inside information, not disclosing relevant facts. Management buyouts are just general fraud. So that is a moral preachment. When I was writing about the Drexel Burnham Lambert junk bond scandal, that was not just a warning to people that the stocks and Drexel were all going to go into bankruptcy, which they pretty much did. But that what Drexel was doing was morally wrong. So there is definitely a moral content.

There's moral content today as well. I am a stock owner of Goldman Sachs, but I think a lot of what Goldman Sachs did during the meltdown in the fall of '08 was morally wrong, and the aftermath in '09 was morally wrong. It was a moral question.

MACKE: Goldman was scummy, but they got out of it more or less intact after AIG paid them off and the government kicked in.

STEIN: I don't think that Goldman Sachs's behavior in getting the government to bail out AIG first and foremost turned out to be, well it turned out to be great for the government because AIG recovered so much more than anyone thought it would, looked better than everyone thought bailing out AIG would work, but at the time it was pure selfishness on the part of Goldman Sachs. I think to the extent Goldman Sachs had control of the behavior of Secretary Paulson, which I don't think you ever leave that fraternity, bailing out AIG to Goldman's benefit but letting Lehman Brothers fail was morally extremely reprehensible.

MACKE: Do you think Hank Paulson bailed out Goldman specifically because he worked there, or did they save Goldman because it was smart to keep Goldman in place given the meltdown uncertainties?

STEIN: I don't think Hank Paulson is smart at all. I think he is a gangster. I don't think he is the slightest bit smart. I don't think Wall Street people in general are smart. I think that's one of the biggest myths in American lore that people on Wall Street are particularly smart. They're not particularly smart. They're tough, they're aggressive, they're greedy, they're often quick thinking, but I don't think they're particularly smart at all.

I've met lots and lots of these powers on Wall Street. The only one I ever thought was particularly smart was not on Wall Street but on Farnam Street in Omaha; that was Mr. Buffett.

They are not stupid, not like they're juvenile delinquents, stupid. They are not great geniuses like Warren Buffett. As far as I can tell, there's only one real genius that I've ever met in the world of investing, and that's Buffett, and I've met very smart people but they're not on Wall Street. People on Wall Street don't impress me as being particularly smart.

MACKE: It's backing up on more economically and trying to learn from history. Do we extrapolate too much from the lessons from the past, then make reforms to regulate behavior that no longer exists?

STEIN: No, I don't think we can ever learn too much from the past. There's one giant lesson from the past: don't try to be too specific and don't try to be too obsessed with what's happening day by day.

MACKE: Ben Bernanke is a historian, and he spent six years fighting the ghosts of the Great Depression. What do you think of the Bernanke tenure and the idea of the government getting involved in bailouts? Buying a global market index fund would have turned out much different, for better or worse, if the Fed had stayed out of the bailout business.

STEIN: If you're talking about Bernanke from the time he had a position in public policy, which is when he was chairman of the Council of Economic Advisers, his record has been dismal. Because he said there couldn't be a nationwide housing crash. He said it couldn't happen. He also said that there was no real retirement crisis and wouldn't be. Those two turned out to be disastrously wrong.

He also said that we didn't need to rescue Lehman Brothers, and that turned out to be wildly, disastrously wrong. I'm not a huge fan at all. I do think that keeping interest rates low and just flooding the economy with money was a good idea, but that was closing the barn door after the horses had escaped. It would have been incomparably better if he knew some history—he's supposed to be a great expert on the Depression—if he knew some history, and if he knew that no matter what, you don't allow a big bank to fail. Never allow it to happen.

Shoot the managers, but you don't allow the bank to fail. What's the benefit in letting it fail? There's no benefit at all . . . If you want to punish the people who brought the bank to ruin, fine. Take Richard Fuld [former CEO of Lehman Brothers] out and shoot him; that's fine with me. But don't let the bank fail.

MACKE: So the U.S. let Lehman fail and bailed out everyone else. Now we've had endless fiscal stimulus for the last five years and counting. How can it possibly be unwound delicately, especially in bonds?

STEIN: We can't get out of it delicately. There's no such thing as getting out of it delicately. Getting out of a bubble of this size doesn't exist as a historical phenomenon.

MACKE: Is that an argument for or against more financial education from economists and Wall Street–connected people on television? Neither group seems to have a clue.

STEIN: I find that a lot of the people that I interact with on television about investing are not at all useful or helpful to the investor. In fact, I would say very few of them are useful or helpful to the investor. It's an extremely rare person that is on CNBC that is saying anything useful to the investor. That's a very unusual phenomenon, and I don't see much of it on any TV show.

I have to say that every time I see anyone make a specific prediction about the future—that is, a specific arithmetic or mathematical prediction about the future—I shake my head because those predictions are useless. There's one guy whose predictions are incredibly useful; that's John Bogle.* That's one guy. He's the only one.

It's maddening to see how useless most of the advice given is for the ordinary investor.

MACKE: You're a smart guy working in a medium where most of the advice given is useless. How can anyone tell the difference?

---

* John Bogle is the founder and former CEO of the Vanguard Group. He is considered the father of index investing, promoting the idea that investors should buy baskets representing the broader stock markets as opposed to shares in individual companies.

Why continue to do this when it in a way promotes a damaging medium?

STEIN: I try not to make useless calls.

MACKE: Of course not, but everyone remembers the bad calls. That's true for everyone. They far outshine the helpful insight anyone dishes out over the year. Your bad calls get put on the front page, but you only get exonerated next to the obits.

STEIN: Well, that's a very good phrase, a well-taken point, and I have learned over the years to just give extremely general advice. And the general advice is, "Buy the indexes and hold on to them forever," and that advice has turned out to be extremely good advice. But it's the "forever" part that's a problem in human life.

People saying they could pick stocks, really, I think are doing a disservice to the viewers, and the people in the newsletters and the newspapers saying they can pick stocks are doing a disservice. And also people who tell you what the big boys are doing—and sort of implying that you should do what the big boys are doing—are not doing you a particularly useful service.

Though as I said, John Bogle did a good thing, and I try to repeat that information over and over and over again; and if even a couple of thousand people have picked it up over the many years of my doing it, then I feel great about it. And I try to repeat that information over.

When I made mistakes, as I did at the start of the financial crisis when I didn't think it could last as long as it did, you're right; I do flagellate myself. I feel bad about it. But I think that there is a particularly hot place waiting in hell for people pretending they can pick stocks.

MACKE: Right next to the people who book them to perform the service. There are really two kinds of pundits. One is like yourself, people who are trying to educate others. A whole different group of people are spouting off with what amounts to very thinly veiled sales pitches for their own books or newsletters. Not just an analyst or investor but guys who come on and make the same hollow predictions largely designed to support their own sales efforts. How do people tell the difference?

STEIN: Well, there are also people trying to get you to be the customers of their money management firms. There a lot of them out there. They're a particularly difficult group. I think particularly irresponsible. If I turn on CNBC and I see some person giving you a pick on a commodity or giving a pick on a bond or on bond interest rates, I just turn it off. It's just comical for people to pretend they can make useful picks in those regards. It's comical.

MACKE: Guys picking bad stocks is one category. A big step below them is the guys pitching sound bites designed largely to scare people into paying a few hundred bucks a month for insurance against being scared. The future's uncertain, and the end is always, permanently, near.

STEIN: Right, it is again irresponsible behavior and protected by their First Amendment rights. There is no doubt about that. But I think people who buy this propaganda get certain psychological satisfaction out of hearing the cries of doom and gloom, so maybe they do get the value.

MACKE: Most people underperform in the market in a big way. Is part of the appeal of the fear propaganda the natural effort to feel less dumb? If the game is all fake and rigged, it's easier to justify not doing better.

STEIN: Not only do most people underperform in the market, they underperform in the market by a great, great deal. When you have underwriters telling you to go in and out of the market or stock pickers telling you to go in or out of particular stocks, they're really not doing much good. I think the ones who are doom- and gloom-sayers probably do more good because they at least are providing some kind of amusement.

MACKE: It's funny, but not when people at home listen. For the past decade there's been a steady stream of people on TV pitching physical gold purchases as a "safe alternative" to cash. Meantime they're making huge, 5–10 percent, commissions and appealing to wildly unsophisticated viewers.

STEIN: Right. I think the people who are flogging gold, generally they are not doing anyone a favor, nor are people flogging the commodities like Jim Rogers. He is an astonishingly smart guy. Even he had trouble getting dates right, and he's the smartest of the smart.

MACKE: I met with him. I agree. Very smart man. The people who are most useful—and the people who tend to not get the biggest microphone and most time out there—are the ones who say "I don't know," the ones who are honest about not having an idea.

STEIN: The ones who say "I don't know" are the ones who say "Just buy the market." There's so much wisdom in the sentence "Just buy the market, and just hold on." It's just mind-boggling how much wisdom there is there. Or you can put yourself in the hands of the Wall Street wealth extraction machine, which just takes money out of your pocket by making you trade.

MACKE: But you wrote a book called *Yes, You Can Time the Market*.

STEIN: Yeah, and we were absolutely right. I wrote that with my friend Phil DeMuth. But we didn't mean timing the market over a period of days, weeks, or months. We said buy when the market is low. Buy when it's low compared with 20-year-long metrics. But just hold on then and don't sell it. When we said time the market, we meant when it's low compared to the 20-year average of the prices of earnings or the 20-year average share price–to–accounting book value or other metrics. And that has turned out to be such good advice. I'm astonished how good it's turned out to be. But we aren't talking about timing the market over short periods by any means. We're talking about literally decade-long periods. And I'm not talking about buying individual stocks using those metrics. I'm talking about buying the index of those metrics.

MACKE: Managers have huge, huge financial incentives to manipulate their accounting data. Accounting is every bit as much art as science. The banks could report almost anything they want. They could report an ampersand, and it would tell me as much as their earnings per share.

STEIN: Well, it's all artistry. I'll give you a very good example of this if I may respectfully do so. The banks hold enormous inventories of foreclosed homes. How do they report the value of those? They could report the value as in time they foreclosed, and then that will give them one value, or they could report the value as of April 11, 2013.

MACKE: When the tide went out in 2009, it turned out they had no idea where their books were, and their exposure to housing was horrific.

STEIN: But now it turns out that I think there is so much more value on the balance sheets than what banks are reporting. I think we are going to have an enormous wave of giant write-ups in the values of the bank assets. I will not speculate on that basis. I won't invest my hard-earned money on that basis, and I won't advise others to either. I would just say buy the index as if it is a big bank from the indexes; then they're the big bank from the indexes. But I'm not going to make investment decisions based on that. And people say you should. I think they are not doing a useful service.

There's just—as you said—too much artistry. This is a lot of artistry, in the accounting that is done on Wall Street. Everything is done in corporate reporting. But if you buy a large index, some of that artistry—which you could also call fraud—gets washed out. Not all of it, but some of it.

MACKE: You're an economist. That sounds harsh, but you freely admit to being one. My objection to economics as a student—probably because I was that good at it—was it seemed like it was just applying a lot of mathematical equations to human behavior.

STEIN: But if they're very, very simple mathematical formulas applied to very simple, basic human behavior, it makes sense. People will generally buy more of something if it costs less, and they generally will offer to sell more of it if it costs more. As long as you can find the formulas to rules of human life that are very basic, you're in fine shape.

MACKE: But we can't do easy things with economics. We can't do M2, which is the speed with which much money changes hands in the economy. We can't get people to spend money. Everyone's sitting on cash right now; we can't get them to use it. There's a certain amount of "We'll chase whatever shiny object will pay off the fastest" to our economic policies. It's hard to get the animal spirits moving when we want to move them. Is it not?

STEIN: Well, the animal spirits are starting to move. It's interesting — for four years we couldn't get the animal spirits to move at all in real estate. Now they're running wild. So at some point, they'll probably start running wild in other areas. Then the banks will be lending like mad, and then we'll be off to the races. But we don't know when that will be. We don't know what the scope of the movement will be. So what we might as well just do is buy the index and hold on.

MACKE: Do you think the economic cycle trumps all this yelling that people are doing at one another? Are managers like U.S. presidents in the sense that they just get way too much credit or blame for the environment at the time they serve?

STEIN: The economic cycle is sort of similar to a news cycle. There wouldn't be much room for people like you and me if people really followed the smart rule of just buying a market and holding on. There would be no need for CNBC. There would be no need for *Barron's*. There wouldn't be much need for any of us if people really did the smart thing. But there is some pretending that little bits of day-by-day information have great importance. And they don't!

MACKE: How does the audience miss that at home?

STEIN: Well, they're trying to get rich quick. Like some kind of primitive tribe in the mountains in New Guinea, they believe there's some magic, and they will learn the magic by watching the magicians on TV. There is no magic. It's just diversification and patience. There's no magic. But people have been brainwashed into believing there's some magic. I see these ads for various brokerages and financial houses. They say, "Stick with us, and through the magic of our highly trained researchers and our deep analysis, we'll help you get to your retirement goals." That's all nonsense. It's just buying the indexes and holding on for a long time. There's no magic.

MACKE: What do you make of these periodic bubbles, these manias? I had a hedge fund in the late '90s, which is largely why I get to do more fun things like talk to you on the phone, because it was a great time to be a hedge fund manager. It was a manic time, but most people knew it wasn't permanent. No one was under the impression that it was going to end well. The housing market was the same way. Most people flipping houses had a decent hunch it wasn't sustainable. It didn't matter. Half the people who survived day trading got killed by house flipping. We never learn anything. Do you play along with this? Bubbles don't, but if people thought they were in a bubble, they wouldn't participate so long, and they wouldn't hang out. What are people missing over and over?

STEIN: People are always missing history. We are endlessly missing history. History tells us that there are no bargains; there are no free lunches in the bond market. History tells us that bubbles don't go up forever. History tells us the directions of the stock market forever. History tells us we have to be patient, but that contradicts the idea of getting rich quick, which also has a great deal of appeal.

If you just had a channel that had a scroll going down the screen that said, "Buy the index and hold on," that would be much more useful than all the shows on CNBC put together.

MACKE: But it wouldn't make you $400 million a year the way the network does.

STEIN: It wouldn't make any money. I mean, when CNBC has some bells ringing and bright graphics on the screen and says we're about to tell you something of great importance, you might as well just turn off the TV.

I've looked that up on my own 68-year-old life, and I try to generalize from my experiences. And generally when I have bought individual stocks in any concentration whatsoever, it has not worked out well. There have been exceptions . . . but not many.

CHAPTER 5

THE *SINGLE MOST IMPORTANT TRAIT*

Who is worth listening to?

The open space and cost-free economics of web publishing have opened up the floodgates of opinion in ways the more expensive-to-create media of television, newspapers, and magazines never could have. The upside of this is that, like on *American Idol*, true stars can be discovered through new channels that are unpoliced by the establishment media apparatus. The downside is that you've got to wade through a sea of untalented amateurs to find your Kelly Clarkson.

The meritocracy of the modern media eventually pushes the cream to the top, but this process takes time. And while the cauldron boils away, all sorts of noxious odors and imperfections in the mix come periodically bubbling to the surface.

Most people think that experience is the single most important thing that a pundit can bring to the table. There is some validity to this. What good is an opinion if it hasn't been seasoned a bit, battle-hardened and galvanized in the crucible of real life and real markets? Can any of us truly profess to have fully formed, postadolescent views on the topic of investing and business with only a few years' worth of experience? Without at least a decade of professional money management, securities analysis, trading, asset allocation, banking, investigative journalism, paid economics work, or some combination of these, one's unqualified opinions are probably best kept away from the public sphere. This is for everyone's good, both that of the speakers (lest they embarrass themselves) and that of the intended audience members (lest they lose all their money listening to the wrong pundit).

And while a lot of people have had experience, that doesn't automatically make their opinions worthwhile. Because sometimes with experience comes arrogance, haughtiness, or rigidity. "This is the way we always used to do it so this is the way we shall do it forevermore." Unfortunately, while the inherent fear and greed dynamics in investing never change, markets, companies, and technologies do. Trends persist and then evaporate; institutions and ideas rise and fall. Not every guy or gal with a smart opinion today will be relevant for whatever is to come.

Intelligence is important too, but not nearly as important as one would think. Even the smartest pundits in print and on air are almost always wrong, despite how well they present themselves. In fact, this is one of the hardest things about interpreting what you hear in the media for your investment purposes—"smart" does not equal "correct," and it never has. This is not to say that we should hope for dummies to come out and share their thoughts, but once a certain level of intelligence is reached, it will avail them not at all in the arena of market commentary. They're all smart people to have made it that far.

And as for honesty, sure, bring it on. But this is a virtue to be appreciated in the real world; it will not change a fallacious opinion into a meaningful one if the speaker of said opinion is unaware of his error.

No, a worthwhile market observer's or commentator's most important trait is not experience, or intelligence, or even honesty.

Rather, it is *humility*: a willingness—*an expectation*—that future events can and will deviate from even the most rigorous thesis, and an acceptance that the markets exist to make fools out of even the best of us. Humility is perhaps the most important trait, and, concurrently, it is the most lacking characteristic among the financial commentariat.

Cliff Asness, the founder of hedge fund AQR, once said, "Seriously, anyone, quant or not, with a shred of intellectual honesty recognizes that there is some chance their historical success is just luck." If only more of us would say this aloud and live as though it were an elemental truth.

The more predictions one makes, the more opportunities there are to be incorrect. The disingenuous pundit conveniently forgets (or wills others to forget) this statistical reality when he beats his chest in the afterglow of a winning call. But over time, this sort of duplicity becomes apparent to the public, and a backlash is the unavoidable result. The line between pundit and punch line has grown impossibly thin in the digital age, as one's previous opinions are all just a click away.

By displaying humility, the market seer cushions his or her fall from grace when the inevitable occurs.

"Kid, you're on a roll," Lou Mannheim tells the young hotshot Bud Fox in *Wall Street*. "Enjoy it while it lasts because it never does."

CHAPTER 6

TOUGH GIG

A CONVERSATION WITH KAREN FINERMAN

Karen Finerman was the first female investor to enter the snake pit of nightly punditry in financial television. None of the rest of the cast of *Fast Money* knew how she really got there. We just showed up one night to find Karen sitting in the middle of frenzied stylists, producers, and lackeys. She was reading financial reports while they were laser-focused on making her a basic cable version of bimbo hot.

It was dehumanizing, as if she were prize livestock before a 4-H contest at the state fair, particularly insulting since Karen was already pretty and no one asks a pig at the state fair for stock ideas.

Karen isn't a trader, a loudmouth, or the kind of female investment banker who tries to overcompensate for perceived shortcomings. She's a successful value investor, the founder, owner, and head of Metropolitan Capital for the past 15 years, and a classy woman from an absurdly overachieving family.

Our conversation took place in May 2013 at the legendary Algonquin Hotel, home to the famous Round Table of pundits and professional wits of the 1920s. We settled into the weathered red-leather and mahogany lounge. We talked for an hour before I started recording. It was a good, deep, funny conversation. I told her my stuff, and she brought me up to date on hers. The time went fast.

MACKE: So, let's start at the very start of your punditry career in 2007. You hadn't done a lot of hits before you came on full-time, right?

FINERMAN: Zero. No TV experience.

MACKE: And so all of a sudden you're there, and the producers did you the great favor of just putting you there and saying, "Hi, this is Karen. She's going to be on your show."

FINERMAN: Yeah, and I had no TV experience or desire or anything.

MACKE: Where did they dig you up? How did you end up on the show?

FINERMAN: I'd never heard of the show; like I said, no TV experience, desire, anything. There was an article, "Women on Wall Street." Someone saw it and said, "Hey, why don't we get this girl to come in?" I think during a hunt for women, that came across their desk, and they found it and said, "All right, why don't you come in and do a screen test?"

MACKE: They didn't exactly debrief us. One day Karen was in the green room; that was our debriefing. "This is Karen. You've done one segment that you did, and now she's a regular."

FINERMAN: No, no, no, no, and I thought . . . Wow, that's ridiculous.

MACKE: And there were no women trading stocks on TV regularly at the time.

FINERMAN: No women anywhere. It was Dylan—the average height and weight of the guys at that desk was overwhelming. They were four big guys. You, Dylan, Pete, and Guy.

MACKE: And no small personalities in the bunch. And there you were, thrown into that group with the producers were endlessly primping you for weeks.

FINERMAN: Endless primping.

MACKE: They were clearly just sucking your blood at first. You were tough and good looking, so, "Let's try a woman."

FINERMAN: And I think, yeah, that's why they chose me even though my style is so the antithesis of what *Fast Money* is all about—trading in and out.

MACKE: It was about trading, and they were still hyping it. They were still hyping the regulars . . . "The Fabulous Four." It was all testosterone.

FINERMAN: I mean, it was when they talk about, what's the show? The show is *SportsCenter* on Wall Street, and I don't know that there are many women on *SportsCenter* (at first). Maybe there are now; there weren't then. It was intimidating, I have to say. You guys are big personalities with some comfort level with the medium, with the format, and with each other. And you were really good at it and really good at good TV. I learned there's a big difference between trying to be intelligent and making good TV. The two can have no overlap, and that was news to me. And I didn't realize that sort of tension is a good thing on TV—the disagreements, the little bit of telling each other, "You're an idiot," but not explicitly.

MACKE: But that was different. That's a tough vibe to get between a man and woman, and particularly if they're putting you in tight sweaters and they're feminizing you. For me to take shots at a woman makes me feel like Ike Turner. I was thinking, "I'm not going to disagree with Karen," and they'd be in my ear shouting, "Take her down!" while I'm thinking, "Forget that" [laughter].

FINERMAN: That's funny. I didn't know that, but it doesn't surprise me to hear it. Take her down. It makes sense, and I remember several disagreements you and I had, and to be honest, the ones I remember I'm pretty sure you were always right.

MACKE: But I was probably a jerk about it, too.

FINERMAN: Maybe, but that's your thing. That's what you're good at. And interestingly, and I think ironically and counterintuitively, the more that I grew to appreciate that, the less heated the exchanges would be because I so appreciated your wit, your style, and . . .

MACKE: But I didn't know how to deal with arguing with a female on air. Pete came on, and I told him, "I'm going to throw something heavy at you." If the show's boring, I'm just going to say something mean to Pete. And that worked, because he's a big meathead but really smart. But I overshot it in terms of arguing with you, and that's not the same as overshooting it with Pete.

FINERMAN: I don't think of it that way — that's interesting, of you overshooting it with me.

MACKE: I thought it looked bad. I'm someone who holds the door for women. It's just not natural for me to say things like I would to Pete. I'll call him a meathead. I would never call a woman a meathead; even if she was, I wouldn't.

FINERMAN: Yeah, it's not good form. That's interesting. What do you think they were looking for in the interaction?

MACKE: God, who knows? I think they just figured it was *Fast Money* and so it was particularly cutthroat. I never looked at it that way because I routinely cut men's throats on any show and never thought twice about it. "Look at that; I cut his throat."

FINERMAN: I think that show probably did need a woman because of the four big guys, and then to have a fifth big guy . . .

MACKE: Oh yeah, just preposterous, and that's still a problem. You can't just have guys sitting there all rigid at a desk yelling at one another. I think that they brought you in because they figured you could handle it, and they figured you were good, and then they threw you straight into the deep end of the deepest, hardest pool.

FINERMAN: I had a tough time in the first month.

MACKE: How could you not? That's an insanely bad position for you.

FINERMAN: Yeah, I think also I didn't realize how steep the learning curve would be. You know the game. I used to way over-prepare for every segment and have the exact sentence I was going to say all fully laid out, and either you don't have the time or you don't get to it, or the conversation goes a different way, and you learn quickly how to wing it.

MACKE: And that winging it is much better.

FINERMAN: Infinitely better, and takes less time, but I didn't know that at the beginning. I also didn't know that you could learn—let's say they come to you with a topic you really don't know anything about—how to punt in a way that doesn't reveal that, and get the ball out of your court. But you learn that you can do that; you don't need to always have what you think is a smart answer.

MACKE: When I get confused I usually go with the ad hominem attack on someone else [laughter].

FINERMAN: Okay, I should have done that.

MACKE: But they want you to have an answer for everything.

FINERMAN: That's the thing about TV. They want people who have really strong opinions.

MACKE: Who would tune in to watch televised *Barron's*? "Five transports you need to own now." "Some blue chip you need to sell."

FINERMAN: I didn't get that at all. I thought, "Oh, they need *thoughtful, subtle, nuanced*"—in fact, that's horrible TV. I'd say things like, "Well, you might do this, but that could go wrong." I would see men on TV, because they were almost all men, who'd say, "The market's doing this!" with this certainty. I was thinking, "How do they know? How do they know and say it with such certainty?" They don't, but you've got to say it with certainty or believe it anyway to make good TV.

MACKE: I approached punditry right from the start like, "I'm just going to kill whomever I'm arguing against." Right, just straight from the jump. Before *Fast Money* I'd do hits with Dylan. And I would argue either side of any topic except stock picks. I truly didn't care; I was just going to out-argue the opponent, and that's why they brought me out. They brought me out over and over, and that's what they liked.

FINERMAN: That's what you're really good at. You are; I always say Melissa Lee is biologically built to be an anchor. She has hair follicles that you can pull on, blow-dry, curl for hours. She can do that; it doesn't hurt. She has the ability to sit still for a month while they style her. She can do it, and you have that same genetic disposition to be snarky, which is what they want.

MACKE: Oh yeah, my snark game is good. You can't fake that talent; it has to be natural. It's not an accomplishment. I'm not bragging. I say, "I have snark game" the way I would say, "I'm 6'1." I'm built for it, but you're not like that. How did you fit? How did you make yourself fit? Because you ended up fitting, and you weren't of the mold.

FINERMAN: I know, and I hate conflict, and I never want to say anyone else is stupid. I am sort of biologically opposed to making good TV. I don't want to hurt anyone's feelings; I try to be measured, I try not to get too emotional.

MACKE: You run real money too. When you do that, you know there are 10,000 stocks, the vast majority of them people shouldn't even consider. You're just better off. And of the remaining stocks, maybe about 20 of them are buys. You went straight into a place where you're supposed to give opinions right away on everything. Anything could come up.

FINERMAN: I would argue, "Well I don't know anything about XYZ Corp." You know what? That doesn't matter. I felt a little bit like Dustin Hoffman in *Tootsie* when he gets some role in a commercial as a tomato or something, and he's like, "But I'm not being true to the character," and they're like, "Forget it; you're a tomato."

MACKE: But you know a lot more than a tomato. You were actually trying to say smart things financially. You're trying to help people; you like the TV side of it, but you're not trying to get people killed, which is why you don't want to say "buy" or "sell" on everything.

FINERMAN: Yes. I think I had a lot invested in showing people that I was smart, whether that's an insecurity of mine or whatever, or maybe it's relative to you guys who had this easy way about you, to convey to you, "All right, I'm smart and I deserve to be here."

MACKE: But why did you want to be there?

FINERMAN: It was fun. We had some fun.

MACKE: We had a great time, but you didn't know you were going to have fun up front, and it wasn't fun for you for a while; it didn't start fun. They primped you like one of the dogs at the dog show. Then you'd get ripped on the Internet for being something you weren't.

FINERMAN: Dylan was helpful. I was on the show for maybe a month, and I had been looking at Yahoo comments, or I think it was Yahoo, and reading the comments, and they hated me; they absolutely hated me. And I said, "Dylan, I'm just getting massacred here; they hate me," and he said, "Don't read it. Just don't read it; don't focus on it." And that was really helpful because—

MACKE: You still know the abuse is out there.

FINERMAN: You know it's out there. I used to read it and take each thing personally, and that is a big mistake. Because you are putting yourself out there, and the thing is, that I also didn't realize, is that you put yourself out there and you remember your calls—and you remember every one of your calls—and you have this assumption that everyone else remembers, too, but they don't, for better or for worse.

MACKE: Oh, it's entirely for worse, because if you make a good call, it's their idea, and if you make a bad call. . . .

FINERMAN: And if you make a bad call, it's all on you.

MACKE: If you're wrong the audience blames it on you and never forgets the mistake.

FINERMAN: That's true; that's true. I guess for me, I took myself more seriously than I should have, and that was a mistake.

MACKE: But you still take the job seriously; you've just adjusted how you take it seriously. It's showbizzy, but you have to be smart within that construct of a show. We were all trying to make good picks within the construct of TV being a showbizzy thing.

FINERMAN: Right, and those two things are often at odds with one another. This notion of what makes good TV is something I come back to again and again.

MACKE: Doesn't it matter, distilling something that is smart and trying to get to the bottom of it?

FINERMAN: Yes, that's a good point. I think that's it, too; if you can try and explain something in a way that people have never thought about but in a way they can relate to, it doesn't need to be so wonky, then that's a benefit.

MACKE: But then you worry about dumbing it down. By implication, obviously just in the term itself—you're calling the audience dumb. It's not like you're trying to insult people at home; you're trying to respect the audience at the same time as you're trying to explain something complicated in three words.

FINERMAN: Even now while I give you that description, I wonder, is that too wonky? Do you lose people? I don't know.

MACKE: And if you lose people, you know they're just going to do something reckless that a more TV-friendly pundit suggests.

FINERMAN: Right, someone's going to do it, and I remember somebody saying to me, "Why are you doing this? You have a good business. Why are you doing this?" Two reasons, it was fun. I love the camaraderie, and I love being on a team. It was really fun, and if some other woman was up there and it wasn't me and I had the chance to be the first, I wouldn't be able to live with that. Why would I pass that up?

MACKE: But when you get the chance to take something really confusing and scary and explain it in a way people understand, it's good.

FINERMAN: When it's good, it's good.

MACKE: The best shows were always really intellectually high-powered. We had to be smart or we'd be screwed. *Fast Money* was *the* show of the financial meltdown; I was really proud of that. I think we did a great job helping people with that, considering the conditions that we had.

FINERMAN: When you think about that meltdown, it's odd that it was dramatic and yet has faded already for me. The idea of, there would be major news every night, and some of it I didn't get in the context . . . that is, how, wow, the politicians and bankers do not have a handle on the business, and it's spinning out of control.

MACKE: Way the hell out of control.

FINERMAN: Yes, way the hell out of control, and that was fascinating. It makes for great TV that there are these events that people are trying to put into context at a time when the world is really unraveling.

MACKE: But there is no context. It was all new stuff. It was exhilarating, but it was maddening, because you couldn't help the audience.

FINERMAN: Yes, remember when there was that woman waiting outside the studio, "I lost $600,000." And just to feel like, "Oh my God, that was her life savings . . ."

MACKE: Bought it the whole way down, because, boy, if you like it at $30, you must love it at $20 or $15.

FINERMAN: And then the overlay of seeing our government have these ridiculous hearings where it was so clear they had no clue.

MACKE: And then people come to us and need help. That woman outside the studio, people would just need help. Or they'd blame me. I'd be negative, and people would think the meltdown was my fault.

FINERMAN: If you weren't talking, then the market would all be fine.

MACKE: Is it harder to take it seriously after the crash ended? It seems like the stakes are so much lower. They matter to people, but it's a whole adjustment.

FINERMAN: You kind of feel like who's going to be there to listen after people having been so burned.

MACKE: Part of what was hard about it then and in general is that you know you're not going to be able to help most viewers. The market is really, really, really, really hard to beat, and so working from that, if you work all day every day it's hard to beat, to keep up with; the people who trade as a hobby get nuked, and the people who do it as a hobby are the ones who watch the pundits.

FINERMAN: I do feel a sense of responsibility. I hate the idea of losing someone else's money. I can deal with losing my own money, but I hate losing money for someone else, and you do put yourself out there, and you do take a little bit of that. You probably remember a bad call you made and feel bad about that.

MACKE: That's never happened to me, but I've seen yours.

FINERMAN: Yeah, I know; there's a lot to choose from.

MACKE: Where does your responsibility end? It's almost this moral hazard, which is way overstating it, but if you're out there punditing . . .

FINERMAN: If you're out there punditing, you realize people want to be led; they really want to be led.

MACKE: But they're also selectively picking where they want to be led towards a conclusion they've already made. They want you to agree with them.

FINERMAN: They want to be led into what they believe is right. If you're a long Apple and you hear a pundit say, "Apple's completely underpriced here," they think, "Oh, she's a genius."

MACKE: With that type of viewer bias, do you feel like you have the power to influence people without just telling them what they want to hear?

FINERMAN: No, not really, actually. I think the fundamental question about punditry, I think, is it entertainment, or is it designed to actually help people? I don't know what the design is. I know what you think the responsibility is, which is to really try to educate people. Not even so much help them make money—it's more help them not to blow themselves up.

I'm curious if you find this, too—that you remember the haters; it resonates a lot more with you than the people who say, "Oh, you gave me a good call on XYZ. Thanks, Jeff."

MACKE: I have people who have told me I saved their life during the crisis . . .

FINERMAN: Really?

MACKE: Yup. And I ignore it and just want to go and pick a fight with someone who is giving me a hard time. It's like, "That's good, thanks. I'm glad you're okay." Now screw that other guy . . .

FINERMAN: Yes, it weighs so much more heavily on you.

MACKE: But not every pundit takes it so responsibly.

FINERMAN: Really? Okay, maybe I shouldn't care . . .

MACKE: I don't know what the motives are of the next generation of people in the chairs. If you think of someone who was watching—if you were like a little baby pundit, if you were 28 years old, watching those broadcasts of the meltdown—that was fun. It looked fun; it was fun . . .

FINERMAN: To be a pundit you mean?

MACKE: To be a pundit at that time. Presidents want to be presidents during war, weathermen want to broadcast a nor'easter ripping up the East Coast, and pundits want to talk during the meltdown. We were clearly having a good time . . .

FINERMAN: Right, and this was the greatest meltdown in the history of the financial world.

MACKE: Then the government stepped in and changed all the rules, and the crash stopped. And no one ever went to prison. Don't you feel like you're talking about a rigged game? To a degree it's a confidence game.

FINERMAN: In the market?

MACKE: In the market in general. I think that it is skewed . . . the big guy is going to win.

FINERMAN: I believe that, absolutely.

MACKE: And the little guy is going to get killed.

FINERMAN: And the little guy's going to get killed. I think Herbalife was a great example of that, and you have these two guys—I don't know if it's just ego or what—but the Icahn-Ackman fight. That was some great TV.

MACKE: That was amazing TV, that was beautiful TV, but trading off that would crush people at home. You know Carl, I know Carl; you know him better than I do. I think he's great. But the truth is if he didn't have multibillions of dollars, he would have just been a dude yelling at his TV about what an idiot Ackman was, setting himself up to get squeezed that way. Instead Carl called in and attacked.

FINERMAN: I know that he got on the phone, and it was amazing. So to me the math for Carl is, do I die with $14 billion, or do I die with $11 billion and having really jammed Bill Ackman—maybe $11 billion is okay.

MACKE: Yeah, and Herbalife to Carl is just a cudgel with which he smites his enemies. Carl seems to think, "What does Herbalife make? Clubs, I think. I think they make clubs, because that's what I'm doing with it." But people at home don't know that game is happening.

FINERMAN: The little guy's going to get in the middle of that.

MACKE: And you know that, and you're kind of part of the process. You know these guys and how they work. You and I look at them; we know exactly what Carl's doing. He's just got a spite thing going with Bill so he's going to kill someone he hates. It was extreme, but that's kind of what the hedge funds have become; it's like showbiz now.

When I ran a hedge fund I wouldn't go to a conference and make a PowerPoint slide presentation on my position. Screw you—that's my special sauce. I wouldn't show that stuff to investors. I would just be like, "Oh, it's a magic thing."

FINERMAN: Right, I'm running my magic box here. But I think it's a different game now; it's all about asset gathering, and to do that, the higher the profile, the more asset gathering you can do, I think.

MACKE: If you're a TV producer and you don't put the Carl *v.* Bill fight on air, you just need a different line of work, and so it has to be there. It's fascinating, and it's fantastic, and it's amusing to you and me because we're not going to touch that with a 10-foot pole, but people are. I keep coming back to the *Catcher in the Rye*, where it's like you're just trying to protect the little kids from falling off into the thing.

FINERMAN: And yeah, they don't know that you can or can't, but I do remember the ones that tell me they sell; I remember that. But I did underestimate how fun it is, though. And when we had shows where really stuff was happening and we had some good things to say—that's exciting; that's invigorating. Even if that was '08 and it was an awful day for me at the fund, to just switch gears and have a totally different experience—it was the ultimate emotional hedge in a way; viewership skyrocketed.

MACKE: But do you think we've created this adrenaline junkie, because that's what I mean: "the next wave," the people who are watching the pundits on *Fast Money* now have escalated the theatrics, and now it seems like these people always act like they're broadcasting the apocalypse.

FINERMAN: Because that's what you have to do.

MACKE: You have to, from a media perspective; that's what their job is. We put big splashy headlines up front involving human tragedy, because that sells papers and that is what your work is.

FINERMAN: I think the media created the Facebook debacle of the most hyped road show of all time just to pander to viewers. Groupies just descending on the Suburban that Mark Zuckerberg was in . . .

MACKE: But I broadcast it, you broadcast it, and it's this helpless feeling, because I'm sitting there ripping it in a broadcast, but people are still watching me broadcast it. You're kind of giving it that sheen just by the fact that you're spending the time to make fun of it.

FINERMAN: Right, right, so it is news. I think it does seem that the attention span of the investor has gotten shorter and shorter and shorter, which I can't help but think is somehow related to financial news and the stories always being like, "Boom, this is big, this is big, now it's big the other way."

MACKE: It's our fault, Karen [laughter].

FINERMAN: Okay, maybe it's not our fault, but come on, there's something there, right?

MACKE: But there aren't enough disclaimers in the world to both broadcast it and stop people from jumping on board. We can scream, "Don't do this trade; we want the pick to be a starting point!" Doesn't seem to matter.

FINERMAN: What do you think—when I think of punditry, Cramer of course comes to mind.

MACKE: He's the godfather.

FINERMAN: I don't know how he's been able to do it with that energy for this many years. I don't know. What do you think it's about?

MACKE: I think he started wanting to save people. I think that he's passionate about markets and he's very fired up on it. And I think it's something he slips on; that's his job. And I think he just looks for twists on it and he's trying to help people. I think he gets a bum rap, but I think a lot of that is the structure of what the show is.

FINERMAN: Right, it's a lot of theatrics and all the noise and whatever.

MACKE: Yeah, and he's created a lot of this, but he's a really smart guy.

FINERMAN: I believe that, too; he's a really smart guy, no doubt, no doubt. He's a really smart guy with a voluminous amount of company knowledge.

MACKE: Oh, it's just crazy, yeah.

FINERMAN: The breadth of what he knows, yeah.

MACKE: I compare him to someone like Jim Rogers who ran Quantum and lived, breathed, ate it, wound it down, then decided he was going to motorcycle across Asia and stuff. He's still in tune with the markets, but it's not this daily obsession. I don't think Jim ever gave up the obsession, and I'd guess *Mad Money* is his outlet. Instead of running a fund, this is what he does. But I don't know the answer. That's why I want to ask him. He still loves it. I burnt out fast. How do you not burn out?

FINERMAN: What burned you out? What do you think?

MACKE: I think that, after the financial meltdown, after all the howling . . . I was the one wailing at people. That became my role because I was genuinely afraid for them. When the crisis ended, I didn't have anything to warn people about anymore, and there just wasn't a great transition by me. It kind of revved up and up, and then by April 2009 the meltdown clearly wasn't getting worse anymore. It was clearly jerry-rigged and obviously, nakedly, openly a rigged game.

FINERMAN: GM wasn't going to disappear, and Citigroup was not going under regardless of how under it really was.

MACKE: Right. Then there's no place to go with my "thing," and so I just wanted out; I just needed to be gone for a while.

FINERMAN: Did you miss it?

MACKE: No.

FINERMAN: After how long? No, you didn't miss it at all?

MACKE: Not at first. I almost came back because I felt like I just wanted to prove to myself, just to show that I could. After *Car People*, I wanted to prove I wasn't crazy or on drugs like everyone was saying; at least not on drugs. . . . Hey! This is your interview. We're talking about you. Not me. How much of what you're doing is a "prove-it" thing? How much of it is just you wanting to prove yourself, to both you and other people?

FINERMAN: Yeah, there's some of that, and particularly my mother for me. Nobody cared about the show like my mother. We used to air at seven and nine. She would watch both.

MACKE: Your mom was great; I loved her.

FINERMAN: Thank you; she was our biggest fan, and I'd get a commentary on my hair every day. I've got to tell you, I think there is an energy and excitement at CNBC whenever I go there, which is very rarely, of the idea of making news, and it sounds hokey, but there's an energy and excitement there of activity, and I'm not even sure, I don't know if the agenda's so clearly laid out that way, to educate people. I don't know that that's the agenda.

MACKE: I think that desire to help is what the pundit has to bring to the party, because no newsroom kid, no journalism major who's 24 years old and just hanging on to this job, they're not going to know anything about the market.

FINERMAN: And have no context and—

MACKE: And nor should they; it's not their job to. Their job is to put on a TV show that people watch.

FINERMAN: But I feel like the CNBC mandate is maybe we need to make ourselves—what's the opposite of expendable? Necessary. You need to be informed. Now I don't know why, why do you really need to be informed about every tick? Do you need to be informed about Apple every percent that it moves up and down? It seems like a lot because it's integers.

MACKE: Are most people better off not ever seeing it?

FINERMAN: Yes, you're better off not. You don't make better decisions because some parts supplier maybe thought they reported something down … blah, blah. You're maybe better off—not maybe; likely you're better off not seeing it. How can it matter every day, all the time, everything, every piece of information? Just by definition every single thing can't be that weighty.

MACKE: But we're regulars when you're a one-off pundit person, you can go to a producer and say, "I've got something to talk about."

You're on *Fast* at 5:00 and it's got to matter somehow. You can't show up and shrug.

FINERMAN: I didn't get that when a guy would come on with a really out-there theory, opinion, price target, whatever, that this was for him a really cheap call on making a career, right? Who's going to remember if he's wrong? He'll just be in the dustbin of pundits who blew it, but if he got it right, he could make a career off that.

MACKE: And particularly if it's bullish; there's a skew to bullish because the audience wants to hear a scold, and the majority of the time the market's going higher.

And so if you're wrong with a huge call it doesn't matter. Just come with a $2,000 price tag, because you'll be the guy who called that.

FINERMAN: Exactly right. Yes, otherwise, "Ah, we're sort of in line with consensus." That's not a guest you're going to have back.

MACKE: But is the machine broken? The machine exists. If you want headlines, you make an extreme call. If you make that call, viewers are going to use it to make bad decisions. Who can come in from the outside, as a pundit, and be a check on that process? You know if it's not you, it's going to be someone else less bright . . .

FINERMAN: I want to be the person; I don't want there to be someone else. To be honest, it's because I want to save investors from themselves. It's somewhat driven by my own interests; I get a kick out of saving viewers. It's fun. That's going to sound terrible.

MACKE: I've got your back. How could it not be fun to be relied on that way?

FINERMAN: It is fun.

MACKE: You always picture somebody someplace who did something nice with your call. Because of your idea they did their own research, came to the same conclusion as you, and were able to send their kid to college because of something you said. Which may not happen.

FINERMAN: That is nice to think about, but I don't know that it happens.

MACKE: Do you watch the show when you're not on it?

FINERMAN: I never watch the show. Never watch the show.

MACKE: Now that'll sound bad.

FINERMAN: Yeah, that will sound bad.

MACKE: When will you have proved your point on TV? When will you have been satisfied that you've climbed your personal media mountain? Because it's not like you want to go anchor *Good Morning America*.

FINERMAN: No, but you know, that is a good question. When will I have proved my point? I don't know. Probably I only will know after.

I do feel a responsibility to women, and I actually felt like that was an important role for me, to create the TV persona anyway of a woman who is capable and can be where the boys are and can. . . .

MACKE: Hold your own and then some.

FINERMAN: Yes, better said than I can. Hold my own and then some. I really feel like that was an important part of why I wanted to do it, and I get a lot of satisfaction from that feedback from women, not as much as the negative from the people who tell me to count tomatoes, but that's life.

MACKE: You did do that. You did that.

FINERMAN: I feel like I did do that.

MACKE: They threw you into a deeply weird testosterone-filled situation, and you didn't bimbo it up; you didn't fall back on any crutch. You just sat there and fought with the meritocracy, the mad men. I've always admired that. I've had a huge amount of respect for that.

FINERMAN: Thank you.

CHAPTER 7

THE MAN WHO MOVED MARKETS

> *There are clear lines separating those who
> swear by him and those who swear at him.*
> **—LOUIS RUKEYSER ON JOE GRANVILLE**

I t is late in the evening on January 6, 1981, and telephones all over the country are starting to ring. Thirty employees of a Florida-based stock market newsletter business are making outgoing calls to deliver a very simple, yet ominous, message to a few thousand subscribers across the nation:

> This is a Granville Early Warning. Sell everything. Market top
> has been reached. Go short on stocks having sharpest advances
> since April. *Click.*

Early the next morning, just after the opening bell of trade rings on the New York Stock Exchange, the market gaps lower and sell orders continue to flood into the trading floor. The Dow drops a total of 24 points that day, or 2.5 percent, on historic volume of more than 93 million shares traded, more than double the daily average. The Dow then proceeds to drop another 1.5 percent the next day; a five-week sell-off is soon under way. Traders and business news reporters are pointing toward Joe Granville to explain

69

the sudden, sharp drop in the stock market, and Granville is more than happy to be pointed *at*.

He tells a news camera from behind his desk in a Daytona Beach suburb that "the market told me, '*Sell*.' And we do what the market tells us to; we never hedge. Only losers hedge." Granville's controversial "Sell everything" call had made instant history, and the debate over prescience versus self-fulfilling prophecy would rage as the losses of the week were tabulated all over America.

It was not the first time that "Calamity Joe" had influenced the price and direction of the market. On April 22, 1980, Granville told his subscribers that he was switching from short to long. Within hours, the Dow had rallied by more than 30 points, an intraday jump of over 4 percent for the U.S. stock market on no other news besides Joe's bullishness.

To market observers of the time, it was both mystifying and terrifying—the age of the market-moving pundit had officially begun.

THE SECRET OF PUNDITRY

How was it possible that one "expert" out of so many could have this much power over the entire U.S. stock market—enough clout to literally *will* crashes and rallies into being with a few words? It certainly wasn't the length of his track record, as Granville's buy and sell calls had performed terribly throughout the secular bear market of the late 1960s and 1970s. Nor could it have been the size of his audience; he had just a thousand or so paying subscribers in the early days, nowhere near the 90,000 people receiving the *Value Line Investment Survey* or the *Merrill Lynch Market Letter*.

No, what Joe Granville had lacked in breadth and depth, he made up for with sheer personality and moxie. He had figured out the secret of all punditry, market or otherwise: certitude.

Granville had made a name for himself and rose above the legions of goldbug letters from would-be stock wizards by saying exactly what he thought at the top of his lungs. There was no hesitation and no waffling. He derided Wall Street's traditional securities analysts as "bag holders" and referred to the *Wall Street Journal* as "The Bagholders' News." His nickname for Louis Rukeyser was

"Crab Louie," and he referred to Alan Greenspan as a "bespectacled prune." In contrast to the buy-and-hold "losers," Joe Granville gave subscribers specific instructions to go 100 percent long stocks or sell the market short with all their money. This was certitude writ large; he frequently made predictions for market moves greater than 10 percent in either direction.

The secret to Joe's influence and rapid rise to the top of market punditry was the absolute resolution with which he foretold the future. It should come as no surprise that he was able to attract such a large following because people have been shown to prefer commentators with unwavering confidence over those who are more reserved and have actually gotten things right. The research shows that in the presence of someone speaking emphatically about events to come, people subconsciously shut off the part of their brain that reminds them this cannot actually be done.

So strong is our desire to know what's coming, that a newsletter writer from Florida could come along and rock the New York Stock Exchange with a midnight phone call.

MATHEMATICAL OR MAGICAL?

In the Spring 1982 issue of the *Journal of Portfolio Management*, the legendary early quantitative analyst Edward Thorpe posed the question, "Can Joe Granville Time the Market?" He then sought to answer it with two other analysts and a stack of Granville's newsletters along with his full cooperation.

For Granville, this was a chance to test his intuition and skill at reading his 18 key market indicators, which had become the financial version of Colonel Sander's secret blend of 11 herbs and spices. Could the Granville edge actually be verified and quantified? If it could, just imagine how much he could charge for his advisory service with actual scientific proof! And if the study could not conclusively prove his timing ability, well, who the hell was going to read the *Journal of Portfolio Management* anyway?

Thorpe and the study's coauthors met with Granville to discuss his indicators and methods. They then got to work testing Granville's calls from the mid-1970s through the end of 1981.

Using "hypergeometric probability distributions" along with many other algebraic equations and ratios, the quants made a startling discovery—they simply could not dismiss Granville's timing abilities out of hand (even though they go through great pains not to confirm them either).

> Granville selected 446 of the 719 market days as up. If his predictions are better than chance, we would expect him to have a higher percentage of up days in his chosen set of 446 "up" days. In fact 57 percent of the days he called "up" actually were up. This is about 23 more than the number expected by chance. Is it significant? Given the number of up and down days in the period as a whole, it seems very unlikely that Granville's "buy" periods would have contained so many up days by chance.

The authors of the study concluded that, while Granville may have had a small statistical edge on his Dow Jones buy and sell calls, some of the indicators he claimed to use could be shown to have no real predictive power. Further, they informed us that most of the stocks his newsletter included as specific buy and/or short-sell candidates had done much worse than the market. Last, we are reminded by the study that Granville had made many other predictions, such as the specific time and date of an earthquake in California, that never happened.

Regarding the earthquake prediction, Thorpe was not exaggerating. In the spring of 1981, Joe Granville was at the tail end of a three-hour appearance in front of a ballroom full of investors in Vancouver. He told the crowd that on April 10 the fault lines 23 miles east of Los Angeles would shear the state of California in half. He was said to have repeated this prediction at another event that week, warning that Phoenix, Arizona, was soon to become "beachfront property." Joe delivered these jeremiads with immense conviction. "I follow 33 earthquake indicators. If you knew what I knew, you couldn't keep quiet."

Of course, no such thing ended up occurring, but Joe was making so many predictions about so many things at this point that it almost didn't matter.

THE CIRCUS

Thanks to his big sell call in January 1981, his fame as a Nostradamus of the markets had swelled the ranks of his newsletter subscription base and turned his speaking appearances into standing room–only events everywhere he went. Estimates put his annual income during this time at more than $6 million—the equivalent of $16 million in today's dollars, about what a star NFL quarterback makes. Granville's company was taking in $250 per year for each of his 20,000 newsletter subscribers and another $500 apiece for the roughly 3,000 subscribers to his telephone "early warning system" that had so notoriously tanked the market at the beginning of the year. There were cassette tapes for sale with trading lessons on them, and Granville claimed that each public appearance he made during his 150,000-miles-per-year trek could make his firm up to $100,000 in fees and new sign-ups.

His appearances and events were becoming a cross between the circus coming to town and a revival show tent complete with feats and miracles. The more outrageous Granville's antics and observations, the more people were willing to pay for them. Professor Robert Shiller describes these increasingly wacky shenanigans in his book *Irrational Exuberance*:

> Granville's behavior easily attracted public attention. His investment seminars were bizarre extravaganzas, sometimes featuring a trained chimpanzee who could play Granville's theme song, "The Bagholder's Blues," on a piano. He once showed up at an investment seminar dressed as Moses, wearing a crown and carrying tablets. Granville made extravagant claims for his forecasting ability. He said he could forecast earthquakes and once claimed to have predicted six of the past seven major world quakes. He was quoted by TIME magazine as saying, "I don't think that I will ever make a serious mistake in the stock market for the rest of my life," and he predicted he would win the Nobel Prize in economics.

With his eldest son, Blanchard, managing the newsletter firm day to day and fleshing out dad's utterances with legitimate technical analysis for the weekly missives, Joe Granville was free to run from one end of the country to the other with his exciting hybrid of market commentary and showmanship. Brokerage firms would set up and sponsor events for their customers, and Granville would show up and blow the roof off the place.

Kristin McMurran had profiled the market seer for *People Magazine* that year and made note of some of his more outrageous entrances. In Alaska he showed up for a speaking engagement driving a dogsled. In Tucson he walked across a swimming pool on a camouflaged board and then deadpanned to the crowd, "Now you know." There were high-wire flying entrances, tuxedos with blinking-light bowties, exploding hand grenades, child singing sensations, animal sidekicks, and all other manner of costumes and contraptions. Granville once emerged from a coffin to let an audience know that the bull market was dead.

Off the stage, he was every bit as wild as he was during his day job. McMurran's article captured the man behind the market prognostication:

> In conversation, Granville is a fountain of dates, facts and figures. Every other sentence is punctuated with "boom"—as in "Truth is Truth. Boom." Though he has lately become wealthy, he still spends seven and a half months a year on the road, bunking in hotels and living out of a tattered suitcase. Separated from his second wife since 1971—their divorce became final last year—he chain-smokes Marlboros, tosses back Margaritas, and disco-dances until dawn. In the company of old or new pals, he unwinds by playing poker or trading purple jokes. With women, whom he often calls "Frisbees," he is forever playing the ladies' man. At a restaurant, he may greet a waitress by chortling expansively, "Do you know who I am, honey?" She rarely does, but often delivers her phone number with his brandy. Says Joe: "Women are interested in men who can make them rich. Boom."

It is important to remember that the ascendancy was taking place after 15 years of moribund stock returns and right around the time that *BusinessWeek* had famously declared "The Death of Equities" on its now infamous August 1979 cover. A brutal bear market had worn out a generation of investors since the market's

1966 peak, accompanied by stagflation, the loss of the Vietnam War, the troubled Nixon and Ford administrations, and the assassination of John Lennon. By 1981, the financial markets needed a hero, someone who could bring humor and a sense of adventure back to the game. Joe Granville's provocative persona was just what the doctor had ordered. While the Wall Street establishment despised him, the public ate it up.

ALL GOOD THINGS . . .

A brilliant and all-but-forgotten analyst named James Alphier took it upon himself to analyze the great market timers throughout history, and he called his 1981 paper "Granville in Perspective." Alphier dissected the records of the so-called Forecasting Giants of the Past to see whether or not any market analyst could consistently maintain forecasting accuracy over extended periods of time. He began with a question: "How often has an analyst, whose research is publicly available, been able to do something like this in the past?"

The so-called giants in Alphier's paper included George Lindsay, whose "repeating time interval" work was able to produce a decade's worth of top and bottom calls, complete with specific dates and price levels. Alphier analyzed 30 years' worth of accurate bull and bear market calls from Edson Gould, who had been calling the beginnings and ends of major market trends with shocking accuracy since the early 1950s. Alphier also reconstructed the unparalleled predictive work of Major L.L.B. Angus, who had correctly forecast the market's 1920s boom, its peak in 1929, and its low in 1932.

Alphier's conclusion upon studying these giants as well as a great many pretenders was that with only a handful of exceptions, great timers could only remain accurate for a run of between three and five years. He notes:

> For periods of as little as four years, there have been many analysts who have been able to (1) forecast the major market averages, (2) nearly coincide with the extreme high or low, and

(3) do this on the significant swings. In these, and most other cases we could cite, there is a tendency after three to five years of near perfect forecasting for the analyst to make one or more major errors. We will not recount the many painful examples of this in our files.

The bad news for Joe Granville was that, by the time Alphier's 1981 paper was published, his massive winning streak was already passing through the midpoint of this three- to five-year time frame that had begun with a bull call at the market's low in 1978.

Following his amazing run of nailing all four major market turns through the first quarter of 1981, Granville's track record had begun to suffer. Whether it was hubris that had done him in or too much time spent teaching the chimp to play his theme song on piano, one thing was clear: the magician was losing his touch.

The U.S. stock market would hit its final low for the 16-year secular bear market cycle in August 1982. Then–Federal Reserve chairman Paul Volcker had finally tamed inflation (running at a rate of 7 percent that year but dropping), and stocks were selling at a highly depressed price-earnings ratio of under 10. Unemployment had peaked, as had apathy toward investing, and all of a sudden, the market had just taken off. Joe Granville, whose novelty and fame had been partly responsible for the public's renewed attention to stocks, had ironically missed the effect he was having on the markets. People were coming back to the game, and a major rally was under way.

"Sell it short" was what Granville's letter had been saying all summer, and the rally hadn't shaken him from his position. By this time, his tens of thousands of subscribers and acolytes had been getting pummeled by the relentless tape as they were either missing the move or, worse, actively betting against it.

By the fall of 1982, the stock market had staged one of its most explosive rallies of all time. From the lows of August through November, the Dow Jones Industrial Average had advanced by more than 275 points, or 35 percent, to a new 10-year high. For the bears, this new change in character was excruciatingly painful. It was the beginning of a new secular bull market, but many market timers, analysts, and economists were simply unprepared for it.

As for Joe Granville, he was off the lecture circuit and had been steadily reducing his public profile all year. The home office was telling reporters that he was quietly working on a new book at his home in Kansas City. Granville's adamantly bearish stance had cost his remaining 13,000 subscribers a fortune, and the stockbrokers across the country who had been running their clients' money based on his forecasts were either despondent or furious.

During his win streak, Granville had been relentlessly disdainful of Wall Street and the brokerage industry, calling them losers, thieves, and idiots at every opportunity. And now it was Wall Street's turn to respond in kind.

The schadenfreude was thick in an October wire story by the *Los Angeles Times* that had been picked up by newspapers all over America. Under the headline "Tarnished Idol," Granville's losing record for the year had been laid bare, accompanied by quotes from the era's most prominent market watchers. Ned Davis, a fellow technical analyst whose research firm was also based in Florida, told the paper that "I think his basic system is sound, but I don't care what kind of system you build, it's going to fail sooner or later. I think [Granville's problem] has to do with ego. He says he listens to the market. Truthfully, I think he thinks he's smarter than the market." As to the chances of a Granville comeback, Davis wasn't optimistic. "No brokerage is going to sponsor a guy who has been bearish for 18 months."

Famed analyst Larry Wachtel was equally critical of both Granville and his subscribers, saying, "I don't see really how he can crawl out of this. The lesson for those getting crucified on the short side is don't follow anybody without thinking things through yourself."

The *Dow Theory Letter*'s Richard Russell summed it up nicely, saying, "The moral of the whole thing is there are no geniuses on Wall Street. There are just people who are excellent for a while."

INTO OBSCURITY

To echo the closing coda to Billy Joel's "Miami 2017," in the case of Joe Granville, there are not many who remember. The majority of Granville's newsletters have not made it onto the web, and in the 1970s and 1980s, we didn't quite have the wall-to-wall coverage of the markets that we do today. But what is clear from the archival magazine stories and newspaper articles of that era is that the man who once moved the markets with his predictions would never recover from missing the flop from bear market to bull. The markets would rise relentlessly for the next 18 years with only sporadic corrections that were swiftly dispatched by the stock-hungry hordes. Even the crash of 1987, a jarring event at the time, hardly shows up on a monthly chart of the 1982–2000 bull market, and once inflation settled down for good under Clinton, multiples began expanding more rapidly.

In this context, no one had much use for market timers or perma-bears calling tops. Every dip was a buying opportunity, and guys like Granville were occasionally ridiculed but mostly ignored.

Granville would surface in the popular press occasionally in the three decades since his heyday, and the success rate of his predictions was as inconsistent as ever it had been. In May 2002 he told *BusinessWeek* that the market's top was in as of March. When asked by the reporter what investors should do, Granville replied:

> They should be short. All my people are short, betting on the downside. My last call was when I gave a bear selling signal right on Mar. 19, at 10,635 in the Dow. The outlook is getting increasingly worse. When I look at the market as a whole, I look at it as an army, with the generals and the troops. And it's very, very disturbing to the troops when you see a number of key stocks—the generals—such as General Electric, IBM and Merrill Lynch leaving the line and retreating. On top of that, smart people have been leaving the market all this year.

Now, of course, March 2002 turned out to have been the very end of the bear market that had begun with the tech bust; stocks would go on an uninterrupted tear for the next five years from that interview. And while Granville was correctly bullish about the prospects for gold beginning a new bull market, he was wrongly bearish on U.S. stocks and particularly tech stocks, which would go on to stage a tremendous recovery from then.

Ten years later, at age 89, Joe Granville would make headlines again. This time, he makes a January 2012 appearance on Bloomberg Television in which he predicts a 4,000-point crash for the Dow Jones to occur at some point during 2012. No such thing happens. The Dow Jones Industrial Average ends up logging its fourth straight positive year in 2012, a gain of almost 900 points, or 7 percent, with virtually zero volatility to speak of.

Mark Hulbert, a *MarketWatch* columnist, has been tracking newsletter recommendations since 1980. In 2005, he took a look back and assembled a ranking of all the newsletter prophets he'd been following. According to Hulbert's analysis, Granville's letter was at the bottom of the rankings for performance over the past 25 years, "having produced average losses of more than 20 percent per year on an annualized basis."

On September 7, 2013, Joe Granville passed away at Saint Luke's Hospice House in Kansas City, Missouri; his third wife, Karen, was by his side. He was 90 years old and had, by then, really and truly seen it all.

Several generations of oracles and wizards have come and gone since those early days of crash calls and faxed financial bombast. Very few of those who have followed in Granville's footsteps have been able to attain his level of market-moving influence or headline-grabbing flamboyance. All of them have eventually failed to hang on to their temporary relevance.

Joe Granville's failure to accurately forecast securities prices is not a personal failing of his—it speaks to the inability of any system or human being (or combination thereof) to do this kind of thing with any meaningful consistency. Markets are, as Michael Mauboussin notes in his book *The Success Equation*, "a complex adaptive system" being acted upon by millions of individuals who do not behave according to any predetermined set of rationales or rules. This plain and simple fact is what condemns all market timers to inevitable failure, regardless of the depth of their experience or the calibration of their indicators.

And when elaborate stage shows and a rock star mentality begin to enter into the equation, you can pretty much hang up your spurs right then and there.

Because that's when the ride is over.

CHAPTER 8

REDEMPTION SONG

A CONVERSATION WITH HENRY BLODGET

I n 1998 Henry Blodget became a very public face of the bubble by putting an audacious presplit $400 price target on Amazon .com. When the stock reached that mark within 60 days, a star was born.

In 2002 that same star was disgraced and publicly lynched when then–New York attorney general Eliot Spitzer published e-mails Henry had written while working at Merrill Lynch. The e-mails rather vaguely conflicted with his favorable published ratings of several of the stocks he was covering as a hotshot Internet analyst. The prosecution was one of the first based on the use of internal e-mails as evidence of fraud.

The complaint was settled when Blodget agreed to a total of $4 million in fines and "disgorgements" and a lifetime ban from the securities industry without admitting or denying guilt.

Though he's quick to point out that he didn't go into exile after the Spitzer affair, Blodget's road back to the limelight didn't truly shine until he covered the Martha Stewart insider trading trial for *Slate*. If getting Blodget to cover the case was a coup for *Slate*, it was little short of a miraculous opportunity for Blodget himself. Not that *Slate* made it easy for him.

Ostentatiously distancing itself from Henry even while openly exploiting his talent and infamy, *Slate* asked Blodget in his first assignment to write an essay justifying his right to opine on a public figure such as Stewart being dragged through a show trial. The resulting column was a minor masterpiece of self-deprecation and spin control with just a dash of contrition.

> I don't want to insult Martha Stewart by drawing comparisons—my "story" is, at its most mythical, only a faint echo of hers—there are obviously parallels. . . . Like Stewart,
> I have had the bizarre experience of watching legions of people I have never met come to trust me, look to me for guidance, regard me as a "guru," and then decide that I am, in fact, a scumbag.

As comeback announcements go, the column may have lacked the drama of Napoleon's post-Elba appeal to the French army, but Blodget's opening missive and subsequent coverage of the Stewart trial were pitch-perfect.

To many people, Henry is and always will be a symbol of Wall Street's endless willingness to cravenly rip off Main Street. It's a preposterous charge made by political opportunists looking to cash in on the public feeling burned by the Internet bubble. As a high-profile analyst at the heart of the dot-com IPO mania, Blodget made an ideal target for prosecutors. What made him perfect wasn't the evidence against him but his positioning in the financial industry. At the time, analysts were exceptionally well-paid celebrities, but they didn't have any lasting institutional power. Blaming the Internet bubble on analysts as opposed to underwriters or the public itself was politically expedient. Blodget had to walk the plank for the same reason a low-level Goldman Sachs trader took the fall for the financial crisis while the SEC largely ignored the bank itself. There's a certain set of rules for how the government conducts its periodic Wall Street reforms. It works like this: banks get fined, guys like Blodget and Goldman's Fabrice Tourre get charged, and regulatory officials run for office.

Because of that cynical but quite practical regulatory pecking order, Blodget was chosen for execution by Eliot Spitzer, an attorney general and future governor who once described himself as a "f***ing steamroller" of ambition.

Blodget is quiet, ambitious, and private. He's built like George Plimpton. Eliot Spitzer is loud, ambitious, and much less private than he'd like to be. He's a steamroller. A decade after their famous showdown, Blodget is the CEO of Business Insider, a company valued at about $75 million when Amazon.com CEO Jeff Bezos invested in it. Eliot Spitzer was forced to resign the New York governorship in the wake of a prostitution scandal. He recently ran for New York City comptroller, losing in the primary despite spending $10.3 million running for a job that pays less than $200,000 a year.

Whatever you think of Henry Blodget's role in the Internet bubble, he's obviously equipped to go the distance. Steamrollers clearly are not.

I have monster respect for Henry Blodget. Whatever you think of him, know this: it takes balls the size of church bell clappers to do what he has done. His target audience consists largely of people who spent years using him as a punch line. He knows it. He also knows he'll always be a joke to many people. As my esteemed coauthor put it, "He'd be great for the book, but just be aware I think Henry might be Satan."

When I decided to do this book, I knew I needed to talk to Henry. After weeks of planning, postponing, and my general badgering, Henry and I spoke in June 2013 on an extended phone call. I agreed in advance to omit any references to family and let him review the transcript to make sure nothing in it ran afoul of his banishment agreement.

MACKE: What did you do during the interstitial between when you sort of disappeared from the public eye and then you came out on *Slate* covering Martha Stewart?

BLODGET: Well, I didn't disappear that long, and a lot of people said to me immediately afterward, "Dude, you didn't disappear long enough." But I was in a situation where when I left Wall Street, I was writing a book and spending some other time writing. I did that for about a year or so. Then the Martha Stewart trial came along, and it just seemed like a great opportunity, given what I had gone through with the SEC and with Eliot Spitzer, to use both the Wall Street experience and my journalism experience and the regulatory experience to cover a trial. So I asked a few friends of mine who were in the industry, "Who would be good to work with?" and they said, "Oh, *Slate* would be great!" That was really only about a year and a half, I think, after I left Wall Street and all the regulatory stuff. So it was not very long.

MACKE: How was it for you personally after you fell out of the spotlight? Did you feel like you were being scrutinized in a whole different light?

BLODGET: I went through this bizarre period in 1990s where effectively I got hit by lightning. I mean, I had an incredibly fast rise as a career. Some credit to me; I was working very hard, but also just was riding an incredible wave in terms of the Internet. So I was in the right place at the right time. I had made a couple of stock calls that had gotten some very big national and international attention. So I had been in the press very heavily. It was all sort of silly how much attention was being paid to me based on a couple of calls and so forth. But that was an era in which stock market pundits were really almost celebrities. I mean, we went way outside just the investor audience.

Then when the crash came, most of the folks who had been visible during the bullish phase were raked over the coals, and I talked about, then, about feeling like a piñata with everybody swinging at me. That was just when the market crashed. That happens every time an asset class breaks down the way the Internet stocks did. But then after I left Wall Street, the regulatory stuff came around, and that was obviously much worse because it went from going to "You're just an idiot and you missed the top" to "You are a scumbag and you weren't calling it like you saw it."

MACKE: Do you think you were a scapegoat for the Internet mania as a whole? Do you think they just kind of plucked you because you became a name brand during the inflation of the bubble? It's not as though you were the only analyst who didn't see the collapse coming.

BLODGET: No. I think that I was visible, which made me a very promising target for people on the regulatory side to look at. That happens pretty much any time the market goes through a crash.

Then I obviously wrote and oversaw a lot of colorful e-mails that helped in that. I think that if you look at market history, every time there is a bubble and then crash, this is all part of the process. We saw this in the housing market as well, and certainly after 1929. People forget that the reason the SEC exists was that after the 1929 crash Congress got involved, and they said, "We've got to change this," and so we created the SEC and most of the securities law and so forth.

So that process is very standard. I didn't realize it until afterwards when I started reading some of the books about bubbles and realized that it was just all playing out according to a script. But that's just simply what happened afterwards. Sure, at a lot of times I felt that it was unfair and directed at me and should not have been. These are just rules that should have been changed beforehand instead of changed afterwards and so forth. But I don't think that it was any different than what happens every time there's a market crash.

MACKE: Did you feel guilty? Or just as though you were the guy the public chose to blame for this particular bubble just as we've found scapegoats for all the others?

BLODGET: Well, I felt like when I did miss the top of the bubble, I felt like an idiot, and I felt like I had let everybody down because a lot of people were listening to me, and it wouldn't have been that hard in hindsight to say, "Okay, this is the top." And of course that's the myth that gets created every time there's a market bubble like this, because really there had been opportunities since 1995 in the Internet sector. People had been saying, "This is a bubble; it's going to burst." And it just kept getting bigger and bigger, but when it finally does, you look back and you say, "How could I not have known?" I was very far from alone in that. Every analyst on Wall Street missed it, and lots of the smartest investors in the world missed it, but I still felt bad. I wish I had seen it.

Then came the regulatory stuff, and so that was a further massive blow to my reputation and to the reputation of the firm and so forth. I felt horrible about that. I have to say that the way I experienced that period really was . . . and where I was getting trashed in the press constantly was just a huge, almost physical weight weighing on me of the public being furious about what had happened and directing their ire at me. That was a very tough period. Obviously in that case I had to get through it, but feeling like you have that many people angry at you and you've let people down is very tough, and the one thing that I did not want to do was go out that way.

I just felt like it was a disgraceful way to go out. I wanted to have a family; I wanted my kids to be proud of me. I didn't want my public career to end on that note. So I determined very early that I was going to do whatever I could do to get back out there and earn back whatever trust that I could earn back. That's what I've been doing for the last 10 to 12 years since then. But especially in the beginning, starting to write as I did, publicly, it was an opportunity to remind people about me and trigger their ire, which I heard full-throatedly, which was again something that I expected—but it's never fun to hear. It always hurts.

MACKE: The public scorn is all but mandatory. The hardest part of coming back is bracing yourself for that hammering.

In 2003 when Martha Stewart went on trial for insider trading, you covered it for *Slate*. Obviously that couldn't have been a more perfect platform. But you knew the trolls were going to be out there exactly because you covering a securities trial was so ideal.

One of the most interesting pieces that you wrote on Martha Stewart was the first one, where it seemed almost like a disclaimer. It was as if *Slate* essentially said, "Here's a pile of crow; you eat this and then you can cover Martha." How hard was it to write that?

BLODGET: It was cathartic to write that. There were a few things that I wanted to remind people of, starting with the fact that I had followed my own advice in terms of investing in stocks and I had also lost my shirt. That was good. And I also wanted to explain that I had been through a similar regulatory situation and had learned a huge amount about how the whole system works. Unlike Martha Stewart, fortunately, I never had a criminal investigation, but just knowing how the SEC worked and how the whole process worked helped me understand things and view them in a way that I hadn't before. So I wanted to spell all that out.

I also just wanted to acknowledge it up front because my name was very big in those days. Everybody had heard of me. I wanted to acknowledge it up front and say, "Look, I know you've heard these things about me, and here I am, and I want to be as direct as I can about them. Now let's talk about Martha."

MACKE: Do you think the audience moved on? If that's the audience, if it's cathartic for you to write that, it's a huge step, God knows, I know, for you to write that. Do you feel like your doing so and your kind of explaining and kind of trying to move on with your life convinced anyone to drop the matter? Do you think anyone that was on the fence about you was moved?

BLODGET: I would hope some people at least decided, "Hey, let me see if it's worth giving this guy another chance." And that's really all that I wanted to do. I thought it was all that I could do to just say that to people, and it's what I say whenever I get hate mail, which is, "Look, a lot of people have given me a chance to earn back their trust. If that somebody includes you, that's wonderful; I'm eternally grateful for that." That's really what I want to do. I knew that I was going to get shelled, but again I just did not want to go out the way I had to go out when I left Wall Street.

Part of the process for me that was very tough was I had always been very public in talking to the press, in certainly writing research and going on TV and everything else. When you get into a legal situation, you can't say anything. I was very handicapped in that, and still am handicapped in that I can't talk about the details of what happened to me and I can't talk about my view of it publicly. So that made it harder because people still felt like they were owed an explanation. I have been able to say more over the years, but I still haven't been able to get into the details. So listen, even today, 12 years later or what have you, I will occasionally say something that makes somebody angry, and they will throw that back in my face, and that will probably last forever. It's an easy thing to bring up if you're unhappy with something that I've said.

MACKE: It seems so disproportionate that these people can e-mail guys like you, me; I don't know what your e-mail flow was like but very ad hominem attacks for me. I've had my family threatened; I've had people write me long, ranting letters mocking me for a short, ranting TV segment. There's no recourse against those attacks. The hostility in some of those e-mails we get is very real.

Contrast that with the way the government goes after insider trading or the case against you where it's all e-mail. There's no context. A snarky comment in an e-mail is a prosecutorial offense.

BLODGET: I think just generally with respect to securities law, I think one of the liabilities for everybody in the industry is that any uncertainty in the present is lost the moment something actually happens. Then it looks as though people knew it was going to happen.

The truth is in the market. If you and I talk about the market today, you might have a strong opinion, but you don't know what the market is going to do. Neither do I, and neither does anybody on TV. People are just giving their opinions, and then something will happen; and some of the people will have expressed opinions that were right, some of them will have expressed opinions that were wrong, and it will look like some people knew what was going to happen. Nobody did.

The problem that people face with e-mail is that e-mail tends to preserve offhand remarks. It tends to preserve opinions that you might have held while you were coming to a professional opinion, things that you might have said in response to something somebody said to you does not rise to the level of professionalism. In other words, when you research a stock, you might start talking to people, and you might say something like, "Oh, you're right. Oh my God, that's terrible. This thing is such a dog." Then the next day you might learn that, well, actually, there's another side to that. Here's what I'm thinking about. Then you might come out and say, "My opinion on this stock is that I'm positive," and then I bring up the old e-mail and say, "But hey, wait a minute. Here you said it was a dog and now you're saying it's positive. Obviously you were lying."

This is the problem with this method of looking at it, but it is a reality. I mean, these e-mails are a reality . . . there are more and more of them all the time. Nobody has learned the danger of them unless they actually go through this. I think it's a reality of regulatory investigations now, and it will continue to be, and it's only going to get more like that. Because now that we have texts and we have Snapchat and photos and so forth, there will just be more and more of an electronic record of that. Again, there's always a defense side where you can explain these things, but the potential for offhand remarks, or temporary opinions, or what have you, to look back at becomes more and more likely.

MACKE: You're fighting what seems to be a damning cutout quote with an elaborate explanation, and it's going to be the sexy quote in bold print.

BLODGET: Right.

MACKE: So getting back to your personal track after you covered the Martha trial, and you could call it exoneration at any point. You could have then; it was a nice, successful series of stories. You could have walked away, but you didn't.

BLODGET: After I covered Martha Stewart, I did other series for *Slate*. I did a series on China, and I did a series on Wall Street and what you need to know about Wall Street for *Slate*. Then I started writing for other publications, too. That was over the course of a couple of years. I wrote a book called *The Wall Street Self-Defense Manual*, which really was developed by having worked on Wall Street for 10 years but then also having the experience of being a Wall Street consumer looking at it from a distance and saying, "Wow, there are things that people ought to know about this."

Also, just learning how to approach investing as an individual investor, which is very different than how a sophisticated professional investor who's managing billions of dollars will approach it. You have a whole bunch of different types of decisions. There are different products that you have to be aware of.

There are costs and fees and so forth. So I actually had to go through the process of learning how to be an intelligent, individual investor, which was not part of what I did on Wall Street. I was a sector stock analyst. I was responsible for coming up with opinions about 10 to 20 stocks that had nothing to do with broader investing and so forth.

So I wrote a book about that, which was very helpful for me, and I also did some consulting. Then in 2007 my partners and I started what we thought was going to be a small New York tech publication called *Silicon Alley Insider*, and right away it got a lot more readership from California and places other than New York, so we figured we would broaden it very quickly.

MACKE: Did you still feel the tension of being a marked man by 2007, or had it been just a number of years and you were over it?

BLODGET: No. I always feel it. I don't like to be criticized.

I hear some people say, "I don't care. I love it when people yell at me and call me an idiot. I just love to reach for the delete key"; maybe so. Especially when somebody has something where it's a relatively sophisticated complaint as opposed to just some idiot sounding off, which there are tons of, I obviously want to respond to that. So I knew I was going to get that. I had written in my own blog called *Internet Outsider* for a couple of years. I had opened up the comments. I had built a community of people where people would always come in, and they would say, "Oh, Blodget. I remember him."

Then some of them would stick around, and they would say, "Look, I know what I heard about you, but hey, this is smart stuff. I'm glad to be a part of this community." So I had been doing that and addressing that directly and been very accessible for a couple of years. Then the same thing happened when we launched the business. People would come in and attack me personally especially if they didn't like something that I said. I don't hear it when people like what I've said, but if they don't like what I've said, then the past is brought up very quickly.

And that continues. It's less now than it used to be, but people will always be happy to post the [settlement] press release when I say something they don't like.

MACKE: But is it that way when you meet them in person?

BLODGET: People have always been great in person. It is the anonymity of the Internet that allows people to treat people the way they wouldn't treat their worst enemy. Certainly political arguments are like this, and stock arguments where people have money on the line are like this and so forth. But in person, no, everyone has always been perfectly friendly to me, which is great.

MACKE: Why do people get so passionate about it? Why does anyone seek advice from guys on TV talking about their latest buy or trade idea?

BLODGET: I think there's a desperate need for good financial advice for individuals. I think unfortunately the incentives on Wall Street and in the money management industry and in the media create an environment where there's very little of that. For example, one of the things that became clear to me over two to three years of studying the best advice for individuals was that it is crazy for individuals to try to pick stocks and it is crazy for individuals to try to pick mutual fund managers or hedge fund managers who can beat the market.

For 99 percent of individuals, it's just devastating to their financial performance. Really what they should be doing is keeping their money in low-cost index funds and only rebalancing once every couple of years, and that's it.

And yet the problem is as a brokerage firm, as an advisor, as a media pundit, you can't just go on and say everyone should just buy index funds. Stop trying to figure out what's next for Yahoo or Google or Apple. Just buy index funds and forget it. Financial TV would just have to fold up the tent. The good news is there are lots of professional money managers out there and there are very dedicated individual traders out there who do, in fact, want to dissect stocks every day and try to figure out where the next trade is. That's where the whole financial media industry is; they're catering to those people.

Obviously the media has to cater to those folks, too, because there's not much news in saying, "Well, today and yesterday you should buy an index fund."

MACKE: There's also an entertainment factor. CNBC, Business Insider, Yahoo Finance . . . they're all ultimately in the business of getting people to watch, not just inform.

BLODGET: I think you do both. It's very true that storytelling is very critical. You hope that both the analysis and the story are based in a study of the facts, which in most cases I think it is. But there's no question that it has to be portrayed as a compelling story. And for good reason, which is that we all have thousands and thousands of sources of information and different things that we can read being thrown at us every day.

You've got to cut through that and say, "Look, this is the most important stuff that you should be paying attention to." At Business Insider, that's what we've built the business on. It is trying to cut through all the stuff that doesn't matter and filter in the things that we think our readers will enjoy paying attention to. But, yes, you have to be compelling in the way that you tell stories.

MACKE: The problem with that is the most compelling way to tell a story is by discarding the facts and just scaring the hell out of people. Having a simple gimmick is easier to market than being thoughtful. Being a perma-bear sounds smarter than having a two-sided opinion, but it's pure shtick. It's BS, but it sounds smart to say things like "The dollar is going to disappear! Buy gold bricks!"

BLODGET: I take it as a given that nobody knows what the stock market's going to do, and nobody knows what Apple is going to do, and nobody knows what Facebook is going to do. But if you go on TV and tell me that you have no idea, that doesn't help me very much.

When I watch I know the guy on TV doesn't know, but what I do want to hear is your opinion and why you have it and what the logic is and why you think the people who are saying the opposite are wrong. That helps me think through and come to my own conclusion. That's why I do think there is real value in smart analysts and smart pundits talking through things.

With Jim Cramer, I think the guy is brilliant on stocks. I don't think that individuals should invest that way. I don't think that's the smartest way for most individuals to invest, but if you want somebody to help you think through where the opportunities might be in the market and think through what the issues are on a particular stock, he's wonderful at that. So are many, many other pundits. So I think that when somebody is using logic that is completely unfounded, we have a big opportunity to say, "This particular logic is ridiculous," and we're very eager to do that.

MACKE: But you can't stop that inanity, and neither can the media. The best way to get attention and become a TV regular is to make a HUGE call. You and I know there's pressure on people making their first appearances to draw a lot of attention to themselves but a network can't run a crawl across the screen saying, "This guy is just making an outlandish prediction because he'd like to come back again."

BLODGET: Ironically, I think it's very helpful when somebody comes out with a very strong opinion that is startling to people, backed by logic that actually makes sense. So now with Apple trading at $450 a share as we're speaking right now, if somebody came out and said, "Look, I still think this can be a $1,000 stock, and here is why I think so"—if that person has very good logic that I can follow, that analysis, even though it sounds outlandish, is potentially much, much more valuable than the 95 percent of analysts who are saying, "My price target is $500." These are all the same guys who had the price target of $1,000 back when Apple was $700 a share, because it seemed so obvious and now they've all taken their price targets down.

Similarly, if somebody said, "Apple is now $250. I think it's going to $200," and then has very, very good logic backing that up, that is also very valuable because it's something you don't hear very often.

It's often the people who are making outlandish predictions who are the most helpful in terms of helping you form your own opinion, because we all hear so much of the "Me too; I'm saying just what everybody else is saying because I'm too scared to make a particular prediction."

We all hear that all day long. So I actually personally find it more helpful when somebody comes out and says something that sounds crazy. Then I want to know why they believe it. If they believe it for some stupid reason that has no basis in anything other than they want to say something that sounds crazy, then I'll dismiss them as an idiot. If they actually come on like a couple of people did at the market bottom in 2009 and say, "Look, I know you're going to find this hard to believe, but I think it has now gotten so bad that it can't get any worse and we're going to go higher from here."

We had a couple of those guests on, like Barry Ritholtz; he was trashed, trashed, when he said that, because everybody had decided the market was just going to go down, down, down, never go any other way, and anybody who had said anything positive for two years had been wrong. Barry came out; he was right. Boy, wouldn't that have been helpful if people had not dismissed him as an idiot.

I think it's often the people who appear crazy who are the most valuable commentators.

MACKE: A lot of people called Barry an idiot because (a) he changed his mind and (b) he went bullish. There are people who have made a personal industry out of calling for the apocalypse constantly, just endless. "We're rallying now, but it's all going to end, and that's going to be a nightmare."

Optimism has been dead right for four years, but there are so many bad things out there that being positive sounds horribly out of touch.

BLODGET: For some reason, being negative always sounds smarter. I don't know what it is about people, but I noticed this when I was an analyst as well. It's easier to sound smart as a negative pundit.

I think the only thing you say about those folks is, look, they're wrong. They could say until they're blue in the face that it is fake or that somehow the Fed has done something that they shouldn't have done in some moral world or what have you, but the fact is that they're wrong. That's the appropriate question for the people who have missed the bull market since 2009. "The market has more than doubled in five years. So what did you miss?"

MACKE: Is there a deadline on this prediction for the imminent apocalypse that's going to come? Because you need a starting point, right? If we get a 25 percent correction now, that's not going to go anywhere near taking back all the gains we've seen.

But most pundits refuse to say, "I was wrong." No one is ever wrong. They're "early." Sometimes really, really early.

BLODGET: Anybody who pretends that being wrong is not part and parcel of trying to beat the stock market—that you're going to be wrong 40 to 50 percent of the time even if you're great—is hallucinating, because the market is incredibly efficient.

The idea that a commentator should be correct all the time— it's just crazy. It's not going to happen. So that's why I find it helpful, again, when people come out and say, "Look, here's my logic; here's the trade that I have. By the way, over the past six months I've been dead wrong."

It immediately raises my impression of them and makes me listen to them more closely about what they say in the future.

MACKE: Do you think that's an insider thing that the people who are professional pundits can appreciate that—the ability to say "I was wrong"—and that laypeople don't really understand that that's part of the equation?

BLODGET: I think laypeople can sense and relate to people who are just straight with them, and I think that that is one of Jim Cramer's strengths—that he is straight with people. I think that there are big gurus who have been held up for a long time as gurus, and some of them are straight with people, and it's clear that they've been wrong. That's okay.

MACKE: I'm a big proponent of getting a good ass-kicking in terms of defining yourself and realizing what kind of character you have. At least personally.

In terms of investing, losing big is also the best education, but it's insanely expensive. Is it possible to really convey through words the real, visceral experience of being wrong on a huge stage so the audience doesn't have to go through it themselves?

BLODGET: I can say personally the only market that I had ever known as a professional in the 1990s was a big bull market where, in fact, it was incredibly smart to buy the dip. That was the mantra in the 1990s, and that was good advice all through the bull market.

I very much appreciated the fact that there weren't always bull markets, and that sometimes things would crash, and that you had to always be aware of that and hedge for that and not have too much exposure as a result of that, but there is a difference between knowing it intellectually and actually having experienced it.

One of the things that I found tough was I didn't have a sense of how a rip-roaring good bull market could suddenly become a disaster. After I went through it in the 1995-to-2000 period, the bull period, and then 2000 to 2002, the incredibly harsh bear market, I then experienced it. So when I saw the housing market starting to bubble up in 2004, 2005, I had a sense of how it could deteriorate.

I didn't know exactly what the cause was going to be or when, but I was no longer having to satisfy myself that good things can turn bad and here's how they do and psychology changes quickly. I don't think that I could have learned that without having gone through it. I think there's a certain amount that you could learn from reading smart people who have a lot of experience, but I also think there is value in experience. I think that's very hard to get any other way.

MACKE: Do you feel you're better at helping people now because you went through not just a financial boom-bust-boom cycle but also experienced sort of the same thing in terms of yourself personally?

BLODGET: I think overall getting just more experience will make you better. I mean, I didn't believe all of the wondrous things that were said about me in the 1990s when things were going very well and they were going relatively easily for me. I took my job very, very seriously. But I was being written about around the world as though I had some incredible skill that other people didn't have. I didn't take it particularly seriously.

I didn't absorb it in the way that I might have absorbed it had I been younger—if I'd been 21 when that was happening.

Because I had already gone through a lot of professional experiences even before I got to Wall Street. So that made the beating a little bit easier for me to take because I didn't have to go from this super high where I believed everything that was written about me in the 1990s and then I just got completely clobbered. I personally was, I think, on a relatively realistic self-assessment through the 1990s and then beyond.

MACKE: But the difference is that when they're saying great things about you, it's easier to ignore. When they're saying crappy things about you, it seems grossly unfair. It's incredibly hurtful.

BLODGET: You are 100 percent right about that. So, yes, I was very aware of that. As I said, it felt like a huge physical weight listening to that. So what has that done for me?

One of the things you learn as you get older and you go through a lot and you see your friends go through a lot is that life is not fair. It's something that has helped me, the whole thing and things that I've seen with other people that are vastly, vastly more serious than anything that I went through and vastly more unfair in so many ways. You see people get through experiences like that, and it's just incredibly inspiring, and it just makes you or helps you value what you have much more greatly.

I didn't just go to Wall Street right out of school and suddenly get on a rocket ride. So I knew that the professional world could be tough and so forth before I got there, but this obviously just made that even more clear. It was a very tough experience to go through. But when you work your way through them, you definitely learn from that, and certainly, as I said, I didn't want to go out the way I would have had to go out if I had disappeared in 2002; that would have been horrifying to me.

MACKE: Is there a finish line for you? Is there a specific point at which you'll feel vindicated, if not exonerated, so you can leave on your terms?

BLODGET: No. I'm definitely not doing what I'm doing now to somehow be exonerated for the past or be past the past. I love what I'm doing, and I would probably be doing this anyway.

But I do think, when I say that, in terms of going out, I just think that there are some people who went through what I did and they just disappear forever, and that's fine. Ten years later nobody remembers anything, and they're living a completely different life, and it's fine, and it's all way in the past.

What I like to do is what I'm doing now, which is be out there and be public and writing and speaking. I didn't want to stop doing that.

I don't know whether that will ever end in terms of being done. I think there's certainly a lot that we can do with Business Insider going forward, but I think if I were to leave Business Insider tomorrow, I would probably get up the next day and start doing something very similar to what I'm doing now. It's just a wonderful thing to do with one's life.

MACKE: So talk to me about Business Insider. I think it's just a fantastic site. One of the reasons is that editorially it doesn't spend a great deal of time trying to convince the reader how erudite the writers are. You have people there who are smart enough to explain complex material in a digestible manner.

In finance especially, it's quite easy for intellectually mediocre people to dazzle an audience with BS. The people who are genuinely smart are the ones who can make complicated points in a way a broad audience can understand. That seems to be what you're doing.

BLODGET: That's right. That's a big goal of the site.

There are plenty of pundits and analysts out there who produce a massive tonnage of work, a lot of which either is devoted to something that's not particularly interesting or important or is in a level of detail and depth that is not going to be interesting to people who are not obsessed with that one little corner of an industry. So what we're trying to do is focus on the big stories, the important things, and relate them in a way that intelligent, curious people can react to and understand and, most importantly, have the time to consume.

When I was an analyst, I was like everybody else, writing these inch-thick reports about different companies and different industries, and then I was mailing them out to fund managers.

Finally I remember going to a fund manager's office on a trip, and I sat down with him, and we were talking about whatever company it was, and I said, "Well, did you read my report?" He said, "I don't know" and he pointed to a stack in the corner four or five feet high of reports just like mine and he said, "It's probably in there. Those are just what came in last week."

It's incumbent upon you as an analyst to distill things to the point where everybody will get your core message, whatever that happens to be. That's a lot of what we do here—just present important information in a way that is very easily digestible for busy professionals, and we are all incredibly busy.

MACKE: The investors who need the most help investing are the ones who don't know where to look. What should people be doing with this overwhelming amount of information that's flowing at them all the time?

BLODGET: It depends whether you're trying to develop an investing philosophy, and if you are, my strong recommendation would be go read Jack Bogle's indexing, and you look at the performance of even the best money managers in the world over the long haul and you understand why that is. I think if you devote a lot of time to that, you will understand why for most people indexing is the way to go. That's the intelligent strategy.

If you are trying to figure out whether Apple is a buy or a sell, that's where I think that reports actually can help you. I think what you're looking for there is to get the widest diversity of intelligent opinion that you can. So you find smart analysts who are negative, and you find smart analysts who are positive; and if you can't find that diversity in the research reports, then read online. There are many commentators who are on both sides of these things online. Read as much as you can in the news, think about it yourself, and then come to an opinion yourself on who is right and why.

Just have respect for the person on the other side of the trade, because there are a lot of smart people on both sides, and these analysts who are coming up with these reports in many cases are very smart and very thoughtful and have a lot of experience.

Yet they're coming to a different view on the stock. But I don't know any other way other than that to go about it.

MACKE: You've been on an unbelievable journey. I've got one last question, and it's the hardest one: What have you learned? Is there anything that drives you out of there? Is there any lesson beyond "Life isn't fair" that you've taken away from this that would help people?

BLODGET: I think the message is very clear: you're going to go through good times, and you're going to go through bad times. You just keep fighting until you can't fight anymore.

CHAPTER 9

DOW 100,000!

*The most distressing thing that can happen to
a prophet is to be proved wrong. The next most
distressing thing is to be proved right.*
—ALDOUS HUXLEY

O n Christmas Eve in 2012, Bernie Madoff sent a letter to
CNBC in which he weighed in on a host of current finance
topics, from the opaque dark pools that had begun to
dominate daily trading activity to the rapid proliferation of hedge
funds—both of which he saw as dangers to investors. I'll pause now
while you rifle through your pockets for that anti-irony pill . . .

Let's continue.

The news media immediately picked up on Madoff's comments
and went live to air and the web with them as though they were
helpful or important. Never mind the fact that the man doing the
opining, in this case, had already pleaded guilty in March 2009
to running the largest Ponzi scheme in history. The simple fact is
that once you've become a Certified Financial Pundit (or CFP), it is
nearly impossible to have your license revoked. You can be wrong
about everything, watch your predictions lose people money
repeatedly, and even steal $50 billion—but so long as you've still
got a recognizable name, you're still in the game.

Of all the ways to stay in the headlines, blustery conjecture
about events to come is perhaps the most surefire method there is.
The more specific these divinations, the better. And being right is
irrelevant, so fire away!

Around the turn of the last century, optimism was at an all-time high as new Internet and wireless technologies changed our lives and the burgeoning boomer generation came into its peak earning and investing years. Europe had agreed to a sovereign merger of sorts after a millennium of internecine warfare and heavy cream sauces. In the meantime, the human genome had just been decoded for the first time, putting science on the threshold of godlike insights into our recipe and ingredients list. The world appeared to be headed into a new era of perpetual peace and profits for all. Goldman Sachs strategist Abby Joseph Cohen had taken to calling our nation's economy "Supertanker America," and the imagery alone made one want to tie the red-white-and-blue flag on like a cape and leap fearlessly from the ledge of a building up into the clouds above.

Into this effervescent bacchanal came a book that has become legendary for both the exhilaration that was so emblematic of the era and its epic wrongness.

Harry S. Dent Jr. had made two financial predictions in the late 1980s that were startling for two reasons. First, like all good attention-grabbing predictions, they were completely unfathomable to others at the time he made them and flew in the face of the consensus thinking. In addition, they turned out to have been right on the money.

Harry's area of interest and expertise was in demography, the study of statistics such as births, deaths, income, or the incidence of disease, which illustrate the changing structure of human populations. Using trends like the household spending cycle of given age groups in a population, Dent had been able to correctly forecast the fall of the Japanese economy and, more impressively, its subsequent decade-long stagnation. At the time of his prediction, Japan had been swallowing up choice real estate all over the world, and its companies (along with their soaring stock prices) had seemed unbeatable. To refer to this call as an outlier would be an understatement. His other prediction, that the Dow would hit 10,000, was also outlandish at the time and roundly mocked.

The great thing about being an obscure economics commentator and making bold calls is that if you're wrong, well, no one really remembers who you were anyway. In other words, there is very little risk. The rewards, however, of getting a bold call right, are incalculable. The book editors come calling, and the lecture circuit is quick to ante up—you become a seer in the public's imagination, "The Man Who Saw It Coming." When Danish physicist Niels Bohr said, "Prediction is very difficult, especially about the future," he was referring to actually getting the prediction right, not playing the prediction game, which is much easier to do given this asymmetric risk-to-reward equation.

Unfortunately, this concept is little understood by those who become excited by out-of-left-field predictions that come to pass. Children need Santa Claus, and as adults, they require just a tad more sophistication in their fairy tales—the professional forecaster who uses statistics to see the future certainly fits the bill.

And so in the wake of his Japan crash and Dow 10,000 calls, Mr. Dent becomes famous. And then goes on to make some of the most spectacularly wrong pronouncements ever committed to paper.

As 1998 turned to 1999, the bull market was entering its eighteenth and final year and seemed hell-bent on creating a fireworks show of speculation unrivaled in modern history. The Nasdaq index was headed up an astonishing 85 percent that year, while no less than 17 popular stocks were recording year-to-date gains of over 900 percent. Nothing like this had ever been seen before (or since), and continued, uninterrupted economic progress became a given amid all the shattered records and unprecedented wealth creation. In an era during which daily superlatives were as common as a bowl of Cheerios on the breakfast table each morning, how was a prognosticator to get anyone's attention? How could a man's message (and marketing) rise above the din? The answer was very simple—use even more hyperbole than anyone else would ever dare to.

And Harry Dent Jr.'s next book, *The Roaring 2000s*, was born, followed by a companion volume, *The Roaring 2000s Investor*.

In the latter book, Dent predicted that the economy would be led by Internet companies into some sort of never-ending prosperity paradise in which demographics and innovation would drive markets and civilization to new heights. It was the perfect message for the times, as its wild-eyed enthusiasm and hyperbolic conclusions seemed to justify, with math and science, the reckless behavior of investors, professional and amateur alike. In reality, the book was merely doing what many others were—extrapolating current trends far out into the future and assuming best-case scenarios at almost every turn.

Dent's prediction for the Dow Jones Industrial Average, which had just broken above 10,000 for the first time in March 1999, was an incredible 44,000 by 2008. He was only off by 36,000 points, give or take. He had also suggested that the tech stock–heavy Nasdaq index would rise to between 13,000 and 20,000. Now, of course, precisely the opposite happened: The Nasdaq would peak a few months into the following year at just over 5,100. Within 2½ years, the index would go on to lose almost 4,000 points, or 78 percent, of its total value, bottoming out at 1,100 in the fall of 2002. A total of $5 trillion in investor capital, much of it from Main Street, had been vaporized by the collapse, and those who had completely bought into the enthusiasm of Dent's "new paradigm" had been handed the education of a lifetime at an astronomical tuition cost.

Roaring 2000s? Dent was close, but no cigar.

Rather than epic prosperity, we got a recession, a four-year recovery, and a gradual expansion in which the majority of the 1999-era technology companies had disappeared while a few had chugged along respectably and quietly matured. In the aftermath, Dent would resurface now and again to reiterate or justify his old predictions, most notably in 2006 when he published *The Next Great Bubble Boom: How to Profit from the Greatest Boom in History: 2006–2010*. In this new tome, Dent foresaw the Dow Jones Industrial Average trading to 40,000 by 2009.

Of course, within a year the Dow was peaking at 14,000, and by 2009 it would actually be trading more than 50 percent lower at 6,500. Dent had missed by 35,000 points or so once again.

Strike two.

Perhaps the third time would be the charm?

Perhaps not. Undeterred by his previous two debacles, in which the forecasted booms had turned to epic bust, Dent would resurface yet again with the investment thesis based on his latest demographic research. In December 2008, three months after the Lehman Brothers bankruptcy, which represented the deepest, darkest depth of the financial crisis, Harry Dent Jr. unveiled his newest prediction. I'm going to need you to empty your mouth of all liquids and to hold one of the armrests of the chair you're seated in before I give you the title of the book.

The Great Depression Ahead: How to Prosper in the Debt Crisis of 2010–2012

I swear, I'm not joking.

The author who had successfully predicted two of the last zero boom times had flipped prodigiously gloomy right at the nadir of the cycle.

In his late 2008 book, Dent predicted that the Dow would ultimately drop to a low of 3,800 during a decade in which unavoidable deflation and impossibly high debt would wreck the economy, taking real estate values, stock prices, employment, and even gold hedges down to the mat.

Now, of course, the exact opposite has happened since his book was first published. The U.S. stock market had put in a generational bottom within a few months and had ended the year 2009 up 25 percent. As of the summer of 2013, well past the "debt crisis" dates referenced in the title of Dent's new depression book, stocks had rebounded by 145 percent. The economy has since added millions of jobs, and home prices have stabilized and rebounded in every region of the country. The once optimistic Dent had turned supremely pessimistic at precisely the wrong the moment, an amazing feat.

Strike three.

I've seen subsequent interviews in which, as late as 2013, Dent was revising his price targets and timetables to Dow 6,000 and a final crash happening sometime around 2019. This moderation of his doomsaying and extension of his endgame is excellent punditsmanship, to be sure—admirable even—in that it gives him more time and more opportunity to make media appearances.

As recently as November 2012, Dent was telling his tale of failed economic stimulus and the spending drought to come to Maria Bartiromo and Bill Griffeth on CNBC's *Closing Bell* program. The formerly optimistic Dent now employs all the tricks of the traditional doomer: He claims to be early rather than wrong. He points to the evidence of recovery all around us that would seem to contradict his negativity and claims that it is somehow proof that he's actually right. He insinuates that what we're seeing on the surface belies what's really beneath. He muddies the waters even more by saying that there are two economies, the one the government and the media are reporting on and the real one, the one that he is actually dead right on.

Dent's theories and research were even incorporated into two failed investment funds. The first, a product launched by AIM that had managed as much as $2 billion at one time, was quietly merged into another fund after 80 percent of its assets vanished. The second was a short-lived actively managed ETF, presumably purchased by those who had been unfamiliar with his prior work.

It's a neat trick, and it works. His big books, which had all appeared atop the *New York Times* bestseller list, continue to sell. His newsletters do as well, and he remains a sought-after, fee-commanding speaker to this day. He is articulate, charismatic, and undeniably smart. But articulate, charismatic, and smart do not necessarily produce positive investment outcomes. Nor does an in-depth understanding of socioeconomic statistics and trends, no matter how intriguing the conclusions. As Allan Roth, who teaches investments and behavioral finance at the University of Denver, notes: "Brilliant research doesn't equate to beating the market. The stock market has outsmarted the likes of Sir Isaac Newton and Albert Einstein."

Roth had the opportunity to witness the Harry Dent show firsthand in February 2009, just a few weeks before the stock market's bottom and a few months ahead of the end of the Great Recession that summer. Dent had been speaking to a crowd on behalf of a financial advisor who had sponsored the event. In an April 2009 article, Roth explains the effect Dent's predictions were having on the audience: "Now Dent is a great presenter, but my attention was often diverted to the 700 or so guests in the room. Their heads were nodding yes nearly the whole time, which seemed fascinating and a tad disturbing. I felt like I had stumbled into a religious revival rather than a financial seminar. My hunch is that the financial planner who sponsored Dent signed up new clients in droves." The people in attendance had become convinced that the end-time had arrived and that Dent was merely reiterating their already formed opinions for them—the confirmation of preexisting bias is a powerful narcotic in book form and is lethal in person.

It is important to note that Dent was not alone in going down this road of attention-grabbing book titles. Larry Swedroe, founder of Buckingham Asset Management, refers to these books as being indistinguishable from the rest of the "investment pornography" that clouds our minds.

Wherever the *Roaring 2000s* book is mentioned, you'll frequently see a reference to the equally histrionic bestseller of the era, *Dow 36,000* by journalist James K. Glassman and economist Kevin A. Hassett.

I'll briefly mention a book called *Dow 100,000: Fact or Fiction*, which was released during the late 1990s' raging bull market. Written by Charles W. Kadlec, then managing director and chief strategist of brokerage firm J. & W. Seligman with a foreword by well-known technical analyst Ralph Acampora, it is filled with elaborate predictions, some of which would defy some basic laws of physics and mathematics. At one point, the author claims that 408 million Americans will take to the Internet by 2002, which would have been quite a feat considering the country's population of under 300 million people. For obvious reasons the book wasn't taken very seriously, so we'll not dwell on it here.

In the Glassman and Hassett book, *Dow 36,000*, the case is made that stocks have been serially undervalued for decades, as price-earnings ratios and other metrics understate the true potential of equity investment. Published on October 1, 1999, during the bull market's final parabolic spike, this treatise came to its largely unsophisticated readers at a time when stocks had undeniably never been more overpriced. But you are told right in the introduction that the book "will convince you of the single most important fact about stocks at the dawn of the twenty-first century: They are cheap. . . . If you are worried about missing the market's big move upward, you will discover that it is not too late. Stocks are now in the midst of a one-time-only rise to much higher ground—to the neighborhood of 36,000 on the Dow Jones industrial average." *Translation:* Only a complete and total f***cking *sshole isn't throwing every spare dollar at the market right now.

One important point of order: While many investors, econo-mists, and analysts believe that the Dow can hit 36,000 "someday," Glassman and Hassett specifically said in their book that it would happen within three to five years. Once again, the media was handed a gift in the form of highly educated, well-respected authors making an extremely bold claim and once again the public were handed a rope to hang themselves with.

Since then, the Dow has collapsed to below 7,500 twice and has not even attained a level half as high as that 36,000 target.

As for coauthor Kevin Hassett, the economist, he eventually found a home on John McCain's all-star team of advisors for the 2008 election. This panel of experts presumably had something to do with McCain's election-losing mantra that "the fundamentals of the U.S. economy are sound" as the worst crisis in 70 years was tearing the nation to pieces all around him. Can't believe they lost that one.

The other coauthor, James Glassman, popped his head up again in 2011, ostensibly to say that he was wrong and to deliver a mea culpa in the form of a *Wall Street Journal* op-ed. A paragraph or two after admitting that his Dow 36,000 forecast may have over-reached just a tad, what begins as an admission of error quickly morphs into something more overtly political. There are conserva-tive overtones in all his reasons for the market failing to have lived up to its true potential.

Among these reasons, he blames "a demographic imbalance, with too few workers supporting too many retirees and other non-workers." Another of his reasons is "a growing preference for European-style security."

Let's see. He blames "demographics" which apparently were unforeseeable just a decade prior. Given the various speeds at which people tend to age (I've just decided that I am still a teen-ager—take that demographers!), this is totally understandable. Then he blames the social safety net, which must account for a 25,000-point differential in the Dow versus his target—what else could explain it?

More excuses? Sure: "Still others include inefficient investment in human capital, especially K–12 education, and an enormous buildup of debt partly meant to prevent financial catastrophe in

2008–09. Meanwhile, developing nations like China, India and Brazil are growing far faster than the U.S." When you hear the term "inefficient investment," that is code for *privatize our schools*, and when you hear that such and such nation is growing faster, this is a stepping-stone on the road to *corporate tax rates are too high.*

At a certain point, the reader of this might conclude that it would be easier for Mr. Glassman to simply admit that the book had been written to make a lot of money while leaving the consequences to be dealt with later. But then we'd miss out on the sequel!

In 2004, the *Washington Post* asked Mr. Glassman if he felt "the need to apologize to someone who read your book, went in and got creamed?"

To which the response was "Absolutely not."

He then hilariously quipped that "I think the fact that the book title is a number—as things have turned out, maybe a calmer title might have been better." This is probably true—but then who would have bought it? Which media outlets would have so boisterously promoted it? Go big or go home, the pundits have learned, and nobody has ever gone bigger.

James K. Glassman went on to hold several powerful positions at news media organizations and think tanks and within the government.

In September 2009, he was named founding executive director of the George W. Bush Institute, and he currently serves as one of twenty-one members on the SEC's Investor Advisory Committee.

The book, now a notorious symbol of poor predictions and part of the iconography of the bubble era, can currently be purchased on Amazon.com for one penny.

* * *

For a media desperate for salacious headlines, authors who write exaggeratedly bullish or bearish economic and market forecasts are a godsend. Therefore, regardless of the track record of his predictions over the last 15 years, you will continue to be exposed to the beliefs and ideas of Harry S. Dent Jr. This will continue until the moment he decides to stop sharing them and not a moment sooner. His Certified Financial Pundit's license, while perhaps dinged a bit over the years, has not yet been revoked. This is the case so long as he continues to supply the journalists with outlier views.

The outrageousness of his opinions virtually assures that viewers and readers will come flocking, like palookas rushing a carnival tent to gawk at the latest spectacle that's come rolling into town. But the provocative predictions of Dow 40,000 or 4,000 are only half of the appeal. What the media truly loves is the fact that it's all grounded in academic research. This patina of erudition gives the producers and editors the best of both worlds—explosively controversial content without the tabloid stigma and loss of credibility.

It's a win-win scenario for the predictor and for the press. Not so much for you in the audience, with your head spinning and your portfolio positioned for extremes.

CHAPTER 10

WELCOME TO THE MADHOUSE

> It's a tough game. There are a lot of times when
> they're writing bad things about you and all, so the
> guy with the big money says, "Hey, who needs it?"
> —CARL C. ICAHN

Y ou can hear the hoots and hollers from the floor traders in the background as CNBC's Scott Wapner stares intently into the camera. From the anchor desk at the New York Stock Exchange, he is presiding over the financial media equivalent of a cage match between two of the wealthiest, most successful hedge fund managers of all time. Scott's not getting many words in as his two illustrious guests, both via telephone, rip each other's throats out live on the air.

There are threats, insults, and f-bombs flying back and forth, and floor activity virtually grinds to a halt on the exchange as the blue jackets crowd around TV monitors to listen in.

Carl Icahn, one of the most storied Wall Street personages in the history of finance, is disemboweling his rival Bill Ackman during an impromptu segment of CNBC's *Fast Money Halftime Report* in the middle of the trading day. This is about money, but it's also about a personal grudge involving lawsuits and perceived slights. It is years in the making, and the vitriol is thick.

It's not every day that two multibillionaires decide to air their grievances live on TV, but here we are. It's brutal, and it goes on seemingly forever, bleeding into the next show, as neither man wants to be the first to hang up the phone. The Twittersphere is going berserk—every trader, investor, and financial reporter with a social media presence is watching and reacting in real time. Thousands of messages and links are flying by; the normally slow-moving vertical columns of the Twitter feed are spinning down like a slot machine.

In the meantime, the stocks that are related to the dust-up between Icahn and Ackman are all gyrating based on who's getting the best shots in—shares of Herbalife, JC Penney, Icahn Enterprises, and other publicly traded entities affiliated with the combatants are undulating with the rhythms of the repartee.

Welcome to the madhouse.

* * *

For a long time, some of the most famous investors in the world were as well known for their obsession with secrecy as they were for their prowess in the markets. Hedge fund managers, especially, were notorious for the lengths they'd go to stay out of the public eye. Hedge fund legend George Soros once famously remarked that "speculators ought to keep quiet and speculate," and most of his colleagues had made that notion a way of life.

In the 1990s, Jim Cramer famously broke this mold and was one of the first hedge funders to begin publishing his market thoughts daily and appearing regularly in front of the camera. He became beloved by the investor class as the dot-com boom turned him into a celebrity. He was disdained, however, by many of his more reserved hedge fund peers for dragging the spotlight toward their general direction. Ultimately, he resigned from his fund, Cramer Berkowitz, in the wake of the dot-com crash to pursue his writing and media career full-time.

A generation later, however, the hedge fund attitude toward the media had loosened up somewhat. William Ackman of Pershing Square, David Einhorn of Greenlight Capital, and Whitney Tilson of T2 Partners had begun to talk about their stock picks and investment ideas publicly circa 2005. One blogger referred to them as the Three Amigos, referring to their predilection for appearing at conferences together and to the fact that their portfolios seemed to contain many of the same investments. Tilson started to blog regularly about his portfolio at the crowd-sourced aggregation site Seeking Alpha. It proved to be a fantastic marketing move for the small hedge fund he comanaged, and it enabled the launch of a retail '40 Act mutual fund product to boot.

William Ackman, meanwhile, arrived just at a moment during which the financial press was desperate for a new superstar to cover in the wake of the dot-com crash and denouement. With his piercing blue eyes and athletic, almost regal, bearing, Bill fit the bill.

The third Amigo, David Einhorn, would ultimately prove to be the most successful of the three. Einhorn's intrepid unmasking of what had turned out to be publicly traded accounting bombs like Allied Capital, Biovail, and even Lehman Brothers, solidified his standing as a formidable short seller and value investor. The fact that he could take huge pots at the poker tournaments of Las Vegas certainly didn't hurt the mythmaking process, and his boyish good looks were just the icing on the cake.

As Tilson, Ackman, and Einhorn showed their peers, there was no shame in taking part in the financial media cacophony, and for the purposes of raising new money, the system could be gamed just like the stock market. Tip just enough of your hand with a well-presented stock idea and the public would come running with checkbooks open. This was accomplished through articles published at Seeking Alpha as well as annual appearances on the conference circuit at events like the Value Investors Congress, the Ira Sohn Foundation, and the SALT Conference.

The combination of solid performance and media accessibility proved to be a winner for the up-and-coming star managers—their brush with fame was having the desired effect, and all three were able to raise their funds' asset levels substantially.

Tilson launched a mutual fund to capture assets from those in his new audience who were not accredited and couldn't invest in T2. Ackman was profiled by the *New York Observer* and told the interviewer that his goal was nothing short of becoming the best investor of all time, outdistancing Warren Buffett's track record through a combination of healthy living and superior stock picking. David Einhorn wrote a book about his adventures in short selling and his eventual vindication against a shady company he had bet against that decided to fight back. The Amigos were at the top of their game.

But as in all aspects of life, you can always have too much of a good thing. The thing about the spotlight is that it picks up our flaws as well, illuminating them for all to see. With notoriety for their funds and personalities came increasing scrutiny of their daily activities in the market and in their personal lives.

The website Dealbreaker began to publish their quarterly letters to investors online. Their appearances at the investment conferences began to garner the kind of media attention once reserved for Warren Buffett alone. When they mentioned a stock they were buying or selling, it would invariably be one of the biggest movers of the day as traders glommed onto the idea. When a market rumor of the next big Bill Ackman trade began to make the rounds, the press would be quick to amplify it online and on the air.

In May 2012, David Einhorn had randomly popped up to ask a question on the Herbalife quarterly conference call. While he had no position whatsoever in Herbalife's stock, his skeptical tone of voice was enough to cause an immediate 20 percent drop in the company's share price, with $2 billion in market capitalization vanishing in just minutes.

Never before had hedge fund managers operated so publicly, with their every utterance carrying such market-moving import. They began to feel a bit uncomfortable about this impact, especially when the pump-and-dump accusations began to fly. The idea of their mentioning a trade purely to benefit from the resulting price action had to have been offensive to the professional investors, especially given the long-term nature of their portfolio positions. They would soon change up their tactics to diffuse all the media attention.

In the summer of 2012, all the media attention being paid to Whitney Tilson and his Buffett-esque value ideas had come to a head. His longtime partnership with Glen Tongue (the other "T") was dissolving, so that the manager could go back to his roots, running a more concentrated portfolio of his own ideas.

Tilson informed his investors of this retrenching in a widely circulated letter that June after a brutal 14 percent drawdown during the month prior. "To ensure that I can focus intensely on in-depth company and industry analysis, I will adopt a much lower public profile and let my investment returns speak for themselves. Specifically, I will dramatically reduce my television appearances, interviews with the media, blogging/writing, and public speaking, both in the investment and philanthropic realms. I also plan to write letters to you quarterly rather than monthly."

In the meantime, things weren't going much better at his vehicle for retail investors, the Tilson Focus Fund. The mutual fund had performed in-line against its benchmark from its launch in 2005 through 2010, but then things had fallen apart. It had lost 21.5 percent in 2011 against a flat market for U.S. stocks, followed by a 6.5 percent drop in 2012 while the S&P 500 had rallied almost 16 percent. In June 2013 the fund was liquidated, which Tilson and the board had decided was in everyone's best interest. True to his word, Whitney Tilson has largely stayed away from the public eye ever since.

David Einhorn had begun to adopt a similar aversion to the spotlight, as the outsized reactions to his public pronouncements had turned cringeworthy for the normally subdued investor. In May 2013, Einhorn came out on stage at the Ira Sohn Conference, a veritable lollapalooza of an event, loaded with world-renowned investors, and addressed this at the top of his presentation. "It doesn't make sense to blindly follow me or anyone else into a stock," Einhorn told the crowd and, indirectly, the media watching from the upper gallery in the hopes they'd pass the message on. "Do your own work."

This exhortation had come a few weeks after the magazine *Bloomberg BusinessWeek* had chronicled the impact he was having with a cover story entitled "When David Einhorn Talks, Markets Listen—Usually." The piece had shown how, while the investor had moved stocks dramatically at first, his influence was already on the wane. This was probably music to the investor's ears. The manager had made it a point to mention that he was a medium- to long-term investor, and he certainly did not "speak about stocks to benefit from any price appreciations that might occur."

But just as David Einhorn's calls were losing sway with the traders who followed them, another famous investor was rising to prominence for his very public, very vociferous market pronouncements.

Carl Icahn was already one of the world's most famous investors in Wall Street history by the time of his late-career resurgence as boardroom instigator and swashbuckling activist investor. He'd built a reputation over the decades as a shrewd investor, a money maker who could sniff out value in any sector of the market, and, more than any of these things, a tough guy who didn't take crap from anyone or suffer setbacks quietly. The so-called corporate raider had been triumphing over giant companies like Pan-Am Airlines and Texaco since before the hedge fund industry had even existed. It's been said that Icahn served as the archetype for the Gordon Gekko character in Oliver Stone's 1987 film *Wall Street*, but a biographical film about the real Icahn would probably be even more interesting.

Icahn's reentry into the public consciousness came at a perfect time. U.S. corporations were flush with over a trillion dollars in cash, and their boards of directors were still shell-shocked from the financial crisis. Many executives were focused on minimizing the risks they were taking as opposed to improving shareholder value. As a result, cash piled up, and opportunities to return it to shareholders or reinvest it had remained unexploited. It was what you'd call a "target-rich environment" for a man of Carl Icahn's talents and stature. He didn't waste much time becoming a force within the marketplace, a salivating media in tow.

Carl began appearing on television, eviscerating the lackadaisical managers at his target companies and even sparring with rival investors. His televised thrashing of Bill Ackman was among the most vicious public airings of dirty laundry in Wall Street history. A run-of-the-mill call-in segment had turned into an impromptu ambush. CNBC's Scott Wapner (nicknamed "The Judge") was almost speechless at his good fortune.

Industry beefs like this one almost never made it into the public eye before. Icahn was now turning them into a source of alpha, as market realities had begun to mirror his opinions on the stocks he was involved with.

The public Icahn versus Ackman battle had begun with a rather grandiose appearance that Ackman had made at a December 2012 investing conference during which he thunderously proclaimed his intention to level a company called Herbalife in which he maintained an oversized short position. It was a brash demonstration complete with hundreds of slides, outdoing every other investment thesis that had been laid out that day.

By the time Bill Ackman had finished giving this negative presentation, Herbalife stock had lost almost half its market capitalization in a matter of hours. As the stock tumbled from 50 to 25, Ackman was offering himself as a savior to the company's poor, uneducated pyramid of victims. He proclaimed the multilevel marketing firm to be a scam and predicted its complete and total demise. This was not just about the money, according to Ackman, and to prove it he was promising that the profits from his bet against the company would be given away to charity.

This was all a bit much to his dumbfounded enemies in the hedge fund industry, most of whom understood the value of secrecy, especially when it came to selling a stock short. The last thing a seller needs, when borrowing shares to execute this kind of bet, is publicity—unless he believes as highly in his ability to influence other market participants as Ackman apparently had.

Except Ackman's hold on the stock's direction would prove to be ephemeral, as other large hedge fund players took the other side of his very public, brazen play. Daniel Loeb and Robert Chapman, two competing activist hedge fund managers who'd had real-life run-ins with Ackman of their own, had bought shares of Herbalife into Ackman's trashing of the company. It wasn't long before the resulting short squeeze had gotten under way. All of a sudden, Ackman had found himself under siege, the narrative had shifted from "can't-lose, blue-eyed billionaire fund manager targets shady stock" to "Oh my gosh, this stock might put him out of business!" Even George Soros, an early investor in Ackman's Pershing Square hedge fund, had taken the other side of the Herbalife trade while the two coexisted in the same Manhattan building at 888 Seventh Avenue.

But no one had been so vocally against Pershing Square's Herbalife bet as Carl Icahn. Not content with the doubling in Herbalife's share price that had occurred by the spring of 2013,

Icahn had announced his intent to take a few seats on the company's board as well. In addition, he'd mentioned that an outright leveraged buyout of the whole company might also be on the table. The stock would go on to subsequently almost triple in price, and Mr. Ackman had found himself caught in a vise of sorts by the summer.

In July, Carl Icahn took his victory lap on stage as the keynote speaker at CNBC's Delivering Alpha conference in New York City. Scott Wapner, by this point the financial media's unofficial "Icahn whisperer," coaxed the following out of the septuagenarian living legend: "I've changed my thinking on Ackman. Anyone that makes me a quarter of a billion dollars, I like . . ." The crowd roared with laughter. Icahn admitted having his hatred of Ackman to thank for the money he'd made in Herbalife, saying he would never have looked at the stock if not for his rival's hubristic pronouncements. "It's stupid to take a short position that big anyway . . . it's stupid to get a room full of people and tell them. He's not the best thought-of man on Wall Street, but I like him now so I'm not going to say anything."

Bill Ackman, like his fellow Amigos Whitney Tilson and David Einhorn, would henceforth be adopting a much lower profile going forward. He'd whispered through that May's Ira Sohn Conference appearance and had rolled out a fairly nonconfrontational, long thesis on blue chip Procter & Gamble. There were no fireworks or sound bites to be had from the run-through, just some matter-of-fact points about the company's profit margins having room to expand. The press largely yawned, but that was probably the point. He'd certainly gotten his fill of media attention by that point.

Carl Icahn, in the meanwhile, ultimately went on to discover an even more direct and potent channel to the masses as his official Twitter account went live. In July 2013, a few weeks after Warren Buffett had sent his first tweet, Icahn had arrived on the scene to say that "Twitter is great. I like it almost as much as I like Dell," alluding to another corporate target of his. The media went wild at the idea of having so august a presence talking about stocks directly to the public.

Icahn's account had garnered tens of thousands of followers almost immediately. It wouldn't be long before he'd be using Twitter as a bullhorn. A month after joining Twitter, Icahn tweeted, "We currently have a large position in APPLE. We believe the company to be extremely undervalued. Spoke to Tim Cook today. More to come." Shares of Apple ran up from $475.76 to a high of $494.66, adding over $17 billion in market value in under an hour! TV had nothing on the power of social media, it turned out, and Icahn had unlocked the secret to Instant Alpha.

By the end of the year, the old lion had become the world's richest hedge fund manager, surpassing even George Soros thanks to high-profile, media-lauded bets on Apple, Herbalife, and Netflix during the course of the year. By December, *TIME Magazine* had slapped him on the cover and referred to him as "the most important investor in America."

Where the Amigos had experienced the pitfalls of market punditry, Icahn had found only more profit.

CHAPTER 11

TALES FROM THE NEWS CYCLE

A CONVERSATION WITH HERB GREENBERG

erb Greenberg spent his professional life roaming between old-school journalism, the Internet, and straight television punditry. If financial punditry were a baseball organization, Greenberg would be an underappreciated utility player with a knack for making everyone around him better.

A Miami native, Herb started at the *Boca Raton News* ("Knight-Ridder's smallest yet probably most innovative daily") and journeyed from the minors of the newspaper world. He covered business for the *St. Paul Pioneer Press*, had stints at the *Chicago Tribune* and *Crain's Chicago Business*, and most notably spent a decade cranking out six business columns per week at the *San Francisco Chronicle*.

It was in San Francisco that I first met Herb. He'd stumbled on something I'd posted online and tracked me down to use me as a source. I was running less than $50 million out of a tiny office on Union Street. Only Herb would have thought to dig me up to see if I had anything worth printing.

Herb's passion has always been for digging into the nooks and crannies of companies, finding irregularities and raising questions most investors and analysts don't bother to ask. He red-flagged issues at EDS, Tyco, Planet Hollywood, WorldCom, Network Solutions, and at least half a dozen other major investing train wrecks well before they flew off the tracks.

In one of his more memorable journalistic sieges, he camped out at a company called Iomega for much of the mid-1990s. An early online "cult stock," Iomega made portable hard-drive types of things for PCs back when those seemed like the future. The stock went parabolic on the popularity of its Zip Drive, rising from under $300 million in 1995 to more than $7 billion in May 1996.

Herb mocked the inanity the whole way. He didn't make a call on the stock with any time attached. He didn't pretend to do so. He just picked away at the story and raised an endless series of red flags about margins and commodity pricing pressure and the suspicious nature of a stock rising 1,500 percent in two years. Most of this seems to have been ignored, as the bubble popped and IOM shares fell all the way back from whence they came.

What he got for his trouble was a reporter's salary and a ton of abuse. Even before the Internet troll was invented, Greenberg was scoring his hate mail with what he called the "Hostile React-O-Meter." As far back as 1996, Herb was locked in firefights with online investors and causing the "Hostile-React-O-Meter" to spin way out of control.

Greenberg only briefly stepped across the line into pure finance when he started GreenbergMeritz Research & Analytics in 2008. His research was great, but despite doing more work than many fund managers, his timing wasn't, and by 2010 Greenberg was back on CNBC, having had a hard time finding a paying market for his deep-dive research.

On March 6, 2012, Greenberg wrote a column called "Questioning Herbalife's 'Research.'" In it he criticized the company for its generally shifty behavior. "I don't like it when companies try to position themselves as something more than what they are and say one thing to Wall Street and something else in their SEC filings," Greenberg wrote. "It just makes you wonder what else isn't quite as it appears."

At the time, Herbalife shares were in the high $70s. To the extent of the reaction to Greenberg's column, it was surprising that Herbalife still existed.

Hedge fund manager Bill Ackman and his team at Pershing Square Capital were also skeptical of the Herbalife business model. Doing similar but more intensive research on the company, Ackman came to the conclusion that, as Greenberg suspected, nothing was quite what it appeared. Also like Greenberg, Ackman shared his suspicions with the world.

The big difference between the two approaches was that Ackman shorted $1 billion of shares of HLF before sharing his work. Because of Ackman's high profile in the investment world, he didn't have to do the actual reporting of the story himself. Ackman gave reporters all the facts they needed and then handed them the headline by presenting his work at a high-profile conference.

Just as he had to have known would happen, Bill Ackman's slide show unleashed hell.

On December 18, shares of Herbalife closed at $42.50. On the nineteenth, word leaked out that Pershing Square was short 20 million shares. On the twentieth, Ackman gave his Tony-worthy performance. By the time he was done, HLF shareholders were dumping shares at any price.

The closing low came on Christmas Eve with shares settling at $26.06 on 6× average trading volume. The huge turnover was notable because trading on the twenty-fourth was shortened by three hours to commemorate the birth of Christ and the death of Herbalife shareholders.

Ackman and his Pershing Square fund got short at an average price of $48 per share. As of Christmas Eve, Pershing Square had a paper profit of more than $438 million. Its price target is $0, and Ackman has vowed not to cover a share until HLF gets there. If Herbalife goes out of business, Pershing Square will book gains of over $950 million.*

Bill Ackman has vowed not to profit personally from Herbalife as a moral stance. He says such profits would be "blood money." Herb Greenberg won't profit directly from raising red flags on the

---

* In 2013 Herbalife shares rose 138 percent. Ackman has hedged his bet by replacing some of his shorted shares with puts, but his Herbalife has been Ackman's self-described "worst bet ever" so far.

company nine months before Ackman because Herb doesn't buy, sell, or short individual stocks.

I spoke to Herb in the summer of 2013 when Herbalife was still unfolding as a story. In the interview he discusses his passion for investigative journalism and the relationship between doing work ("being a journalist") and being a pundit pulling trades out of the air.

I expected to find some resentment over his work having infuriated so many and launching millions' worth of trading activity without ever generating big-league money for himself.

What I mostly heard was the desire of an ink-stained wretch to go back to the ocean and start writing again. True to his journeyman's soul, on August 15 Herb announced he was leaving television, moving back to San Diego and going back to work for TheStreet.com.

For the moment at least, his "Mellow-React-O-Meter" is greenlining...

MACKE: Your type, the guys who are straight reporters in a way, are the most interesting to me. I mean, it's because you actually like going through all these filings. You hang out with smart people, and you're not obsessed with making a billion dollars off it, which...

GREENBERG: No. I can't make a billion dollars off it, because I can't buy individual stocks.

MACKE: Yeah, I know. But I've known you for what, 14 years? A long time. And I know the level of research you do, and it's valuable research in the right hands. You could've done something in the ring by now, if you were interested in going to the other side.

GREENBERG: What do you mean?

MACKE: You could've taken a shot at a hedge fund, a mutual fund...

GREENBERG: But I've tried it. Remember, I tried the research business. And we did that for two years. And it was a wildly successful business. But in the end, it was a broken model. And we had the wrong model. And as you know when you're a journalist, you get pulled back into journalism. But I probably don't have a certain level of skill set [for trading], or you have to be in there with the right team that really wants you. And you have to be willing to put up with that. And you lose a level of control. So it depends.

MACKE: But working for media people isn't really less controlling. They're kind of as demanding as clients, in a lot of ways.

GREENBERG: Well, the media business—it depends on what your role is in the media.

MACKE: It seems so; you're doing a lot of reporting, which I know you enjoy.

GREENBERG: And for one minute, you spend hours hoping to get the information, so when you're on, you don't sound like a total idiot.

MACKE: Well, you do that preparation. Not everyone does.

GREENBERG: And that's probably the difference between what a journalist might try to do going on TV and a trader, who might just be able to pull it out of thin air because that's what they do all day, is they look at companies and look at names. I'm looking at an aspect the way the longer-term investor might look at a company as an investment. But, yes, you're right. I've tried that route, but it just didn't ever work for me. And I always seem to be pulled back into journalism.

MACKE: Do you think it's the timing? I mean, you go deep research, and you can wait forever. Traders don't have that kind of patience. Most fund managers don't either. But, see, you've done this on Herbalife; you're doing it on Starbucks; you've done work that a hedgie will use as legwork, trade off of, and make money on.

GREENBERG: Right. He can. I can't and don't pretend to. And I don't pretend to in the way I look at things, because I'm not taking a position. Now, my viewers are taking a position. But there are many different types of viewers. The markets have changed considerably.

MACKE: You're doing investigative journalism effectively. And there's not an audience for a lot of it. I don't mean that negatively—I just mean, if you're going into the nuts and bolts of something and you get too smart, the entertainment value kind of necessarily gets obliterated.

GREENBERG: Yeah. So you know the world of media—look, you know TV as well as anyone, because you were [at CNBC] and you are doing it online. And it's not that much different, what they're trying to do. They're not the pure entity they used to be, because in order to keep people's attention, you need—and this is a bigger issue, you know—you need to talk about and overkill the story of the day. I mean, look, our—Apple was our most searched company by far even a day ago.

MACKE: And so that's what you give the audience because that's what they want to see. Financial media does what a business should do: give customers what they want.

GREENBERG: That, to a journalist like me, is the problem. Everybody wants to know about Apple; but it is but one company. And so all the other companies fall by the wayside. Frankly, most people, I guess, don't care about some of the companies I'm looking at. And that's the entire news industry; whether it's print or broadcast, it has to cover the things people are interested in at that moment as opposed to things they might be interested in down the road. So I've always done—other than when I pulled into TV—I've always written and talked about the things no one cares about at the moment. And, hopefully, they will at some point in the future. So if you get ahead of the curve, you've served your reader—your audience.

MACKE: Like you've stuck your flag in a story.

GREENBERG: Yeah, because I think there's real value in that. And I think that sets you apart from everybody else. And it doesn't make you the most popular guy in the world at the moment. You're not on air all the time, or people aren't clicking on your stories. I can show you stories I wrote. I mean, I wrote a piece in October; it was "What Every Apple Investor Should Know."* And I went on air at the time and talked about subsidies for Apple products and how the technology was losing its edge. But do you think anyone cared at that point that there was a fervor to that item I wrote? No.

MACKE: You were on the Herbalife story before anyone was there.

GREENBERG: I was there. If you went back and looked at the Herbalife story I started with, it was about a claim they had made about research and development and it just sort of mushroomed after I wrote that piece. And it was an old, almost innocuous piece that no one would care about. But it took a long time to do the work. It took us nine months of work in between everything else we were working on.

MACKE: You're meticulous about your work. You know these companies backwards and forwards. And then you wait. You're reconciling the two; because you're in a business where you'll go on *Fast Money,* and you'll have so much research and such in-depth stuff. And it's some kid who's trading it just because of the momentum. He'll sit there and make money in the short term. And he's a hero. And you know you're right, but you have to wait for the story to break and hope someone remembers you were already there . . .

GREENBERG: And you're right.

MACKE: Right. You touched on it. It's the idea generation in which you've got five blocks to fill; you want 20 different companies in there, and you're fast learning four of them, five of them, backwards and forwards.

GREENBERG: You could bring anyone on air to just talk about things. I mean, there are a lot of smart people out there. And what I think the Internet's proved is that there are so many smart

---

* "What Every Apple Investor Should Know," October 2, 2012, http://www .cnbc.com/id/49253311. Between the time the article was written and the time of our conversation on April 25, 2013, Apple stock fell over 38 percent.

people—whether they're writing on Seeking Alpha, or they've got their own blogs, or they're on Twitter, or whoever they are, people we never knew about before—there are a lot of smart people. All of them could come on TV; all of them could talk smartly about companies. But what I've always tried to do to separate myself is to take an idea, usually from somebody I'm talking to, and then be able to add to it.

MACKE: Then you see where else the story can go or come up with an idea.

GREENBERG: And then you go out and you try to prove it. And that's everything working absolutely correctly when the stars align; that's the wonderful part about what I do. And, yeah, even in an environment like this, you hope it works. But then again, when you get down into the mechanics of a company, you wonder if it matters anymore? But I still think people need to know about companies. As long as there's a public market and there are companies that trade, I think that there is a role for people to try to raise red flags over them if they deserve to have red flags raised over them.

MACKE: How can the audience separate the articulate pundits from the ones who are actually smart? The people who are good versus the people who are just out there for PR reasons or whatever other agenda.

GREENBERG: I don't know that they can necessarily do that. I think the journalist—and I have to be careful what I say, because I mean, I know the journalist—if the journalist is on talking, hopefully the journalist has done work. When I worked for the arbitrage firm, I learned a very important lesson, and that was we would know more about the companies we had invested in than anyone in the press. So there are people who are in the investment community who come on, and they've done their work; or they have people who work for them who've done their work. And they know more than any journalist because there are fewer investigative journalists today.

MACKE: So where does a journalist come into the picture?

GREENBERG: It's a tough call. And it depends on who you're listening to. Nothing's a hundred percent. Stocks will go up. People will say—look—look at Netflix. Well, I raised red flags. And the stock collapsed. I raised red flags pointing out off-balance sheet things. Well, that doesn't matter anymore. But it might matter in the future.

MACKE: Right.

GREENBERG: It's a matter of trying to figure out who really is smarter, who is really thoughtful. There are people here we have on air who I think are really smart and I'll listen to every word they say. And other people I'll turn the volume down on, or I won't turn it up because I don't really care one way or the other.

MACKE: Does it bug you as a journalist that doing your homework and making money aren't necessarily related? There are people that just almost have feral intelligence in terms of trading these things successfully.

GREENBERG: But they have an innate instinct. And they're not hampered by trying to be too smart. And in this environment that's, I think, how a lot of people have made money. I mean, look at the Herbalife story.*And those are very smart people on every side of that story. But when Dan Loeb and Bob Chapman†

---

* Herb Greenberg, "Questioning Herbalife's 'Research'" (http://www.cnbc.com/id/46639027).

† On January 9, Ackman's "frenemy" Dan Loeb reported a long position in HLF of 8.9 million shares at an estimated cost basis of just over $31 per share. In response HLF stock rose 26 percent from the close on January 8 to January 15. The stock rose over $7 in 4 days following the news, closing at $46.19 on January 15. Loeb's total paper gains on HLF as of January 15 were more than $130 million, more than $50 million of which came after the public disclosure of his position.

Later in the month Carl Icahn interrupted an appearance by Ackman on CNBC's *Fast Money* to ridicule him and suggest Herbalife's stock could be subject to "the mother of all short squeezes" because of Ackman's position (http://www.cnbc.com/id/100408608/Icahn_Ackman_in_Epic_Showdown

bought the stock it was based on the psychology of the market, not the quality of Herbalife's business. Buying shares was just a smart trade, even if it has nothing to do with the underlying business model.

MACKE: Yeah. Carl Icahn was great with that, by the way. He was nakedly personal about jamming that stock higher with Ackman short.

GREENBERG: He probably goes in and he buys—he's going to buy up to 25 percent of the company. Based on what I know, I would say that's a riskier bet for Icahn at these levels and based on what could or could not happen to the industries. It's more of an industry thing to me than it is a company thing.

MACKE: Well, Carl, he wanted to crush Ackman on Herbalife, and so he did it. I'm not sure the company had much to do with the trade.

GREENBERG: Yeah, I get it. But it's like—but now he has—you know, he's a big investor in a company that may have an underlying risk of going to $0 that may or may not come to fruition. And that's the other thing. I mean, I can't tell you what's going to happen with the government. I don't know.

MACKE: And do you think that's just a binary bet that traders are often making, one that you can't research your way out of? I mean, there's going to be a law someplace. At some point a judge is going to make a ruling for or against Herbalife. As an investor it's almost impossible to game if or when an investigation could happen.

_of_Billionaires). Icahn then created the very squeeze of which he spoke, purchasing the equivalent of more than 13 million shares.

Realized gains and losses are unavailable, but on paper the gains of the triumvirate's positions totaled over $1 billion. Individuals "playing along" with the very public spat almost certainly fared much worse.

GREENBERG: You know, how many times have I heard people say the SEC is in there, or the Justice Department's in there? That's meaningless these days. That means nothing to me anymore.

MACKE: In the big scheme of things—if you're an individual in an investment that comes down to regulators busting a company or some huge investor coming into the picture, you're probably going to lose money. The big guys always have the edge.

GREENBERG: Well, I think that's the concern with the markets, in general—that the average investor doesn't have a leg to stand on. That's why I'm not a big fan of following institutions in and out of their investments. I think that's silly. You never know. You never know what somebody's really doing.

MACKE: Take Carl and Herbalife. He supposedly owned 25 percent of the company, but he can do that with call options or common stock, and it can all be hedged dozens of ways. He's got all kinds of different exotic things on that. So it's much easier—he doesn't have to go out and sell shares, all those shares, in the company. He can just sell his calls or buy puts or do whatever he wants to get out of that. The individual has no idea what he's really doing. The filings are old, the press releases are self-serving, and the rumor mill is nuts.

GREENBERG: Jeff, look. Look, here's the deal: I think that—whether it's television, the Internet, Twitter—I think information is valuable. The more information, the better. When active investors say they don't read social media, I don't know how they keep up, because that's where dissemination is occurring rapidly. It's a question of knowing how to use the information you see, you get. Who do you trust? You can never trust anybody exclusively.

MACKE: Right.

GREENBERG: You know, my whole thing is helping people avoid losing money; it's always been sort of the MO. You know, just, it's a risk-reward thing: look at risk first, then reward, and then make up your own mind. Investors have to do their own work. I mean, you've got to go out and still work it. And if you can't do that, and you're just listening—I mean, you don't have the judgment to make that call and make it intellectually. You know, this should be aired on TV for people, or things you want to think about, to think about an investment if you already have one; rethink it.

MACKE: Media should be at the beginning of the research process for the audience. It's just silly to buy a stock just because Carl Icahn or someone else says he bought it.

GREENBERG: Or just because somebody raises a red flag over a company doesn't mean you should sell it; it means you should be aware. Just because somebody says this is a good stock to own, this may not be the time to buy the stock. But this is the kind of stuff you and I know, Jeff, from doing this for so long. Half the people in the world are looking for a free pass; they're looking for a hot tip from Uncle Eddie over there.

MACKE: Right. Then there's confirmation bias and having someone else to blame for your lousy decisions. If an investment craters, they blame it on the guy on TV; and if it moves higher they give themselves credit for being brilliant.

GREENBERG: But I think there's value in financial media. I can go down a list of people, pundits, the whole bit; there's value in all of it. But you have to know how to sift through it and understand what the message is.

MACKE: How do you "sift"?

GREENBERG: You can't assail the concept of media, but you can be smart about when you're watching media, what you're reading, who you're listening to. There are a lot of people in the hedge fund community who hate journalists, because they think they're smarter than journalists. But I could argue that you get great information when you go to any journalism, newspaper, online publications, or different columnists; there's a lot of smart stuff out there by journalists.

There's a difference between fund managers who just like to hear themselves talk and those who really deliver really good information. There are people on CNBC who are really smart. And we get some really great people on air. And you want to hear what they have to say. And sometimes listening is really good.

MACKE: When you and I met, I was paying, what, $1,500 a month or something to get Bloomberg. Just to get information, just to get the basic stuff that I can get from 9,000 different places today. You used to have to fight to get an analyst report. It was ridiculous. Now there's been a 180; information is everywhere. There's a fire hose of information and people are trying to take a sip out of it. It's too overwhelming.

GREENBERG: There's been a commoditization of content. And a lot of content is correlated to itself because, again, there's so much information. When I was first doing this in the late '80s, early '90s when The Street.com started, there was no Seeking Alpha. There was no Twitter. There was no nothing. And so online journalism was this broad, brave new area you went into. And you could disseminate the information. You didn't have to worry about the space. And you could get it out without a deadline and without waiting for the morning for it to be published. And it was this really brave new world that really made a difference. But since then, in the span from '98 until here in 2013, the world of information and content has changed dramatically, because there's so much of it. When you go to Seeking Alpha, there's some really smart, smart, smart fun writing there. Sometimes, you don't have a clue who the writer is. But they're really smart.

And then there are some really dumb people writing there; and you say, how the hell does their stuff get on major sites? Go on Twitter and you find and start following someone, and you say, man, this guy's smart. What a great insight this guy has in 140 characters; you want to follow that guy. Guys like you, who I would use as a source, are now in media. I don't even know how somebody figures out where to go to get unique information. So much of it is available online.

MACKE: It isn't a matter of getting it; it's easy to get anything you want. It's a matter of trying to filter it.

GREENBERG: You get anything you want now. It's all out there. I remember we had the research service. I was talking to a hedge fund guy

I knew in San Diego, really smart guy, friend of mine. And we were trying to sell it to him, and he said, "Look, I've got to be honest with you; I can get all of this stuff for free," because he can go to the Value Investors Club, or he can go to any of the things that have sprung up that are even behind paywalls and get good, solid analysis on almost any company anyone would talk about. That's the most remarkable part of all this, of what's happened. There's just so much information. I don't know how people limit it.

MACKE: Well you've had to figure out some sort of filtration technique. How do you do it?

GREENBERG: I think it's real easy. I have a limited group of people I follow; and I'd say two-thirds of them are probably really smart people. And when they tweet, you want to pay attention—assuming I'm watching Twitter, because I'm not watching Twitter all day long, because I'm too busy working.

If there's something I want to see, I can go to StockTwits. If I want to see what's going on, I can do a quick run-through on the tickers, just to see if anyone's saying anything smart. You can go to Twitter and see a feed from smart guys listening to a conference call, and it's picking up on the key facts, you know? That's the commoditization, democratization of good content.

MACKE: Some of it is suspiciously good. When does it become insider information? Information everywhere; it just floods in. Anything that happens in a corporation somewhere, somebody's already posted it, talked about it, and tweeted it. Does illegal inside information as an idea go away when almost anything you want to know about a company is floating around the Net? Can the SEC prosecute based on Twitter?

GREENBERG: Yes. One day, there will be a good case of somebody on Twitter who used Twitter to post false information or used it to trade and pass on information. That's obvious; that will happen one day, of course.

MACKE: They'll pass information, but what if they just do it because it's, "You know, I heard something interesting today," and they pass it along?

GREENBERG: I don't know. One day, someone will really be stupid. It'll be obvious. But you can't catch them all. Somebody will do something. It's like the message boards. There were always people on in the days of the message boards, that were posting stuff. They worked at companies. It was actually valuable information. They could tell you what was going on inside their companies. And if you knew that person was posting, that was value. I think there probably were some people nailed on message boards for posting insider information. And if there were, that same thing will happen; and it won't be a big, big case, but it'll be a case.

MACKE: Someone will do something that will get them indicted. But it's not going to stop anything.

GREENBERG: No, of course not. I've seen stuff from people I know; young people I know post stuff, they put up blogs, and they say things I could never say, that would never pass muster. If people only knew. This is one thing about the media that people don't understand. I can't just go out with anything. When it's something that is significantly raising questions, it needs to be run through a lawyer. It doesn't mean you won't be sued but you need to make sure you're not outright lying—I mean, I've seen people accuse. I've seen bloggers accuse people of fraud. You can't do that writing for a major publication.

Without naming names, I see a hedge fund manager going on air and accusing someone of fraud; that's a gutsy thing to do. It's gutsy, but I could never say it. I can't get away with saying some of that stuff. I just can't. But that's the difference between journalism and everything else, anyway. Journalism still does exist, by the way.

MACKE: But the reaction to journalism has changed. The way journalism relates to the world of financial media has changed entirely. Do you think the level of scrutiny toward your work, maybe even the level of anger, has gone up? You take heat all the time. How do you deal with it?

GREENBERG: You really ignore most of it. I sometimes look to see who the person is, if it's on Twitter, to see if it's somebody who's significant or a nobody. And I don't mean to mean nobodies are nobody, but I really look to see where the criticism's coming from, what kind of person—if there's any history. If there's really harsh criticism, and usually you realize that it's some stockbroker who's pissed off at you, I basically look at it as the Hostile-React-O-Meter, the nastier they get, the more the Hostile-React-O-Meter spins. I just generally have to overlook all that stuff. I don't even see half of it anymore, just because it could drive you nuts. It could drive you nuts. So if I get a bad tweet, as I think you've probably done—if I get a really absurd tweet, I'll retweet it and, just because it's so stupid—sometimes I've got to. One day I got a bunch of nasty stuff, and I just started retweeting each and every one of them.

MACKE: Sometimes I'll retweet the funny ones just because they're funny.

GREENBERG: Yeah, but sometimes they're just stupid. Some are people after you, and they don't have a clue what they're talking about. Often, I'll say about the critics I hope they know more, especially when the conspiracy theories start.

MACKE: TV is where the anger is the worst. It's always the toughest fit for a real journalist covering finance. The big question is why do you go back to TV? You were off the air for a few years. Why did you go back on the air?

GREENBERG: I was getting out of research. I had an option to go with a hedge fund with my former partner. I had a choice; I had a chance to do that. And I decided not to because I felt a strong pull of the journalism in my DNA—the newsperson in my DNA. TV—regardless of what you think of it, where it's going—is still an important form of communication.

TV is a great form of communications; it's morphine. I'm a strong believer in digital. I believe what is TV will be TV and be what you're doing at Yahoo and others are doing online. It's all part and parcel of the transformation of—in financial media, certainly—of how things are going to be communicated. But being here when there's news and when you're engaged in something, there's nothing better. You know that.

MACKE: Sure, but finance pays a lot better. You're really good at the research. You could make a dump truck full of money being not as good as you are at this if you got hooked up with the right hedge fund.

GREENBERG: People have told me that. But, see, over the years as a journalist doing the kind of journalism I do, I don't know that I have the skills to run money. I know enough about both sides of the trade. I watch it. You watch it, because you're writing about this stuff and you watch how it trades. But if we're talking about Herbalife, how it trades has nothing to do with whether it's a fraud or not. It has to do with whether the stock is going to bounce over if it's oversold or what the big funds are going to do. It's not the same.

MACKE: What do you think of the mix between the journalists and the hedge fund guys? When we started *Fast Money*, the journalists weren't crazy about the hedge fund guys, who already had their own money and were coming on and being celebrated like they were conquering heroes of TV. Do you feel like that mix has gotten better with the serious hedge funds now going on air?

GREENBERG: Well, I think they get along. I think they've added reporters here, so there's a level, a high level of journalists here. But there are hedge fund guys; look—I mean, I don't know who you like or who you don't like, but when I talk to someone like Keith McCullough or I talk to someone like Joe Terranova or any of these people, there are a lot of smart people. Because I've been on the other side, I just respect really smart people.

This Herbalife thing has totally flummoxed me because smart people, I think, are making decisions irrelevant of some of the fundamentals.

MACKE: Icahn is in there because he doesn't like Ackman. And Ackman, I don't know the guy from Adam, but to say you have 20 percent of this company short and you'll never cover was one of the dumbest things I've seen a smart person do in quite a while.

GREENBERG: Yeah. But, and then I could turn it around and say a guy's willing to say, "I have 20 percent of the short." I mean, damned if you do, damned if you don't. When I saw his presentation, knowing what I knew, I thought it was a really good presentation because, having done the work myself with a team here, I thought, man, he really hit these things and even deeper than we knew, on some levels. On some things, he just knew more than we knew. And so I looked at it, and I said, that is really good work. I wouldn't have gotten up and said it's a fraud and it's a this; there are things he said I don't agree with. But I thought it was a gutsy thing to do. And I thought taking on that industry was a really big deal, the whole industry, whole industry.

MACKE: The way he presented the trade was dumb. The research was smart. Everything was smart except for the part where he disclosed the size of his position and the fact that he was never going to cover it. He hung a huge target on himself to get squeezed. Other hedge funds almost had to squeeze Herbalife higher. It's just because you're insulting him if you don't. It's like saying you pity him.

GREENBERG: I can understand it. I definitely understand it. But at least Ackman's out in the open with Herbalife.

I think you're raising a question about pundits. It's who are these people? Who are the people? What are their backgrounds? What do they do? Why do they do it?

MACKE: I'm trying to help people use it.

GREENBERG: Let me leave you on one thing, though, that I have a problem with on all of these guys—not all of them, but many of them. And, again, it's the difference between a journalist and a pundit making stock picks. My name is used. I'm out there. Everything I write is a public record; you can find it and I'm held accountable, my reputation is held accountable. I lose readers and I gain readers based on the way I write, because I write with a point of view. But I don't say buy or sell, then just disappear. A lot of people aren't held accountable, and they don't hold themselves accountable. And I think that's a problem. When you don't operate with your name, you can say whatever you want.

Even when the pressure is coming down, I always stand behind the fact that it's my name on the column.

CHAPTER 12

THE *WANDERER*

A CONVERSATION WITH JAMES ALTUCHER

A gifted student as a child and a financial success by age 30, James Altucher ran headlong into the problems that tend to plague such financial versions of child prodigies. It's the manner in which he rebuilt himself and how he continues to tell the story that sets Altucher apart in punditry circles.

Plenty of people love Altucher and follow his *JamesAltucher .com* blog religiously. The appeal of his advice is the same thing that enrages critics. Altucher simultaneously stayed within the belly of the financial beast while openly rebelling against the "brainwashing American religion" foisted on the semi-witting public 10,000 ad impressions at a time 24/7/365.

Not surprisingly, these observations are polarizing. Anger is a natural response to people being told their frustrations and misery are tied to their having been unwittingly brainwashed into cultural serfdom.

Beyond his countless blog entries, Altucher lays out his philosophy most clearly in his book *I Was Blind but Now I See*. In it he swears off voting, makes a case for abolishing the presidency, suggests quitting your job, and says he'd rather blow his head off than buy another house. He also embraces, or at least accepts, a significant amount of anger and other universal failings most self-help gurus wouldn't cop to at gunpoint.

It's all the result of when—in response to hitting his personal bottom—Altucher started mentally from scratch on everything pumped into his brainwashed mind since he was a child. It wasn't nihilistic teen rebellion. Being different for the sake of difference is the ultimate conformity. The goal was mental freedom. Money, one of the American religion's basic tenets Altucher still openly embraces, affords us the opportunity to discover ourselves.

Altucher looks around and sees too many miserable, angry people running toward abstract goals for reasons they haven't fully considered. One of those people was him, but he didn't know it until he found his personal bottom and rebuilt from scratch and did so in public.

Altucher shared his personal story and offered some free psychoanalysis over the course of an extended conversation from mid- to late 2013.

MACKE: Just for the sake of folks who don't know, walk me through your experience. How did you start going into finance, then becoming a financial pundit, then mixing money and a kind of spiritual and capitalist philosophy?

ALTUCHER: I was very much interested in a finance base, and I didn't know which direction to go in terms of managing money. My goal was I wanted to manage money just like I think your initial goal was. One way to do that is to obviously work at Goldman Sachs for 10 years and then spin out of Goldman Sachs and raise $600 million.

The other way is to what I call choose yourself, which is build your own personal brand. You do that by sharing your opinions and ideas freely on sites that are popular, like TheStreet.com or Yahoo Finance or CNBC or wherever. And that's what I started doing, and I had the skill set to both write my ideas in a persuasive manner and have good ideas. If you don't have good ideas, you don't get to stick around. If all you have is bad ideas, people realize that very quickly. You have to have good ideas so people keep coming back to what you're saying, and you have to have the ability to argue it persuasively.

MACKE: Making money the first way is more conventional, or at least much less public. Until recently, ex-Goldman guys running $600 million, which used to be a lot more than it is today, wouldn't say two words in public. They were part of the "highly secretive hedge fund industry." If you're charging 2 percent of $600 million, you're taking in $12 million before you even turn on a machine. If you can actually make a lot of money for people and get 20 percent of the upside as fees, you didn't need other ideas to prove you were brilliant.

Strictly in terms of being a pundit, it doesn't seem like the public keeps score very well. All you seem to need to become a regular talking head is a good story. Is substance at all important for the guys just building brands?

ALTUCHER: I think it is. I think two things are required. One is your ideas have to make people money. Not all the time, which is impossible, but at least some of the time. And you also have to have an ability to be persuasive. So you have to be both an entertainer and intelligent.

MACKE: That's pretty slippery. Being an intelligent entertainer doesn't necessarily mean you know how to make money for anyone except yourself. There are some folks who have really helped the public make money with financial expertise. God bless them for it. There's a whole other group, the vast majority of pundits I'd say, who are selling a gimmick of some sort. Either they work for a bank and just spout platitudes about being cautiously optimistic, or even worse scaring people out of markets for years on end with crash calls.

ALTUCHER: There are two ways to be a successful pundit. One is with greed, and one is with fear. If you work with greed, you have to make people money.

Or you work with fear. There are always going to be people who want to be afraid because that's sort of evolutionary psychology. We get a lot more chemicals firing in our brain when we're in the jungle and there are things moving around that are scary. So if you can keep people afraid, then you don't have to make them money. But if you want to appeal to people's greed instinct, you have to make them a lot of money.

For better or for worse, I've always fallen on the side of greed rather than fear. I'm an optimist. I've been put in a position where I have to make people a lot of money for them to be happy. It's about a three to one ratio. In order to be a successful pundit, you have to make people three times as much money as you lose. That's an important, you know, statistically proven ratio.

MACKE: Fear is easy to sell as a pundit because it has so many faces. The ad campaigns with lions or whales or basically any apex predators are just simple messages implying a firm has control over the wild. It's less complicated than a Disney movie, but it obviously works on a pretty base level. People are already scared over money. A guy with a deep voice speaking over images of powerful animals is just as fear-based as ads for books warning of the coming crash. In either case, underperformance is all but pre-excused. People are terrified of losing it all. Assuaging fear is good business whether you're selling guns or mutual funds or newsletters.

But you stepped away from fear entirely. If anything, you're the opposite now. You're encouraging people to reject everything they take for granted. That's a tough thing to sell, but it speaks to life as a whole. Your work is more about life as a whole. When did you start the transformation?

ALTUCHER: Writing about money, my philosophy always was that I'm not the smartest investor in the world but that I will take ideas from people a lot smarter than me who are essentially giving those ideas out for free.

The whole basis of StockPickr was that I look at Warren Buffett's ideas, George Soros's, Carl Icahn's, and so on, which are always released in public filings that are for free. I built a whole site around those; then I write articles and make recommendations.

But after doing that for almost 10 years, I decided that what people really needed was not money. If you ask them how much do you need, nobody really knows the answer to that, but they know that they're unhappy.

I wanted to approach the deeper issues of this, which is what is making people fundamentally unhappy. What was making me fundamentally unhappy throughout the past decade or two of my career? That's what I started focusing on in my blog, not as a self-improvement blog but more, "Here are my stories. Here is what I did. If you relate to them, that's great. If you don't relate to them, then enjoy them because they're entertaining."

MACKE: I related to a lot of them too much to be entertained in a conventional way. The stuff about your physical health and the connection to happiness was particularly close to home. You suggest eight hours of sleep a night. I've got one of those wristbands that measures how long you sleep. If I can get more than five hours a night, I feel like I can conquer the world. That's a good thing. When I get under four hours for more than one night, I'm on the verge of total collapse. Eight hours is totally out of the question.

I was probably pulling two or maybe three hours a night in the spring of 2009. I didn't sleep for a second the night before the "Car People" segment when I crashed on national television. I stayed up and watched the movie *Michael Clayton* three straight times. I had it on my TiVo and watched it all the way through all night. There's a scene where Clooney is talking to his mentally ill legal partner, trying to save him from himself and their whole corrupt case. I watched it over and over again. "How do I talk to Arthur so you hear me? Like a child? Like a nut?" For whatever reason George Clooney's little speech wedged in my head.

I love that movie but it's amazing how screwed up I had to be to think I was Clooney and not Arthur in that particular scene. What the movie got right, and the hard part about breaking down with that mix, is the funhouse mirror aspect. It was two months after the end of the financial crisis, and I was doing a segment featuring the economic recovery as seen through the eyes of Toyota dealers in Denver. There's something genuinely horrible about how lightweight that type of segment is in the context of a global meltdown. I could recognize that but, wow, I blew myself up trying to explain it.

The most surprising thing in the wake of it all was how vicious it got. I totally understand the network making it "viral." I wanted out so desperately at that point and was acting like a jerk to a lot of powerful people. What amazed me was how harsh the abuse from the public was overall.

People were amazingly mean. Even by Internet standards.

ALTUCHER: Right. You can't take any comments or Internet trolls seriously. They're just unhappy people. I don't quite feel pity for them because it makes me angry. But I do feel that these are not the kind of people I want to be hanging out with. So I don't hang out with them. I don't respond to their comments.

MACKE: But you read them. You admit you read Yahoo's message boards. I love my viewers, but holy crap is the mood on the board ugly. I read them every once in a while when I know I've done a controversial segment. I wish I could say I thanked the people who are cool more than I get into it with the trolls. Sometimes I just want to fight back.

It's really just an online problem, though. Arguing with someone with a fake name isn't like getting yelled at in the street. Do you find people are much cooler in person? No one comes up to me and tells me I suck.

ALTUCHER: I've never had anyone come up to me and tell me that I suck. I usually have people come up to me and thank me. Maybe the ones who think I suck are just like, "Oh, I'm not going to talk to that guy." I don't know.

MACKE: What gets people so upset about pundits? We're guys talking about stocks on TV. It's finance, generally really dry stuff.

ALTUCHER: I think 99 percent of people want to blame others. And I see this all the time. I take personal responsibility for my wins and my losses, but it's hard to get people to do that. People, in general, don't change. Most people are just angry and unhappy for all the reasons I talk about, but they don't want to change. They set goals that are either unreachable or not in their best interest. They blame other people for their problems. They just get brainwashed. Ultimately it eats them up to the point that they get sick and die.

MACKE: If they're torturing themselves, isn't trying to help its own form of abuse? We've known each other a long time, but I couldn't be helped until I found a bottom on my own. Is punditry, both financial and mental, almost futile? Why do you do it? Is it narcissism? Is it selling something? It's an inherently thankless deal. So why does anyone do it unless it's a day job? Why do you do it?

ALTUCHER: To be clear, I haven't been paid for being a pundit in years. Nobody pays me. I also have shifted more from financial punditry to just general articles and posts about life in general. But the reason I do it is you do build a brand. You do become a trusted source, and the people who that's important to will eventually help you find opportunities. Because my name is out there, because people know that they can trust me because they can see everything I've said, the smart people out there will always open the doors to you and give you opportunities.

MACKE: Did your audience go with you as you migrated into more big-life advice as opposed to stock picking things? Do you think they understood the connection between finding happiness and getting rich when you put them in that sequence?

ALTUCHER: I think half did and half thought I was completely crazy. I had breakfast with a person I hadn't seen in a while, and he told me everybody in the office said I had a heart attack. I said, "No, I'm perfectly healthy. I didn't have a heart attack." And he said, "No, the word's out that you had a complete heart attack and then a mental breakdown." So I think that half think I went completely crazy and the other half stuck with me and enjoyed what I have to say.

MACKE: After the "Car People" incident, I kept reading stuff online about my being a drug addict with a mental breakdown. Which was only half right, at best.

ALTUCHER: What happened to you?

MACKE: I collapsed. The viral video side of it is the defining moment, but it was much worse behind the scenes, at least for me personally. The biggest mess was family stuff. My dad died of a degenerative brain disease that led to him getting into some bad deals with shady people. My dad was the closest thing to a hero I ever had, so I tried to help him and lost my temper. I think I said something in an e-mail to the effect of wanting the company in question to be swallowed in the fires of hell. Anyway, my dad died and I got sued for $113 million for "business interference" because I stopped him from mortgaging his house.

As a number, $113 million may as well have been a gazillion. It was absurdly over the top. It was absurd on the face of it. What sucks is that defending yourself from that kind of thing is brutally expensive. I was watching one of those *MTV Cribs* shows or something one day and realized my monthly legal fees cost as much as a new Escalade.

I'm not sure why it always seems to come back to cars with me. I don't even like cars.

ALTUCHER: How did you come out of it?

MACKE: Having a psychological break in general is pretty terrible. Doing it on television is probably worse than normal, but I can't say firsthand. At first it's all just about you trying to save your own life. Then you start feeling people looking at you. It's not like I thought the majority of the world cared one way or the other, but among those who did, it was a fairly newsy thing. I could feel people looking at me for weeks. Months. Once I got used to that, I remembered the way it would impact my kids. I live in an area where a lot of people are in finance. I realized I was probably the crazy dad. That raised the stakes. I'd lost everything. I'd rejected all my friends, gotten divorced, gained 50 pounds, and was drinking two bottles of wine a night. I wasn't killing myself. I was going off the grid. There wasn't a big "bottom" moment. I just woke up and realized that whatever it was I was punishing myself for had gone on long enough. I was so unhappy that I had to either die or find myself again and stop being such an embarrassment.

I was crushingly lonely and terrified about going back into the arena, but I had to. I couldn't go down as the "Car People" guy. It was humiliating.

ALTUCHER: Everybody is afraid. Everyone's a little bit lonely, and everyone's got problems. If you're as honest as possible about what you went through, people say, "You know what? I went through that also." And they start to respect you more.

It's good that you're writing with this, but if you totally described everything that happened, you would be a huge hero to your fan base. I know this for a fact.

MACKE: You're better at discussing your failings. You can do it without it ever seeming as if you don't have perspective on the fact that you're still a pretty blessed person. I mean, seriously, there are people who have real problems. There are so many people with sick kids and dying spouses and hard, hard lives. I was a guy who threw away a ton of natural gifts and made an ass of himself. It seems self-indulgent and a little clueless for me to dwell on what happened.

ALTUCHER: Not unless you're being totally exploitative of your past experiences. But if you do it in an honest and sincere way, again, your audience will shift. Some people will think you're crazy. The benefit is that you become this trusted source that stands out among all the other people who are just kind of spouting their BS while you're being honest and sincere, and what you see is what you get. For instance, I don't talk about my ex-marriage at all. But I do talk about losing enormous amounts of money and how I bounced back from that. That's my way of sharing the right pieces of information without hurting anybody.

I never write anything bad about anybody because also I don't want anybody to write anything bad about me. You put out what you get back. There's always going to be critics, but in general, like I said, you're going to be a trusted source. Your own, your trustworthiness is going to be recognized by the people who are important to you or people you don't even know yet. That's going to create opportunities. You don't do it for the opportunities but that's what happens naturally.

MACKE: We'll see. I'm not so sure, but you know more about it than I do. But it's an interesting point, and it brings it back to the real topic, thank God. Punditry is a business. I'll only get opportunities from this because it'll get viewers or at least will get me a seat at the table. It's not that producers will feel bad for me, and I won't want them to. They'll want the story and maybe a stock idea. TV isn't a therapist's couch or an investment advisor's office. It's a little bit of both but not really either. It's a product. Does that create such a toxic punditry environment that it minimizes the value?

ALTUCHER: It does. There was one particular news show that I was on quite a bit, and the producer said, "Hey, why don't you join us backstage on one of the shows and you can see how the show is produced?" And at one point during the show, he basically said, "Listen, we're just trying to fill up the space between commercials. That's our only job."

The only way they fill up the space between commercials is by having either extreme fear or extreme greed. And I would say the past five years it's been more extreme fear that they focus on rather than extreme greed. But no matter what, it's all bad. So I don't watch any TV. I don't really surf the Internet that much. I think it's much more valuable to read books or to find the one or two trusted sources on the Internet that you can really say, "Oh yeah, I like to follow this guy."

MACKE: Who are the people you follow?

ALTUCHER: There's a lot; there's actually quite a few people. I don't want to go through the whole list because I don't want to forget anybody. But there's a few good bloggers and sources out there. And look, Jeff, you've been through your own stuff. I like watching *Breakout* on Yahoo Finance. I'm not kidding. I watch that whenever there's an interesting story that I'm compelled to watch.

MACKE: Well, thank you. That's because of our excellence, but we still have to make things people want to watch. Compare it to parenting. If you want your kids to be happy, you can give them nothing but ice cream all the time because kids like eating ice cream. If you want to actually raise kids, you got to give them broccoli. Left on their own, kids will take the ice cream, and not many people tune into TV or click on the stories for lectures and brain food. C-SPAN is broccoli, and no one watches it.

ALTUCHER: What the audience thinks is that they want to learn something. But what they don't realize is that they want the ice cream. It's just like people in general. People think they want to eat healthy. Nobody wants to eat unhealthily. But at the end of the day people eat ice cream all day. What financial media does is give people what they really want, not what they superficially think they want.

What the audience really wants deep down inside is to be scared to death. And it's hard for people to overcome that because that's part of our biology. People naturally always want to be on the lookout for predators because we're prey. And so what people have to do to get over that is to kind of change internally. But that's very difficult. Financial TV knows that, and they just keep feeding the audience fear.

MACKE: There are valid reasons to be a little afraid if you're a small individual investor. It's not wrong to think perhaps the big guys have an edge on you and take advantage of the little guy.

ALTUCHER: You can be afraid of it, but unfortunately, there's nothing you can do about corruption. Unless you're actually going to be one of the manipulators, you might as well go to where the manipulators aren't. It's like the opposite of Wayne Gretzky saying, "Go to where the hockey puck is going." You want to go away from where the hockey puck is going.

There's tons of innovation, creativity, inventions, entrepreneurship happening. By focusing on the positive things and investing in those or investing in yourself so that you can be innovative, that's how you make real money. That trumps the business cycle. Focusing on those things is how Bill Gates made the real money, how Warren Buffett made his real money. They didn't care about the business cycle, nor did they care about the government manipulation. They just kept betting on innovation and successful entrepreneurship. Focus on innovation and demographic trends.

Everything else you should not even think about. It's all noise. You have to cancel out the noise. You have to have faith in entrepreneurship and innovation. And you have to make sure you're not being scammed because there's a lot of scammers out there, too.

MACKE: How rigged is the system in terms of helping the bigger guys? Are people right to trust Wall Street, or is it just the big guys are never really going to be taken down?

ALTUCHER: The big guys are never going to be taken down. Wall Street is filled with criminals, and yet Wall Street also funds a lot of the entrepreneurship and capitalism that takes place. So it's got its good side and its bad side.

MACKE: How much of investing is a confidence game? Is the regulatory system just set up so the public has confidence in the market being at least a somewhat level playing field?

ALTUCHER: It's definitely not a level playing field. Who makes money on Wall Street? There are really only three kinds of people. There are the high-frequency traders who trade trillions of times a second. You can't beat them. They make money every single day. There are the guys who buy and hold one stock forever. Bill Gates owned Microsoft forever and made, you know, $50 billion. Warren Buffett held Berkshire Hathaway forever and made $50 billion.

Then there's this third group in the middle, which is the people who trade on illegal, inside information. They've always been around. They're always going to be around. There's no way to beat them. They get more and more clever every year. So they stay ahead of all the security every year.

MACKE: Isn't it a pretty gray line? Where does the line between insider information and research get drawn?

ALTUCHER: It's totally a gray line. The answer is to do away with all of the laws of inside information so at least the regular investor at home will have a chance to see how stocks are moving and think to themselves, "Oh, there must be inside information happening."

It's too hard to enforce, so it's never going to be totally enforced. All the laws of inside information need to be rewritten. It's just another way Wall Street manipulates the masses.

It's better for the SEC to go after the Madoffs of the world that actually steal $60 billion as opposed to a somewhat victimless crime where people are trading on hunches or things they've heard. But it's really, really hard to find Bernie Madoffs. Despite all the people who said after the fact that they knew—"Oh, we knew Madoff was a scam." Nobody really knew until he turned himself in, you know, 20 years after he started or longer. There are a lot of Madoffs out there that are on a billion-dollar scale or a $500 million scale. And so it's really hard to find those guys. And those are the guys actually stealing from people, but the victims are usually rich, so the average American doesn't care that much.

There's kind of a weird relationship between enforcement and the scammers. The truth is you could potentially make a lot more money in your post-enforcer career if you play nice with the scammers now. That's not an accusation but the conflict is structural. And they go after the easy targets that might not mean anything—you know, like a random e-mail at Moody's eight years after the fact. I think maybe one rule is if you decide to work for an enforcement agency, you can't for a certain period of time work for, you know, a major hedge fund or analyst or whatever. But then you might not get the smartest people off the enforcement agencies.

I think the answer for the individual investor is to avoid it all and to focus again on entrepreneurship and innovation and demographic trends and also self-improvement, because that helps you buffer yourself against the noise that's out there.

MACKE: Regulators can't protect people from themselves. In 15 years we've seen, geez, two or three huge meltdowns. They both came from people basically being greedy, then blaming it on someone else. The banks couldn't have made things like liars loans unless they had a liar to borrow the money.

ALTUCHER: Yes. And look, many of those liars were average Americans who wanted to be on a mortgage and they wanted to buy.

MACKE: Right. And before the bubble burst a lot of people were flipping houses and making money. They were the same people who were chasing dot-coms 10 years before. There's always a bubble being formed somewhere, and it's always someone else's fault when it bursts.

ALTUCHER: It's always going to happen. And it's going to happen again. But again, everybody does want a scapegoat. It's a natural reflex. So the key is to improve yourself to avoid that instinct and to focus on how to make money regardless of the economic environment. Cash is always out there, and there are always opportunities to make money. But if you waste time scapegoating or blaming or being angry or being frustrated or regretting or being anxious, you're not going to make money.

The focus is to make money and protect yourself and protect your family and have financial freedom. Everything else will prevent that for you.

MACKE: The real American dream is to have the liberty to do what truly fulfills you. It's freedom. The dream is to be able to do what you enjoy. You can't divorce that dream from money. Even going off the grid requires resources. For a lot of our audience, Wall Street is about acquiring that kind of freedom; even people investing for retirement are doing it so they can eventually do whatever they want.

Even self-actualized, Zen-like investors are pretty much just trying to accumulate profit. Money is always out there, but sometimes it takes a lot more risk to get it. How do you separate that from "gambling," in a sense? It's the same risk-reward setup. It comes down to greed. Can you make greed healthy?

ALTUCHER: Well, you just have to make sure of two things: One is that you're not going to go broke, which I've done many times. And the other is that you're not going to go to jail, which fortunately has never happened to me. If you're a big client of Goldman Sachs and Goldman Sachs then says hey, you can get into this IPO and flip the next day, you absolutely should do that.

So if you can develop strategies that work that are legal and make money, you should do them. But never expose yourself to either illegal risks or risk being not so undiversified so that you have a chance to lose all of your money.

MACKE: Ideally, people won't have to make big decisions unless they're in a positive emotional place, but the truth is that's not entirely possible. No matter who you are, there are going to be times where you're under massive stress—whether it's a death in the family or divorce or whatever—and that stress will drive you into making bad decisions.

You can't always be in a good mental place, but you still have to make financial decisions regardless of whether or not you're happy.

ALTUCHER: You can't be happy all the time, because, look, it's the nature of the universe that all things decay. We're all going to be dead eventually; it's only an illusion if we think that we could somehow avoid that. For instance, my father died in the past 10 years. It was a horrible thing, but everybody dies eventually and you get over it. I'll die. My children are going to die. So, again, the key is you can't be happy all the time.

The world is not about happiness but it's about trying to be peaceful and settled and acknowledge when things feel horrible—being able to say, "Oh, I'm feeling horrible right now but this also will pass."

MACKE: When you put it that way, seeking profit seems pointless. Or at least crass. People seeking financial pundits aren't doing it because they've checked out of the game. They're looking for money.

ALTUCHER: Right. So there's something I refer to as basically my daily practice. Every day I have to make sure I check the box in four areas:

Physically, am I eating well and sleeping well? These are very important things, and it's always possible, no matter what the situation is, you have to make sure you sleep well and eat well. Emotionally, am I surrounding myself with positive people who inspire me as opposed to people who are going to put me down? This is always possible to do. At the very least, engage only with people who are positive toward you, even if you have to see negative people on a daily basis.

Mentally, I always make sure I'm generating ideas. This way if someone gets sick, for instance, or in trouble, I have lots of ideas for how to help or ideas for businesses I can build or whatever. And then spiritually, I always cultivate a sense of gratitude for the things I do have.

I try to always check those four boxes, and that helps me build a foundation on which I build my house. If you build a nice house on top of that foundation, it'll be able to survive the acutely horrible moments. Many times I didn't survive those moments, but over time I realized the best way for me to be successful was to build this foundation every single day.

MACKE: You and I both went through tough periods, and it cost us a lot both financially and spiritually. Now we feel better, but it was horrible and expensive. Is it possible as a pundit or author or guru to show people how to build a foundation under stress without them having to learn the hard way?

ALTUCHER: I think it's very hard. I think they could easily do what I just said without having terrible moments, but it's really hard in general for people to change.

There was a scientific study where some guys at Harvard asked thousands of doctors, "Do patients change their lifestyle after you tell them that if they don't change, they're going to die?" These are people, let's say, with heart conditions or other serious illnesses where they needed to change their diet or else they were going to actually die. All these people said they wanted to live, but only one out of seven would actually do the things the doctor said to stay alive. And that kind of shows you, even when death is looming, it's very hard for people to change.

Hopefully it's possible to push that number up to maybe two out of seven. A few will become more aware of how important this is. But, you know, there is statistical proof that people in the worst circumstances can't even change.

MACKE: The audience probably won't change no matter what you or I suggest. All you can do is serve as some sort of example. But what is your purpose out there? Is it selling books? Is it your brand? Is it that you just are trying to be an example for folks who are looking to rebuild? What's your goal?

ALTUCHER: My personal goal, to be honest, I don't really know. I enjoy writing. I like to entertain. I feel the best entertainment is to also help people by sharing my own experiences and how I got through them. I love doing what I do, and I do like to help people.

CHAPTER 13

THE *CONFIDENCE* TRICK

Doubt is not a pleasant condition,
but certainty is absurd.

—VOLTAIRE

In May 2013, a research paper—written by a pair of grad students from the Washington State University economics program—proved what many of us already knew: he who comes off as the most sure in his opinions will attract the most attention.

Using the tweeted prognostications of baseball fans and professional sports commentators, researchers Jadrian Wooten and Ben Smith determined that people who predicted the outcome of games with the most certainty gained far more followers than those who were merely more correct in their predictions.

The study's authors believe that this has to do with people's natural aversion to uncertainty and their utter discomfort with not knowing what will come next. Those who offer them the surety they crave—"Here's what is about to happen!"—will have a leg up on those who hedge their outlooks or deliver an expectation attached to a caveat.

"In a perfect world, you want to be accurate and confident," Smith and Wooten tell us, but "If you had to pick, being confident will get you more followers, more demand."

This goes a long way toward explaining the extraordinary popularity of the select financial and economic pundits who seem to always be able to deliver their views with an extreme sense of certainty. It is this variety of "expert" who is most sought after by reporters and producers, because the audience response is a positive one, regardless of the accuracy of the opinions expressed. Confidence is contagious, says football coach Vince Lombardi, and we actually desire to be in its presence.

Our ears will prick up when we hear an opinion being espoused in a brash, persuasive manner. There is a physiological explanation for this in that anxiety is the emotional manifestation of uncertainty and it is an unpleasant state of being for humankind. We want to alleviate it as soon as possible, even if we must turn off some of our cognition in order to do this. Researchers have been explaining this phenomenon for decades, beginning with Berger and Calabrese's work (from 1975) on the uncertainty reduction theory as it pertains to interpersonal relations.

In the run-up to the 2012 presidential election, we saw a predilection on the part of the cable news networks to repeatedly book a small group of talking heads who were willing to propound their predictions with the type of fearlessness that viewers crave. It was fascinating to watch this continue as the actual data invalidated their views week after week. It seems as though the more wrong these guests became, the more forceful were their exclamations to the contrary. By election night, former White House chief of staff Karl Rove was essentially claiming the sky was red, not blue, and doing so with an almost ethereal staunchness. Megyn Kelly, the network's anchorwoman, had to physically get up and trek down into the bowels of the Fox News headquarters building to show him where the intel was being compiled that invalidated his claims.

And it still wasn't enough.

If there's ever to be a Pundits Hall of Fame, this performance would guarantee Mr. Rove a berth.

We see this in the financial punditry arena on a regular basis. Those who actually believe that they can consistently time markets or pick outperforming stocks are in high demand because this belief translates into the kind of conviction on-screen that the audience craves. Media laps up the statements of the cocksure commentator because certainty sells papers and engenders click-ability in a way that hesitant realism never could.

Nobody is interested in an ambiguous opinion; the shelves in our psychological storehouses are already groaning with the weight of doubt and uncertainty, so why add more? No, we want to be told exactly what's going to happen and what to do about it, and we're willing to suspend our disbelief that anyone truly knows what the future holds provided the man or woman delivering this guidance is doing so with confidence.

There's an old saying that Wall Street guys like to trot out on the heels of a successful trade or transaction: "It's better to be lucky than smart." I have no idea why people feel this way, as it's probably much easier to be smart twice than it is to be lucky twice, but fine—we'll let them have the maxim for their own. In the context of our discussion here, let's also add that it's better to be confident than accurate. The public has shown a clear preference for the former over the latter time and time again.

Knowing is not the thing—it's acting like you know. Good enough, this is exactly what the public wants anyway. But don't be fooled. Do your research and know the good pundits from the bad. Be alert enough to the fact that the amount of confidence with which a forecast is delivered does not add to its probability of coming true, even though your brain has evolved to see it that way.

CHAPTER 14

THE *BULL MARKET* FOR *OPINIONS*

A CONVERSATION WITH BARRY RITHOLTZ

All pundits like to talk, and most of them are pretty good at it. Barry Ritholtz is a freak on both fronts. Barry absolutely loves to talk and can sling BS at an all-star level. Barry is smart, savvy, funny, versatile, and unfiltered. Networks have slightly different preferences, but as far as other pundits are concerned, Ritholtz is a five-tool player.

Ritholtz is a Bloomberg contributor and author of the financial meltdown book *Bailout Nation*. His work can be found scattered all over the Internet in the form of columns for dozens of different publications and interviews with every major financial or news network. He's also the force behind *The Big Picture* blog at Ritholtz.com.

The conversation below was taped in two different sittings at Yahoo offices in Midtown Manhattan. As is his wont, Ritholtz arrived with his mouth and mind at full speed. One doesn't interview Barry so much as throw a running tape recorder in front of him and attempt to wrestle the conversation in the general direction of the topic at hand.

By the time we sat down to begin the formal interview, we'd already covered the pressing matters of the relationship between dieting and machismo ("Men should never lie about their age or weight") and come to the conclusion that a dieting man should give away clothing the instant it becomes too large as a way of burning bridges on the road back to fatness.

The conversation picks up at the moment I was able to hit the "record" button. The first question was "Okay . . . what's your approach to being a pundit?"

Barry seldom needs more than one invitation to start offering his opinion at length.

RITHOLTZ: So all this goes back to my first appearance on CNBC. CNBC's complex is gorgeous now; it's like one of Saddam Hussein's lost palaces, but it used to be just this dump in Inglewood. It was Larry Kudlow, myself, and [market strategist] Liz Ann Sonders, and we're sitting in this crappy building on a set with a huge glass table.

I had a buddy who told me I should find one thing to focus on so I wouldn't look twitchy during the segment. So I was sitting around the table drinking sodas and looking around the room for my one thing to focus on so I could relax.

I had just finished a second Diet Coke, and I'm getting up to go to the bathroom, and a producer jumps in and tells me I don't have time. I'm like, "What? I got 20 minutes." He tells me no, we're going live, and he's got to wire me up now.

So now I have to pee; I'm sitting around this glass table, and I have to pee, and we're going on air any second. Then I realized that Liz Ann Sonders has the whitest teeth I've ever seen in my life. Immediately those teeth become my focus. I'm just looking at those white choppers and hoping I don't throw up on the glass table from nerves.

MACKE: This is all particularly awkward in front of Liz Ann Sonders, who in addition to having white teeth is quite lovely in general.

RITHOLTZ: She is, absolutely. It was just the three of us for an hour, and it was over before I knew it. Boom, we were done. I didn't really know how it went.

I walk into the office the next morning, and everyone cheers like I'm Romulus coming back from the dead and they're Roman legions. They go crazy. It's so funny how people respond.

With the cheers still echoing in the office, I called my father-in-law—who is no longer with us—who was watching the show. I said, "Harry, what'd you think?"

He says, "I don't know. You looked uncomfortable and kind of nervous."

"Oh, all right. Thanks." For the first half a dozen times I'd do a show, I'd talk to Harry, and he'd tell me what I did wrong. I didn't look comfortable, or I had a lot of stammers, or there was something wrong with my hair.

Somewhere around the sixth or seventh time, I said to Harry, "So, what'd you think?" He goes, "That was good! You sounded sharp; you knew what you were talking about. You really had fun with it; you laughed. You seemed to be professional." I'm like, "No, really. What'd you think?"

MACKE: All of a sudden you're a grown-up pundit in the circuit. You became one of those guys who goes on once a week almost no matter what. Did you get to come back because you were smart or because you got good at running your mouth, even without Liz Ann's teeth to help you? You don't exactly have to be both smart about markets and good at TV to get in the circuit. Just going good at TV can be enough.

RITHOLTZ: That's because a 24-year-old fashion graduate is doing the booking for those shows. Being a booker doesn't pay enough to attract people with a finance background or experience investing.

The bookers and the producers on many of the television shows know nothing about markets. They would just call me and say, "Hey, look, we want to have you on the show; you bull-ish or bearish?"

"So, we're only 75 percent long with 25 percent cash."

"But are you bullish or bearish?" They don't know to ask anything beyond that. That's a person who has no business working in finance.

MACKE: No, but they're not working in finance; they're working in entertainment. No one is fooled. This is not a big revelation for readers—

RITHOLTZ: Lots of people are fooled!

MACKE: But if I'm running a network, who am I going to hire? I am going to hire the person that can get a ton of people to watch my network.

It's entertainment. If it wasn't entertaining, it wouldn't matter if it was smart because no one would watch. You can be the smartest guy in the world, but if no one can understand you or wants to watch you on air, your view doesn't matter even a tiny bit.

RITHOLTZ: You can be both. Look at my partner, Josh Brown. Josh is one of the funniest people you ever want to meet. I'm not just saying this. He's legendary in the Twitter community, because in 140 characters, he can say something insightful and witty and brilliant.

I'm not saying you need to be a wet rag, but on the other hand, look what happened on CNBC with Dylan Ratigan and Erin Burnett. There's a guy who came up from Bloomberg, a lot of experience, really hard-hitting stuff when it comes to finance; and Erin—who I think is wonderful, but not a heavyweight like Dylan—she's the one who gets tagged for the Sunday shows.

There are great people there. I mean, look at Herb Greenberg; look at David Faber. Some of the producers are amazing. There are a lot of really smart people there, and every now and then they put out fantastic content. I mean, they'll do an interview with Buffett or Chanos or Einhorn, or someone and you're blown away by how smart it is.

The problem when they do stuff right is, how much it reminds you that they're not doing stuff right the rest of the time. Look, you have 16 hours a day to do filler.

MACKE: They have to do filler. Eventually there's not that much stuff to talk about during a normal business day. Business wasn't ever supposed to be a 24-hour show. It can be quiet as a funeral on the floor, but the network still has to find something to talk about all day.

If it's a boring day, that's a perfect time to bring on a guy like you. You're entertaining even if it's slow. That makes you a perfect booking when there's nothing to really discuss. That puts you in the role of filler.

RITHOLTZ: First of all, I always try and bring substance. I just won't do filler material. I won't make big stupid predictions for the sake of it. If they ask me where the market is going to be a year from now, I'll just say, "How the hell do I know?"

MACKE: They hate that answer.

RITHOLTZ: I love that answer! I've been giving that answer any time I can for years! It's only backfired once. I used to do *Bulls & Bears* on Fox before there was a Fox Business. I think it was '04—it was after I'd written a piece about how most people analyze the markets backwards from politics. When the market's doing well, the people think it's because the incumbent must have done things that led to a rally—things that drive a market, namely, strong earnings, improving consumer spending, which typically means high employment and high income growth; those all work to the benefit of the incumbent.

MACKE: It's the Joe Flacco effect. Flacco won a Super Bowl, so he got a huge contract, and they let him keep his job. They assume he's good. In the same way if the economy is doing well it must be something the president is doing. Most of the time the guy didn't do anything great other than play for a good team or get elected at the right time in terms of the economic cycle.

RITHOLTZ: The guy in charge gets too much credit for when stocks are going up, and they get too much blame when it's going down, but people try and draw the conclusions.

Anyway, I write about all of that and then go on *Bulls & Bears*. Brenda intros it with "Here's what the history looks like when the market's up this much in the six months before, and here's what it means for the incumbent." She finishes all that and asks me who's going to win the election.

The problem was at the time the market wasn't going anywhere, so the impact on the election at that exact moment wasn't clear. They bring me on to essentially say it's not conclusive. I said, "I don't know," just like that.

She had no idea what to say other than "Well, you've got to tell us" . . .

MACKE: Like you know but you're holding out on her. You've got an envelope under the desk with the winner's name in it.

RITHOLTZ: I said, "Brenda, I'm a market guy. I'm a math guy. I could give you the numbers, I could give you the analysis, but my forecast on this is irrelevant. It's meaningless."

She goes, "Well, if you don't give us a forecast, you can't come back." I said, "Well, thanks for having me," and that was the last time I ever did that show.

MACKE: Really?

RITHOLTZ: Swear to God. I wish I would have had something pithier than "Thanks for having me."

MACKE: An empty prediction would have been much better. If you would have said Thomas Dewey was going to win, that he couldn't beat Truman in 1948 but he's going to take down W, they would have had you back on the show.

RITHOLTZ: The whole point of my piece was using empirical evidence to make intelligent decisions and not allow nonmarket factors to influence you. Politics is the absolute worst influence on people's investment decisions.

When Bush got elected, all my Democratic hedge fund managers in New York would say to me, "This guy's tax cuts are going to be a budget buster; it's not going to create jobs; it's not going to do anything. He's going to be bad for the market," Stocks were up 92 percent over the next four years.

Fast-forward to after Barack Obama got in the White House. Republican hedge fund managers go nuts about how Obama is a Kenyan, a Muslim, a socialist. The day of the generational bottom in March of 2009 Michael Boskin wrote in the *Wall Street Journal* about how Obama was going to "destroy the Dow." The market is up more than 100 percent since then.

If you let these irrelevant, nonsensical factors affect your investing approach, it's going to cost you money. I want to reflect that in the appearances. I don't want to say, "Here is what my forecast is," if I don't know, and I'm running money professionally; I want the viewers to know, "Hey, I don't know." I don't always need to know.

MACKE: "I don't know" is a viable answer to specific market questions. The most honest answer usually is, "I don't have an exact take at the moment." It's inane to think professional investors would flip stocks just to have something to do.

RITHOLTZ: Our clients have a 10- to 20-year perspective. By the way, that doesn't mean you buy stuff in 2000 and you just ride it out for 15 years. That's just stupid. Valuation is important—

MACKE: But markets people are horrible at understanding what that means. Having a long-term perspective doesn't translate into doing nothing in the event stocks get folded in half or triple in value. If you have a bullish long-term horizon, you should be buying those crashes, not hiding behind your long-term theme.

RITHOLTZ: That's right. The most misapplied term in all of finance is the "100-year storm." Every time there's volatility, it's called a 100-year storm—a rare event that won't happen again in our lives. We get one every two or three years. I think there's an issue with that name, which reminds me of the banks of the Mississippi. The guy's house flooded away. They're doing an interview: "So, what's next for you?" "Well, we're going to rebuild. This is a 100-year-flood, and we're going to rebuild." "Really? You're not concerned about—" "No! This happened in 2000; we built then also."

MACKE: They've got at least 190 years to go because it just happened twice in 10 years.

RITHOLTZ: Right. "Statistically we are good for the next 200 years!"

You want to reflect some form of empiricism, objectivity, lack of emotion, but that makes for difficult television. They want you to guess exactly where the market will be. I had a conversation with Tom Keene on the air. "Where's the market in a year?" "Tom, I have no idea." He goes, "Come on, you've got to give us an answer." I go, "I'd be wrong, and a liar like everybody else who pretends they have an idea." None of these guys have an idea, and if you think that's the basis of investing, you are asking for trouble.

Look, the reality is the market's up three out of four years if you give it a long enough timeline. These secular bear markets that we get are punctuated with these wild cyclical rallies, so during half of the secular bear market stocks are actually going up. And then the other half of the time we're in a secular bull market where we are practically going up for 10, 20 years at a time. So if you have a bullish leaning, statistically the long term is in your favor.

But saying that or knowing that doesn't do anybody any good. Networks want you to say the emotional thing. I was on Larry Kudlow's show with Herb Greenberg one night during the crisis, and stocks had gotten hammered all day. Being the voice of reason, Larry tells the story about how when asked where markets would go, J.P. Morgan said, "Markets will fluctuate." And after you do television enough, you're not nervous. Being on air starts to feel like you're just a having a conversation with a bunch of guys. So I heard Larry, and I said, "Well, it looks like we got fluctuated pretty good"—television career is over.

And it's like, "Did you just say 'f***' on the air?" Well, I said, "fluctuate." Herb got it; nobody else heard me right. It was one of my favorite moments on TV because there's that instant of terror. Well, there goes your career. You're done doing television. Which, not that that's a bad thing, but it was just a momentary—oh, was I too honest there for a second?

MACKE: Do you think pundits aren't giving an honest answer most of the time if they say anything other than "I don't know"? Are they being intellectually dishonest? Are they just dumb?

RITHOLTZ: Well some of them are clearly stupid. If you've been on— you know, it's mean to go out and say half the people on TV are stupid. But my experience is that there is a substantial percentage of people speaking on television who have no business speaking.

We can talk about a whole run of people who've just lost people ridiculous amounts of money, but rather than focus on any one particular person, you just have to recognize Sturgeon's law. Ted Sturgeon was a science fiction writer who was once asked why so much science fiction is junk. He said, "Look, 90 percent of science fiction is crap, but then again 90 percent of everything is crap." You're not going to fill 16 hours a day with the parade of Nobel laureates and top performers. It's not Lake Wobegon—everybody can't be above average.

MACKE: Is it stupid, or is it the matter of focus? In terms of mental horsepower a lot of these guys are not stupid; they just don't do their homework, and they haven't made a study of it, and they are not qualified. There's that anyone who's smart in general can simply apply that to investing without much work.

RITHOLTZ: Let me ask a question.

MACKE: Flop it out there.

RITHOLTZ: If I bring a person in here and say I want you to do open heart surgery on him, you would say, "I'll kill that person. I have no business doing that." You draw that distinction . . .

MACKE: That depends. Are we still on TV in this story? Is it a reality show or life? If it were a reality show, I'd do it. That what the patient had signed up for . . .

RITHOLTZ: That's the exact answer! If you are willing to do it on a reality show, now you understand the Ben Steins of the world. They'll go out, and they'll say anything. They have zero expertise, and what they say is forward looking enough and ambiguous enough it won't get held against them.

I'll never forget reading in the *New York Times*, Ben Stein saying subprime is such a tiny percentage of the overall economy that it was meaningless. And I just wanted to say, "Imagine if your oncologist said, 'Well, we found a tumor, and it's malignant, but really, you're a 200-pound guy. It's a couple of grams—I wouldn't worry about it.'"

MACKE: He's a very smart guy. He just had the wrong analogy. He was comparing subprime to the junk debt. He was comparing it to junk bonds and how they imploded.

RITHOLTZ: That's because he doesn't know, and he has no business talking on the subject. You hear those types of calls from guys who are especially political.

MACKE: A huge number of people were blindsided by the crash. Half the people running around today claiming they saw the meltdown coming are full of crap. Warning people of a coming crash in 2003 didn't help investors in 2008.

RITHOLTZ: No, that doesn't count. Here's the thing—these appearances are permanent; they're on the web, and the print version survives. I don't want to beat up Don Luskin, but Luskin has a *Washington Post* piece [http://articles.washingtonpost.com /2008-09-14/business/36917060_1_great-depression -delinquency-rate-depression-comparisons] complaining the day before AIG and Lehman blow up that the economy is fine and everything is okay. Maybe the single worst-timed piece of economic forecasting ever, on par with Irving Fisher in 1929 writing that stocks are on a permanently high plateau. The next day the whole world went to hell.

It was politics. Conservatives didn't want to think housing was as bad as it was. You look at that, and you have to laugh. You have to say, "This guy has other priorities and other goals, but making people in the market isn't one of them." The great tragedy of economics is how it's been completely co-opted by the political wankers that are out there. I pulled up Joan Robinson out of Oxford—her great quote is—and I'm paraphrasing—"We learn economics not to understand economics, but so as to not be fooled by economists."

That's the problem with all these political pundits on financial television. They have a tendency to fool people while they're promoting something unrelated to investing. They will literally be selling a book or mutual funds or whatever. Their goal isn't to help make people money. Their goal is to fill airtime. The beauty of Twitter or the beauty of blogs, the beauty of social networking, is that you can find this stuff. All the crap these guys were saying in the 2000s and late 1990s still exists online. Guys who are full of crap can get called out on it.

MACKE: You can get called out inaccurately. If you talk in public long enough, people will take you out of context and accuse you of saying all kinds of things. I cite something you said in 2008 to prove you're a perma-bear.

RITHOLTZ: Well, that's something completely different. That's why you go at those people hard and you trash those people. I just had some jerk on—so I wrote the "12 Rules of Goldbuggery." Really critical of gold and maybe the single most viral thing I've ever written.

Based on a comment from a reader on what are the fundamentals of gold—was a blog post and basically took this guy's concept, blew it up to a full post, and it went nuts. Some schmuck's response on the blog was to yell about how I was really bullish on gold in 2011.

Complete crap, but because of the Internet I've got proof. I immediately linked the post where I said "gold hit our upside at $1,350 and we were selling half. I don't know how to value it. I've said this a hundred times. I don't know how to value gold." When people lie about what you've said, you have an obligation to respond fast and hard.

MACKE: What about changing your mind? Everyone has been wrong, but smart, useful guys actually admit it and explain what they got wrong.

RITHOLTZ: Well, that's the other side.

MACKE: But you talked about Ben Stein missing subprime. Six months later on Yahoo Finance, Ben wrote an entire column saying, "You know what? I messed up. I misunderstood. I compared subprime to junk debt and that was completely wrong."

Doesn't explaining mistakes add value?

RITHOLTZ: So, two things. First, every year I publish my mea culpas. I've been doing this for five, six, seven years. Not only do I publish it on the blog; it ends up in the *Washington Post* as well. I expect to be wrong. Ned Davis had this wonderful quote— we spoke to him yesterday, so it's fresh in my mind. He said, "Everybody in this business makes mistakes. The difference between the winners and losers: the winners make little mistakes; the losers make big mistakes." When you're wrong, it's okay be wrong—it's not okay to stay wrong.

MACKE: Other traders know that but—

RITHOLTZ: That's right, and most of these guys only own up to a very small percentage of their mistakes—the mea culpa from Ben

Stein was about one horrific and obvious thing. Now go back through the past thousand columns he's written, and dissect each of those. Half of them are horrifically wrong.

MACKE: Which makes him about par for the course. You have people that—

RITHOLTZ: Oh no. He's much worse. It's not that he's a dumb guy. It's that he presents himself as if he knows what he's talking about in investing, and if you look at his track record, he doesn't.

You guys used to do this on *Fast Money*. Here's what we got right and wrong. It might have been the only show in finance where people owned up to "Hey, we got this wrong." I don't know any other show would have someone come on and do that.

Do you remember that guy who had a mutual fund of nothing but Internet stocks? The Internet Fund—I think that's what it was called.

MACKE: Ryan Jacobs.

RITHOLTZ: Right. I'll never forget this promo I saw on CNBC right before my partner threw the TVs out of the office. "Up next, the tech fund manager who's doubled his returns this year. Up by 98 percent."

And that fund, I go, "Wait, that can't be right." This was in about 2003. The Internet Fund, which had been down to 95 cents a share, whatever it is, was at $1.92.

It's up near 2. Maria neglects to tell the audience that two years earlier it was $12-and-change a share. Hey, he's only down 86 percent. Woo-hoo!

I lost my mind, and I did a blog post about it and said, "This is why financial television loses you money." It was just horrific.

MACKE: So did Ryan lose his right to speak? Does he get to talk but you have to lead the segment off by hurling abuse at him? "You know what, Ryan, you're a moron. It's nice that your fund has doubled off the lows, but you're still down 86 percent since inception. Your recent performance does nothing to offset the damage done in prior years. In effect, you drained the entire ocean of money for 2 years and have now peed on the bedrock over the last 12 months. You're a loser; get off my show until you refill the ocean." ·

RITHOLTZ: No, but you need to do more to offset the cheerleading. You could have guys like Herb Greenberg who are investigative reporters tell people about the scam of the week. Financial television shouldn't spend most of the day kissing the butts of the CEOs of banks. "Here is a pair of kneepads and lip gloss; welcome to financial television." It should be investigative journalism. It should be comforting the afflicted and afflicting the comfortable.

MACKE: I love Herb, but not that many people who dot their *i*'s and cross their *t*'s are going to be able to string together a sentence. Herb's nice looking, keeps himself in shape, but reporters can make lousy guests. If all you put on TV were uptight investigative journalists, you'd lose to C-SPAN every damn day in the ratings.

RITHOLTZ: That's why you watch selectively. On *Squawk Box*, when Becky Quick sits down with Jim Chanos or Warren Buffett, that stuff is gold. That's the stuff you grab the transcript; you read it; you reread it a week later. There's wisdom there. There's intelligence there. There are people who have made lots and lots of money for their clients over the long haul—those are the people you want to sit at their knee and learn from.

On the other hand, I don't really care about some kids who are floating a new start-up. That's just fluff. It's not offensive, but there has to be some gravitas. It's not just CNBC; it's CNBC, it's Bloomberg, CNN, and Fox. There has to be a little more intelligence. There has to be a little more thoughtfulness, a little more understanding that there are people who are watching these shows and making decisions with their money based on what they see.

As a network either you can say, "Screw 'em. We don't care; we have to entertain the people," or you could say, "Well, let's try and put more and more"; and, by the way, to Bloomberg's and CNBC's credit, they've been rolling out more and more of that stuff. My opinion is, not nearly enough. There are still too many talking heads, too much nonsense, and too much bumper sticker stuff. Do you remember the Octabox? I don't know if they do that anymore because they threw the televisions out. You have a four-minute segment, eight people plus the host. It's like just flinging catchphrases at a camera. It's asinine.

MACKE: That's a nice idea, but running a network, any network, is a business. You get paid to get eyeballs. To make money it has to entertain. Viewers don't pay attention to people who seem boring or totally unable to communicate. You can't just be brilliant; you have to seem that way within the format.

It's always been that way on financial TV and in life. Think of Steve Jobs. He acts like Wozniak didn't invent the first Apple. Jobs threw tantrums until his designer Jony Ive figured out how to bezel an iPod and most of the other things that made it so appealing.

What about Tesla? The guy, not the car. You've written about Nikola Tesla. Tesla was the man. He was Edison's protégé until they got in a fight over Edison basically stealing Tesla's work.

RITHOLTZ: Right. Did you know Tesla invented the electric starter in your car?

MACKE: No, but that makes sense. Tesla invented everything. Tesla actually invented alternating current electricity. That was one of his fights with Edison. Edison wanted direct current electricity transmission. The problem is the wire basically lights on fire if you don't alternate the current.

There was a ton of money at stake on how the country got wired. Tesla was a crap businessman. He might not have even cared about money. He was about the science. Edison wanted the credit, the money, and his name on the building. That bastard actually electrocuted an elephant using AC to try to prove how dangerous it was compared to Tesla's DC, even though Edison had to know it was crap.

RITHOLTZ: It's fair to say Edison was a bastard of the worst degree.

MACKE: Right, but Edison would've slapped around Tesla in a four-minute debate if you put them in a bull versus bear debate.

Tesla came off as a lunatic. Tesla looked like Doc Brown in *Back to the Future*; only he's more insane and not at all entertaining.

RITHOLTZ: Sixteen gigawatts!

MACKE: Exactly. Doc Brown was the brains of the operation, but Marty McFly would have done better on CNBC.

I think there's a point in this. Okay. Got it. Tesla was actually concerned about human beings. He was advocating what was right and good for society. Edison was the worst kind of bastard in that he was pitching an electrical system he knew could kill people! It doesn't even matter if Edison did it out of greed or because he hated Tesla or was just a bastard. Edison was just a much better talking head type of person than Tesla, even though Tesla actually cared more about the public.

People who are smart about markets and articulate enough to hold an audience's attention are rare. The vast majority of pundits are just shilling something, which is fine as long as it aligns with viewers' self-interest, and that's usually not the case. People in general are lousy at exposing con men, and they're really bad at doing it with money on the line. How do viewers tell the difference between a polished guy who's an empty suit and a smart guy coming off as a lunatic?

RITHOLTZ: That's a great question. The answer is, it's not a snap judgment you make after watching some guy talk for 2 minutes on television. Unfortunately, that's the nature of financial television.

But let's bring this over to Twitter and StockTwits and Facebook and LinkedIn and all the social media. The beauty of these is that they're curated in a way by people you either like or follow or chose to watch, and you can see how much credibility they have by who their audience is. I got a question from somebody on Twitter the other day. The guy had 96,000 tweets and 900 followers. I immediately think this guy is a crank.

I don't believe the crowd is always right, but there is some wisdom in the collective experience of lots of relatively smart people.

There's an old joke about certain stand-up comedians play to the band and they might not make a lot of money as a stand-up but all their friends think they're really funny and the comedian cares more about the band's respect than he cares about the audience.

A lot of the pundits play to the crowd. I like to play to the band. I'm looking to speak to the educated person who doesn't want to be lied to, who doesn't want to be told things just to make them feel happy. You know what—people every now and then, they're really not happy when you tell them bad news, even if it's the truth.

I'll tell you a story. We've been uber-bulls on Apple since 2001. When a new account comes into the office, we liquidate everything but Apple. That's how much we love it.

By last year Apple was up to almost 96 percent of institutional ownership. Every analyst on the Street had it at either buy or strong buy, and it was up more than a thousand percent in three years. Huge institutional ownership, tons of strong buys, and huge trailing gains is not a good combination. That's a bad sign for the long term.

Then the uptrend on the price broke when the stock fell below $635. So we put out a note announcing that we were selling Apple at $635 and that we recommend that if you own Apple away from us, you sell some or do something else to hedge.

MACKE: Don't be a moron. And give back your gains, basically. I assume your clients got furious. They all owned Apple and had made money on it. They wanted to hear you say you loved it and it was beautiful and it could never go lower.

RITHOLTZ: That's exactly right.

MACKE: That's how it always ends for the cult favorites. Even the ones that turn out to be great companies have stocks that make insane moves, then break down and do nothing for decades at a time. The charts look like Walmart, where they spike and then they drop and settle in for decades. The whole time people hold on out of loyalty when they could be putting money to work elsewhere.

RITHOLTZ: Right. Look at Cisco. Look at Intel.

MACKE: And that's the best outcome. That's what happens to the great companies. Half the companies that spiked with Intel and Cisco have disappeared over the last 10 years.

Most of stocks that go parabolic never come back. And people don't get that a lot of these stocks just go to zero. The companies disappear.

RITHOLTZ: Go back to the original Dow. Most of them don't even exist anymore. But no one understands that. Our clients don't want to hear us say bad things about Apple. They think that we don't understand how great the company is or that we're missing the story. We end up shouting at them: "Look, this isn't our forecast; this isn't our prediction. However, after all these gains, it's not time to get more bullish. It's not a bad company, but none of these things go on forever, not even for Apple. At the very least, buy an out-of-the-money put to cover your ass in case this possibility happens."

Then what happened on Apple? It went $400. It was worth the trouble of telling people something they didn't want to hear about Apple. It added value.

A friend of mine who's really sardonic would say, "Well, we tend to nail truth tellers to planks of wood." Being honest on TV isn't that extreme. It is a little less . . .

MACKE: Less Christlike?

RITHOLTZ: Yes. People don't want to hear it—diverging opinions. That's purely a cognitive emotional problem. They can't help it. We had to say to clients, "Look, we love Apple; we're huge fans of Apple . . . but this is a piece of paper that has nothing to do whatsoever with the stock, and let me remind you," And all that most of them would do is argue about keeping shares. "But, Apple's cheap."

No one wants to hear the truth if it doesn't agree with their view. That is the nature of the beast. But that is if, again, there's punditry online, there's what you do on Yahoo where it's got a back and we're finding your audience. You're writing smart stuff; you're putting it out there. This is my view. Over time you'll have a reliable audience who's going to come back, going to become a core audience because you're offering what they've been looking for. A lot of the same things could be said about the cranks out there in the sense that the audience finds them.

Financial television is halfway between ESPN 4 and the weather channel . . .

MACKE: What does that make you then? You are always on my financial television. Are you like a clean priest in a cathouse?

RITHOLTZ: No, no, no. You can rail against financial media of all sorts from the outside, or you could say, "I'm gonna try and do this a little smarter and not give up on the whole idea."

Look, you've been doing this for a while. Your stuff is very different than the typical person I always got . . .

MACKE: I've gotten a lot of abuse for being this way.

RITHOLTZ: Well, to thine own self be true. If you have to adapt to different personas, if you have to go along to get along, you're just another jerk.

The world is filled with jerks. I don't think this is any great insight. You have to make a conscious decision not to be one of those jerks. If I'm going to go on television, I look at that as a burden and a responsibility, and I want to bring something intelligent and bring some insight. I never just talk my book.

A few weeks ago I was on Bloomberg, and they asked me, "What do you like? What do you own?" Well those are two different things. What do you mean? Well, we own Visa; it's been a house of fire, but we bought it at 90. It's like almost 200. I'm not going to go on TV and tell people I'd buy everything that's in my portfolio no matter where it's trading or what's happened since I bought it.

Viewers look at me and say, "This guy is not the most handsome guy, so he has to be smart." But I am going to say to people, if you are making financial decisions based on a 2-minute clip of television or 30 seconds of radio, you have to really rethink the entire way you find stocks.

MACKE: We've been talking for a while and covered a lot of ground. Let's put the pieces together. Give me the bullet points of what's wrong and tell me how it's possible to derive anything useful from this circus.

RITHOLTZ: Well, people seem to misunderstand the whole point of financial media. If you look around the world—if you look around prints and magazines and especially television and also radio—there's a lot of bad financial reporting going on.

I did a *Washington Post* column two weeks ago, called "How to Get Less Noise in Your Media Consumption." One of the things I do is, when someone says something that I think is either outrageous or foolish, I diary it. I use a program called followupthen.com. It's just a little app—you send yourself an e-mail.

So back in 2010, a bunch of guys had put out a letter in the *Wall Street Journal* saying, "This QE is going to cause massive currency debasement and massive inflation." That was November 15, 2010, so I sent myself an e-mail—to "November 15, 2013 at followupthen.com." I included the link and the body of the letter that was published in the *Wall Street Journal.* And the day before—this is the anniversary of it—I get an e-mail showing me this—so I post it on the blog and said, "Hey, look what these guys were forecasting three years ago."

We still don't have currency debasement, although we had huge currency debasement in 2000. These guys—where were they from '01 to '08 when the dollar lost 41 percent of its value? And we don't have inflation anywhere near like we did, or if anything, there's a fear of deflation.

MACKE: So they were completely wrong, but you're the one who had to figure it out. It's up to the consumer. They've got to understand what they're watching or reading. Financial media is a commercial product. CNBC and Bloomberg and Yahoo Finance aren't just good service deeds. They're businesses. If someone is making big financial decisions based on what they hear without doing other work, it's sort of their fault if it doesn't work out well.

RITHOLTZ: To a large degree. So the first article, two weeks ago in the *Washington Post*, was "How to Get Less Noise." The article this past Sunday was "How to Get More Signal." I give five or six tricks and tips to get the most out of financial media. The frustrating part about it is that there are a lot of great lessons floating around if you can separate the dross and find the gold within it. You can separate wheat from the chaff.

So some of the advice I give is: Take people that you've read over the years and respect their process. Respect their judgment and their track record, and consume what they write. That includes people like Zweig over at the *Wall Street Journal* or Morgan Housel at Motley Fool, Dan Gross or Mike Santoli over here at Yahoo—guys that you've been reading for a long time, who've proved themselves. Hey, there is Jesse Eisinger in the ProPublica who was the other person in that list. These are guys that are really smart and have really ferreted out useful data and put it into the context of information and knowledge that is valuable. As opposed to someone else just going blah, blah, blah.

MACKE: Set up a pantheon of people you always want to follow and notice. A top tier of folks who rise above the daily noise.

RITHOLTZ: Your own little research team. Follow them on Twitter; get their RSS feeds; subscribe to their e-mails. You see what the output of somebody who's insightful and savvy is.

The flip side is guys who've shown themselves to consistently be wrong. You just sequester them and don't read any of them.

MACKE: You cast the losers out in shame. Make the guys who murdered viewers' portfolios roam the earth like Cain, if I can mix my God metaphor . . .

RITHOLTZ: Yeah. There's too much good stuff out there to waste time. The way to improve your television watching habits—what I do with CNBC is a perfect example. I never watch live CNBC, except when Josh is on *Fast Money*. It's mostly appointment television. I'll go to CNBC.com, and I'll see who the guests are that are worth seeing. I'll watch 5 minutes of William Ackman. I'll watch 15 minutes of Warren Buffett. Every day, I see whatever Art Cashin has to say. I get more wisdom in a 30-second hit from Cashin than I do from the next 10 pundits combined.

But to sit in front of a TV for six hours a day, with it even in the background, is just a colossal waste of time.

MACKE: There you go.

RITHOLTZ: So you could take advantage of the financial news, if you're smart.

MACKE: There's the rub. You've to be smart to use it, but you can't get smart watching it.

CHAPTER 15

ALL YOUR INVESTMENT RULES CONTRADICT EACH OTHER

The golden rule is that there are no golden rules.
—GEORGE BERNARD SHAW

F inancial experts love lists of rules. They are clicked upon anywhere they're published, and they make for delicious television segments that producers just lap up when planning the day's broadcast in the network's morning meeting. "Ooooh, did you see that so-and-so just wrote this '12 Rules for China-Proofing Your Stock Portfolio'? Let's get him on this afternoon!"

The problem is that all the great investing and trading maxims contradict each other. All the so-called wisdom of Wall Street can be twisted to fit one situation and then ignored when it becomes inconvenient in a different one. These storied sayings can all be shown to be either worthwhile or dangerous, depending on the context you put them in.

Some examples:

- Always seek out differing opinions and challenge your beliefs. Except when you know you're right, then that other BS just becomes a distraction.

- It is very important to be flexible and open-minded. But invest with set rules and an iron discipline.
- Technical analysis and charts only tell you about what has already happened in the past. It's much better to use the information from the future that we have when making decisions.
- Never run with the herd. It's much better to be all alone on open ground, running in the wrong direction and wholly conspicuous to predators.
- Take your losses quickly. But don't get scared out of a good position.
- Amateurs trade in the morning, pros trade in the afternoon, junkies trade overnight, and lots of guys on TV just trade on paper.
- Be tactical, stay informed, and watch your investments closely! But don't try to time the market, and the less you do, the better.
- If you missed the 10 best days in the market over the last 50 years, your results suffered. If you didn't miss the worst 10 days in the market over the last 50 years, your results suffered.
- Never listen to someone who is talking his or her own book. But also never listen to someone who has no skin in the game.
- Don't fight the Fed. Except when the Fed is wrong.
- Pigs get slaughtered, and no one's ever been wrong taking a profit! But let your profits run and don't sell your winners.
- No one ever made money by panicking! But your first loss is your best loss, and it's better to be the first guy out rather than the last guy.
- Know your investments inside and out; study the management team and fundamentals and balance sheets and income statements until you know the company better than anyone. But don't know it too well—because then you've got a "sunk cost" syndrome happening with the amount of time you've spent and you'll be too attached.
- Buy the rumor; sell the news. Except if the rumor is false or the news is just a rumor.

- Buy when there's blood in the streets. But never catch a falling knife, which could lead to more blood in the streets.
- Look for cheap stocks with cheap valuations. Except when they're going to get cheaper—that's not going to be fun.
- The trend is your friend and stick with what's working. But skate to where the puck will be and buy what everyone else hates.
- Be passionate! But don't get emotional.

Good luck investing with that gobbledygook clanging around inside your head all day.

Unfortunately, this is what many professional financial pundits have to offer when asked for an opinion. They'll reach for the one that fits the point they're making at that very moment. As you can see, there's no shortage of rules for them to choose from and use to promote their point of view and pull the wool over your eyes.

CHAPTER 16

MARTIN ZWEIG AND THE BIGGEST MARKET CALL OF ALL TIME

To me, the "tape" is the final arbiter of any investment decision. I have a cardinal rule: never fight the tape!

—MARTIN ZWEIG

When Martin Zweig passed away in February 2013 at the age of 70, there were two types of articles ricocheting around between those who had vaguely remembered him and those who were curious as to what the fuss was all about.

The first type consisted of stories about his penthouse in Manhattan. It was said to be the most expensive private residence in the entire United States, and it's currently listed as being worth $125 million. But more fascinating than the stories of where he lived were the stories of what he did. In these tales, traders and investors who may not have been aware of Zweig began to redis-cover perhaps the biggest market call ever made: the almost real-time prediction of the crash of 1987.

Martin Zweig obtained degrees from both Wharton and the University of Miami, studying at night and working as a stockbro-ker by day. He began his professional career as an investor after getting his PhD in finance from Michigan State University in 1969. He had also taught finance at both Baruch and Iona College.

What's interesting about Zweig's career as a pundit is how early on it began. He was already writing investing articles for *Barron's* by 1970 and generally getting the market's short-term moves correct. Upon launching the *Zweig Forecast* newsletter and advertising it in the magazine circa 1972, his career as a market forecaster had taken off.

Before CNBC and before Bloomberg Television or the Fox Business Network, there was *Wall $treet Week*, or what everyone called "The Louis Rukeyser" show, on PBS, a weekly roundtable looking at the market week that was and the outlook for the week to come. It featured some of the most famous and brilliant investing minds of the era and aired across the country on Friday nights. There was nothing on the air like it, and both sophisticated investors and professionals never missed an episode.

On the Friday night of October 16, 1987, a sallow, visibly rattled Martin Zweig appeared on the Rukeyser show, and he looked "physically ill" in the words of one journalist. You can see him uncomfortably leaning forward throughout the segment with downcast eyes, the reluctant bearer of bad news.

By that night, the market had already been reeling, the Dow Jones having dropped 235 points that week to below 2,300, erasing months' worth of gains. To many, who had been conditioned to buy every dip over the prior five years, it looked like a buying opportunity. But not to Marty Zweig. As a pioneer in the burgeoning field of technical analysis, Zweig had been looking at his put-to-call ratio, a measure of bearish versus bullish bets indicative of the nerves of the crowd, and had seen the signs of a potential panic. He had placed his bets accordingly using options.

When Rukeyser finishes his monologue, he sits down at the table and turns to Zweig at his right elbow and asks him what he feels about the statement "The bull is dead."

Zweig then shocks the viewing audience—all of them watching it live and concurrently in a time before YouTube and DVRs—with the following: "I haven't been looking for a bear market per se. I've been, really, in my own mind, looking for a crash. But I didn't want to talk about it publicly because it's like shouting 'fire' in a crowded theater, and there are other ways to play it. You tilt your strategy negatively, and you shut your mouth." Zweig can barely meet

Rukeyser's eyes and certainly isn't looking to the camera. Despite the fact that he is positioned to benefit from the disaster scenario he is espousing, he appears to be anything but thrilled about the prospects for it.

This kind of commentary had heretofore been unheard of in public; certainly nothing like it had ever appeared before on television. People who had watched live still recall its haunting effect on them, their investable assets and life savings trapped with the markets closed for the weekend.

Zweig continued, "I think we're in the middle of something reminiscent of 1946 or 1962 which were very similar, and to some extent '29, but it won't be as bad. And I think we're in the middle to somewhat beyond the middle of this break."

Lou Rukeyser posits whether this crash call would then mean that Zweig's longer-term bullishness would need to be revised. The pundit then looks up for the first time and deftly makes the nuanced argument for a crash and then quick recovery. "There'll be some violent rallies, though; in fact, probably early next week I expect a violent rally. I don't look for a long bear market here; I only look for a brief decline, but a vicious one. In 1962 the damage was done in two months, in 1929 it was done in mostly ten weeks, and I don't think it's gonna drag on here any longer than that."

To say that Martin Zweig's prediction that night was accurate would be an enormous understatement. It was note-perfect; the exactitude with which he had correctly forecast the events and the timing were indistinguishable from magic. Three days later, when the markets opened in New York that Monday, the Dow Jones dropped a mind-boggling 23 percent, just as the man had said it would. On the heels of the decline, the "violent rallies" he had prophesied came rumbling up from the depths as if on cue, as if conjured by the wave of a wand. In hindsight, it was perhaps the greatest piece of market punditry of all time—the prescient call, delivered with the perfect amount of humility and proven to have been shockingly correct almost immediately. Nothing like it had ever been seen before, and we have yet to witness anything on a par with it since.

In the wake of this predicted crash, Martin Zweig's apotheosis had become complete. His book *Winning on Wall Street* flew off the shelves, he was hounded for autographs at industry events, and the funds he ran were bought into voraciously. A decade later in 1999, he would make the now-famous real estate purchase in New York for which he'd be forever remembered. The 16-room triplex condo atop the Pierre on Fifth Avenue had cost him a then record-breaking $21.5 million. By 2004 its value had tripled according to *Forbes*, and it has since almost doubled again, despite two recessions since his initial purchase. The purchase of this home may have been his second greatest call ever.

In her eulogy for her friend and early mentor Martin Zweig, Liz Ann Sonders, chief investment strategist for Charles Schwab & Co., reminds us that he had coined two of the most used (and overused) pundit sayings that have persisted even into the modern parlance of market commentary. Zweig, she notes, was the first to use "Don't fight the Fed" and to turn it into the now ubiquitous truism it is today. According to Sonders, he had also come up with the statement "The trend is your friend," which has since leapt from the parlance of the technically inclined into the popular consciousness; not a day goes by where you don't hear or see it repeated in one venue or another.

Mark Hulbert, editor of *Hulbert Financial Digest*, has been tracking the performance of investment advisory newsletters for over 30 years, and had the following to say about Martin Zweig upon his passing: "First and foremost, Zweig brought a rigorously empirical and scientific approach to beating the market, which, surprisingly, was not the norm among advisers when he began his career. That's because almost everyone whose path traveled through academic finance, and who therefore was particularly skilled in modern econometric tools, emerged convinced that it was impossible to beat the market. Zweig somehow escaped this academic orthodoxy. While a professor of finance at Baruch College in New York City in the 1970s, for example, he started publishing an investment newsletter, the *Zweig Forecast*. One can only imagine the sneers that elicited from his academic colleagues."

Zweig was one of the first market watchers, and certainly the only well-known academic, to begin incorporating technical signals, sentiment indicators, and historical chart pattern analysis into his work. He was a trend follower and typically despised taking risk, although he did believe in betting big when all the factors were lined up on his side. He was a huge acolyte of the wisdom of Jesse Livermore and a student of the tape. He also took financial punditry very seriously and was very supportive of up-and-coming experts like Ms. Sonders, offering simple and crucial advice prior to the tapings of *Wall $treet Week*, where he had become a regular panelist. He had a flamboyant side to him too—his collection of memorabilia included the suits the Beatles wore for their appearance on the *Ed Sullivan Show*, a Jimi Hendrix guitar, the original costume worn by Arnold Schwarzenegger in *The Terminator*, Marilyn Monroe's "Happy Birthday, Mr. President" dress, and countless other artifacts from the world of sports, music, movies, and history.

Before Martin Zweig, there were very few market pundits whose process could be accurately described as having been rigorous or particularly scientific. And of those market timers and forecasters who've emerged since, none have been anywhere near as fascinating, as high profile, or as brilliant.

CHAPTER 17

THEY DON'T GET CRAMER!

I think that stocks have been this tremendous, tremendous equalizer for people in this country. Guys who can't make a lot of money at their jobs have been able to make a lot of money in the stock market.
—JAMES J. CRAMER

*O*ne Sunday morning in the fall of 2003, I had walked a few blocks from my Upper East Side apartment over to the 92nd Street Y for a daylong event at which James J. Cramer would be holding court, speaking to and with individual investors about the stock market.

On the way over, I thought about the fact that I'd read just about everything Cramer had ever written up until that point, beginning with his online columns at TheStreet.com and culminating with his bestselling autobiography, *Confessions of a Street Addict*, which had just come out that summer. I was the original Cramer-holic, maybe the very first member of the cult that would eventually be christened the "Cramericans." I tell you this now so that my biases are laid out on the table.

The auditorium was packed that gray morning, the crowd ranging from young adults to seniors. Ticker hounds of all ages had come to hear their high priest speak. A handful of sponsors had set up tables in the foyer with brochures for life insurance and whatnot, but the audience shuffled by without even a sidelong glance. These were *stock market people*, retail investors who had caught the fever and were there to worship at the altar of equities.

Cramer took the stage and ran through his presentation. It contained no slides or props or charts of any kind. Just a where-we-are-now monologue on the state of the stock market, punctuated with stock picks from every sector, from shippers to microchips, banks to brokerages, software and hardware to autos and packaged food. His encyclopedic knowledge of the stock market had, until this point, only been hinted at in his columns. And then here it was, on full display, leveling the room with gale force. After his prepared remarks, Cramer then did something truly remarkable, bordering on magic. Without the aid of a computer (and there were no smartphones back then), Cramer proceeded to dissect each audience member's brokerage statement and tell people things about the stocks they held as though he were reading directly from the companies' 10Qs. But he was not. He had a working knowledge of virtually every single public company that people could throw at him that day, and he had details to spare.

From the back of the darkened theater, I watched as Cramer went one by one through people's actual positions as the crowd lined up in front of the stage. "Coke is great, but I like Pepsi better because of the snack food unit," he counseled one woman. Without even a pause, he was off on a jag about Voice over Internet Protocol and packet switching in response to a man who had presented a portfolio full of telco equipment names. I'd say it was a trick except he was sitting at a folding table with only a stack of papers on it containing his speech.

He must have gone through a couple of hundred stocks in the course of that day and answered dozens of direct questions about every aspect of investing you could dream up. When the event had run its course and all the books had been signed, Jim stayed an extra hour just to shake hands with the rest of the audience and to say hello to those who hadn't had a chance to bring their statements up. I sat there in silence, utterly floored. Jim Cramer, my earliest idol and biggest influence, was crossing over and becoming a star.

THE CROSSOVER

Keep in mind that this predated his daily appearances on CNBC, his own show *Mad Money*, and the dozens of college tours and *Good Morning America* appearances. What had earned him this initial burst of renown was *the writing*. In the columns, which came out at a rate of five or six per day, James was honest about his own trading flaws and investing regrets to the point of it being painful—and yet simultaneously cathartic—to read. We in the industry had all made these mistakes and gotten the same things wrong, but Jim was actually *publicly* flogging himself over them! It was authentic and spoke to the universal condition of the investor's psyche in a way that nothing being written by newsroom journalists ever could. And it took off like wildfire, the very genesis of the financial web.

Before there even was such a thing as blogging, Jim Cramer and TheStreet had invented the trading blog. He'd also become the first web-native pundit to cross over into traditional print media; his 1990s columns for *New York Magazine* and *GQ* are still legendary. Cramer was an oddity in that he was actively running money at a hedge fund while simultaneously discussing his investing ideas in print. This was totally unheard of 15 years ago but is now par for the course—we take financial and trading blogs by practitioners for granted these days as tens of thousands of them are updated every morning.

At the brokerage firm I first interned at in the late 1990s, my job was to stand at the photocopier and run off packets of articles to hand out to the retail brokerage sales force. These packets would contain a sampling of articles from our industry's trade magazine *Registered Rep*, the *Wall Street Journal*'s "Heard on the Street" column, and, invariably, a page or two from James J. Cramer, printed right off the Internet (a novelty at a time before e-mail and when brokers' computers were only capable of displaying stock quotes, not websites). Invariably, as I handed this stapled catalog of intel out to each guy on the floor (and they were all guys), the recipient would tear out all the sheets until he found what he was looking for. "Hey kid, you can keep the rest of this stuff. *I only want Cramer.*"

That grassroots adulation would enable TheStreet.com to become a force within the financial media realm despite its never having been a print magazine or newspaper. Jim was hiring talented market practitioners to write like columnists and journalists. His site was churning out what would become a galaxy of stars who had gotten their start there. He even hired real journalists to flesh out the site's coverage of nontrading-related news items. TheStreet would eventually go public, as had every other web property in existence during those early days of the World Wide Web.

His growing popularity with traders, analysts, brokers, and other denizens of the investing biz would eventually land Jim on CNBC. He'd paid his dues knocking out high-energy segment after segment, and at a certain point, it had become clear that he was the network's main draw. In March 2005, Jim Cramer's very own show, *Mad Money*, had premiered at 6 p.m. This was the precise moment that longtime readers and fans (like myself) had officially "lost" him to the masses. And some of us, like die-hard fans of an indie rock band, resented our hero's newfound stardom.

The format of *Mad Money* was unlike anything that had ever existed before. Its overarching message of "You can do this!" to the mom-and-pop retail set had garnered Cramer a massive following—from college campuses to retirement homes across America. More books would follow as well as live touring versions of the show, which featured frenzied crowds of cheering do-it-yourself investors and would-be professionals.

"THEY KNOW NOTHING!"

This fame would come at a cost, however. As Jim Cramer's star was rising in pop culture, an unhealthy culture of speculation was developing alongside it, in mortgages, in structured credit vehicles, and in real estate around the world. As more retail investors flocked to the investment markets seeking to gain their piece of the action, Cramer became a symbol of the bull market and the idea that investors could score. Within a year and a half of his show's launch, a pair of Bear Stearns hedge funds that were heavily levered to the riskiest parts of the mortgage markets were starting to unravel. Pockets of volatility began to infect and then shut down trading across various bond market sectors, and this would begin to manifest itself in the equity markets soon after. By 2007, debates about whether or not these risky mortgages were a danger became a nightly affair, and many stock market pundits blithely waved these concerns away with a recitation of the latest earnings reports or rally in stock prices.

Cramer was all over television in this era, the face of finance in the eyes of many viewers. His initial dismissive comments about the tremors in the bond markets or the shares of investment banks—"Bear Stearns is fine!" is one of many direct quotes—are what many choose to remember, but this would be far from a fair recounting of what actually happened.

On August 3, 2007, in what would come to be known as one of the most important moments in the history of financial television, Jim rang the alarm.

Appearing on set with his regular afternoon segment counterpart, Erin Burnett, who was inexplicably dressed up in a giraffe costume, Jim went on a rant to end all rants about the utter cluelessness at the Federal Reserve while credit markets were freezing up around the world.

Against the backdrop of a screen showing the stock price of $20 billion investment bank Bear Stearns plummeting (on its one-year journey from $160 to eventually $2 a share), Cramer went wild. Referring to new Fed chairman Ben Bernanke, Cramer bellowed at the top of his lungs, "It is not time to be an academic . . . open the darn Fed window. He has no idea how bad it is out there. He has no idea! He has no idea! I have talked to the heads of almost everyone single one of these firms in the last 72-hours and he has no idea what it's like out there. None!!!"

Erin jumps in with a hesitant "Cramer . . ."

But Jim is rolling now: "My people have been in this game for 25 years, and they are losing their jobs, and these firms are going to go out business . . . and he's nuts! They're nuts! They know nothing!!! The Fed is asleep."

The Giraffe Girl is stunned; she has no idea how to react. It's live TV, and no one put instructions for diffusing a bomb onto her teleprompter. Nobody watching at that moment will ever forget the intensity and the anger with which Cramer had delivered this missive from the trenches.

Unsurprisingly, this incredible moment in financial media was largely ignored by policy makers (and most investors). Within six months Bear Stearns would be wiped out, as would Lehman Brothers some months after that. Goldman Sachs and Morgan Stanley would suffer a near brush with death as well. Complete and total destruction was averted for most of Wall Street once Bernanke and his counterpart at Treasury, Hank Paulson, began overcompensating to make up for lost time, bailing out everything in sight more than a year after the Rant Heard 'Round the World.

Years later, in January 2013, we got to see the transcripts from the internal Fed discussions from that moment. Jim Cramer and every single thing he said during that explosion were vindicated. The Fed was largely out to lunch in terms of the way credit market issues were contaminating the financial system, and the agency certainly hadn't been planning anything to defend Main Street from a possible problem. Atlanta Federal Reserve president Dennis Lockhart had even openly mocked Jim Cramer, and in the August 2007 transcript the stenographer had noted the peals of laughter that filled the room at the mention of his name.

Years later, we now know that the Fed was hopelessly behind the curve, worried about inflation as the global economy teetered on the precipice of a deflationary depression. Cramer was right.

THE SELL CALL

In the fall of 2008, Jim Cramer appeared on America's most-watched morning show and told people the truth. After Lehman Brothers had gone down, the government was in the midst of saving AIG, and by extension, the entire system. There was fear in the air and with good reason—it was all entirely unprecedented, and anyone who was claiming to know how things would turn out was a liar.

During this time, enormous banks like Washington Mutual and Wachovia were going out of business over weekends and being handed over to the walking-wounded banks like Wells Fargo and JPMorgan on Sunday afternoons, so great was the desire to get these things in order before the markets would open. The Lehman people had emptied their desks and marched out of the corporate headquarters on Seventh Avenue one morning, only to be summoned back days later as Barclays had taken over the U.S. operations of the largest bankruptcy in American history. Congress, in the meantime, was fumbling and stumbling over a decision of whether or not to backstop the system or let it burn to the ground. The lame duck president, George W. Bush, was popping up here and there, but his credibility was already gone. John McCain, the Republican candidate, had simultaneously been claiming that "the fundamentals of our economy are strong" while making the mavericky (and fatal) decision to suspend his campaign to deal with the financial crisis. This prompted even more confusion and fear, which Barack Obama and his supporters took advantage of and used as a battering ram into the White House. Americans were undecided on a lot of things, but the one thing we agreed on was that everything was screwed.

And into this morass, Jim Cramer appears on NBC's *The Today Show* on the morning of October 6. It's a month since Lehman's collapse and a few days after the $700 billion TARP plan finally makes it through Congress. Jim walks viewers through a plain-English explanation of why banks won't lend to each other and markets are gyrating wildly. He is in a dark suit, standing soberly across from host Ann Curry, in front of a flat-screen monitor with a graphic reading "After the bailout: What should you do now?" in block letters. Ann parrots the screen, asking Jim, "For investors, what is your advice today?"

Jim says the only responsible thing he can, given the circumstances, and in as calm a delivery as the excitable trader can muster: "Okay, whatever money you may need for the next five years, please, take it out of the stock market. Right now. This week. I do not believe that you should risk those assets in the stock market.

"I don't care where stocks have been, I care where they're going, and I don't want people to get hurt in the market," Cramer told Curry. "I'm worried about unemployment; I'm worried about purchases that you may need. I can't have you at risk in the stock market."

"Very dramatic statement, Jim." Ann has her "concerned" face on, the one she reserves for human interest stories about conjoined twins undergoing separation surgery or kittens stuck in trees.

"I thought about it all weekend. I do not want to say these things on TV."

Jim will be endlessly hounded about this appearance for years to come. Many will say he was fomenting panic and causing people to freak out. But if you listened to what he had actually said, it was the precise right advice for a vast majority of individual investors saving for retirement. Jim explained that he could envision stocks dropping another 20 percent from that October's level and that investors should pull out the funds they needed to live on in the near term. He clarified further by explaining that those with longer-term time horizons or the ability to grit their teeth should ride it out.

The next day Jim Cramer appeared on national television again to further discuss his rationale for advocating that regular people make some sales. This time, he got to explain himself to comedienne and world-renowned financial markets expert Meredith Vieira. "Do you think I'm causing a collapse? I worked at Goldman Sachs. They almost went out of business. My insurance was with AIG. It did get nationalized. Lehman Brothers is a place I traded with for years. It's disappeared, as has Bear Stearns. I've sold a lot of Freddie Mac and Fannie Mae bonds. They don't exist anymore. I could sit back and say, 'None of this really matters. Everything's fine.' Or I can say, 'Take some off; ride it out; put it in a savings account that's insured for $250,000.' To me, that's better safe than sorry. Only in a jittery time would someone who says 'better safe than sorry' be pilloried. I like the stock market. I still recommend defensive stocks. I do one every night on my show. But I think I'm irresponsible if I tell you everything's fine."

Jim's clarification wins him no reprieve from the press. A whole brigade of CNBC haters comes out of the woodwork, knives out. This was the moment that many of them had been waiting for. John Crudele attacks mercilessly from his perch at the *New York Post*'s business section. He calls the Cramer sell call "12 months too late" and mocks the idea that stocks could drop a further 20 percent.

But Cramer will once again be vindicated. The S&P 500 stood at 1,037 during this first week of October while the pundit and punching bag was warning America. Within six months, it would drop to as low as a weekly close of 680 in early March 2009. What

Jim thought could be a 20 percent decline actually turned out to be around 40 percent. But rather than be remembered for this accuracy, the *Mad Money* host would soon find himself climbing onto a cross.

THE MARTYR OF THE MARKETS

Jon Stewart, the host of Comedy Central's *The Daily Show*, had seized on CNBC's coverage of both the credit bubble and the subsequent crash as a kind of ground zero for the crisis. Night after night, *The Daily Show*'s staff had woven together selective and hilariously assembled clips of financial journalists and guests saying ridiculous things. Some of the commentary Stewart showcased was politically charged, and some was just hyperbolically silly. In a crash or a panic, no one looks or sounds their best, and clever editing can do just about anything. In Stewart's eyes, CNBC in particular deserved heaps of scorn because of its standing as the financial news network of record. And in the person of James Cramer, CNBC's most famous personality, the comedian-turned-social commentator saw an opportunity to give the American public a catharsis for all it had been through.

On March 12, 2009, just days after the U.S. stock market had hammered out a bottom for itself, Jon Stewart had Cramer as his "guest" on *The Daily Show*. It had been a heavily promoted appearance, as Stewart had been popping up everywhere, critiquing the network in the days leading up to it. The promos featured Jon Stewart training like a boxer for his showdown with the market pundit.

But if viewers had tuned in for an epic brawl, they were to be highly disappointed. Jon began the show that night with four separate video clips capturing the very worst Wall Street-y statements Cramer had ever made in his years in front of the camera. By the time Cramer got to the desk to sit face-to-face with Jon, the audience was a hissing and seething snake pit. But rather than fight back or make an impassioned defense of his and the network's actions, Cramer was contrite. He admitted that big-bank CEOs like Jimmy Cayne (Bear Stearns) and Bob Steele (Wachovia) should not have been trusted or taken at face value. He sat at the *Daily Show*'s desk and absorbed all the criticism and frustration that Stewart could muster. You could sense that his lack of fight was taking some of the wind out of Stewart's sails, and the segment ended with a handshake.

That day, *The Daily Show*'s website had broken an annual traffic record. The show itself was watched by 2.3 million viewers, the show's second-largest audience ever, behind only the January presidential inauguration episode a few weeks prior. But instead of witnessing a battle or a debate, America got to see something else that night—the spectacle of one man single-handedly shouldering all the blame for the worst financial crisis in 70 years. All the anger and frustration and grief and hatred of the crash had been channeled, like lightning and thunder, and hurled directly at James Cramer before a live studio audience and millions of viewers at home. He was the scapegoat that night for trillions in losses, millions of dashed retirement hopes, and an ocean of foreclosures and lost jobs, things that he could not possibly be responsible for other than symbolically in the eyes of a hanging judge who presided over the show.

But Cramer just took it, without deflecting one iota of blame toward anyone or anything else. It was, in a strange way, more remarkable than any defense he could've mounted. It was perhaps the single greatest barrage of abuse directed at any stock market or economic pundit in history, and Cramer just endured it.

And the next day he was back on TV doing the thing he considers his life's work—explaining the stock market to regular people and helping them become more educated investors.

CHAPTER 18

THE KING OF COMMENTARY

A CONVERSATION WITH JIM CRAMER

CNBC HEADQUARTERS—MAY 2013

Josh and I met with Jim on a clammy afternoon in Englewood Cliffs, New Jersey, between his afternoon on-air segments and the taping of that night's *Mad Money*. His office is an extension of Cramer's hypomanic mind. Framed magazine covers, souvenirs from the show, gift bottles of booze, and branded bric-a-brac of every type are slowly claiming any available surface area. CNBC is playing on a small TV hanging in the corner, just above a growing stack of reading material and gifts sent to Cramer by friends and admirers.

Cramer had been an icon for nearly 10 years by the time *Mad Money* launched. TheStreet.com's founding in 1996 marked the beginning of the marriage between the Internet and investing. Information that was once restricted to Wall Street insiders was being made available for the first time. Cramer was the first real-live hedge fund manager to embrace the idea of throwing back the curtain and letting the public see what really went on at a buy-side investment operation. Everything you know about modern financial news coverage has been influenced by the work of Jim Cramer. Whether or not you regard that as a good thing is up to you.

The sheer endurance Cramer has shown over the course of nearly 20 years in the spotlight is astonishing. He's survived dot-com implosions, a handful of "tell-all" books, and Jon Stewart. He's iconic and wealthy, but Cramer has also had every embarrassing personal and professional failing of his life documented for a generation. He's an open book that refuses to close, cranking out *Mad Money* episodes and educating investors every night.

For more than two hours, Cramer entertained us from the middle of his chaotic den. The only time he held still physically was when listening to questions or pausing in the middle of a story. He was generous and thoughtful in a way that made it easy to forget why he still inspires so much vitriol on and off Wall Street.

MACKE: It's been on the air since 2005, and yet *Mad Money* is still the most polarizing show in financial media. You've got incredibly loyal fans and you've got critics who have been trying to take you down for almost a decade. What gets people so worked up?

CRAMER: *Mad Money* is a controversial show that shouldn't be controversial 'cause the essence of it is . . . well, it's self-selective. The people who watch the show are people who have already determined that they want to have a handle on their finances. Either they want to be with a broker and discuss the ideas, or they want to run the money themselves.

The idea is this show is dedicated to the proposition that if you want to invest your money yourself, let me at least make you better. I distinguish that as versus a professor who might just say, "Cramer's got it all wrong. He should never be doing this because they should all be in index funds. Can't beat the market."

My viewers are people who obviously have chosen not to be in index funds. They want to find, ah, the next Google. They want information, and they want to know how it works.

The show protects. The show informs and it educates. And if it were a market failure, we'd be canceled. They canceled tons of shows in the six o'clock time slot.

What I'm trying to do is help the home gamer because that person wants help or else they just wouldn't bother to watch.

MACKE: People still watch, and you've defied the critics since the '90s. The question is, why do you do it? Because you take a ton of abuse online and in other media for what you do, and I know you take it personally.

CRAMER: Yeah, of course, I do.

MACKE: But you don't need to do this for the money. Why do you put up with the heat?

CRAMER: Okay, that's a great question, because I'm 58 and I think a lot about "all right, wouldn't my life be easier if I didn't do the show?" And I come back and say it's a total labor of love. I think that this is what I was put on earth to do—to inform and to educate.

MACKE: Is that the labor of love, though? Is the labor of love helping these people, or is it the thrill of putting on a show?

CRAMER: It's the satisfaction of knowing that I can help people. I was talking to my dad, and he was saying, "How much do you miss the hedge fund world?" I said, "Dad, helping rich people get richer, really not a higher calling. Helping the people like that bus driver that you have, who says, 'Mr. Cramer, how you doing?'"

Regina Gilgan, my executive producer, says it all the time; it has to do with the satisfaction of being involved in the money business in a way that can be helpful. Now the flipside is like, okay, listen, I get it wrong. It's not in the privacy of my home.

BROWN: Is it more or less stressful than real losses in the hedge fund? Different kind of stress?

CRAMER: Well, no, the hedge fund is really stressful. There was a viciousness to the people who had money in my hedge fund, where you really didn't know that they were your bosses.

Doing the show, I can say who is that guy that's criticizing me now; he follows me on Twitter; he pays me nothing. Forget him. There's a particular boss-to-slave relationship in the hedge fund.

BROWN: You're only as good as your last trade no matter what you've done for people.

CRAMER: There's a certain amount of money immunity; you get to a certain level of money and there's an immunity. You can just go "Listen, I'm running my own money."

MACKE: Well, no other real hedge fund managers were going on TV until recently. For a long time no one who actually ran money was going to show their special sauces and strategy on national television.

CRAMER: No, and that's been a dicey thing to do. At TheStreet.com we do this thing with Action Alerts. We'll buy. We'll say, "Buy CBI," and it'll be at $60. Then we can't buy until everyone gets the alert. We pay $61.50 or $62, and you say to yourself, "Okay, well, look, how can we compete with performance?" We're like, we beat the market but we're moving the market to make it even harder.

BROWN: You're tying your own hands behind your back and then getting audited based on returns.

CRAMER: But you know what? Here's what we do. We show people how it works. We show people what we do. We like play with an open hand. Now, when I started doing *Mad Money*, Mike Holland, whom I love, he gave a quote to the *Daily News* saying, "He'll be able to do this for just a few months, and then he'll realize it'll just be too hard because no one ever wants anyone to see the warts and all." And he's my friend. But you know, we make mistakes, and you call out your own mistakes, and then people respect.

MACKE: But you know people will abuse your advice. There's a percentage of the audience who just wants to hear you say something positive about a stock like Tesla so they can load the boat and say you told them to do it.

CRAMER: It is so interesting that you say that because, whether it be Solar City or Tesla, you'll get people saying, "Jimmy, Jimmy, Solar City [laughs]. It's like squeezed. You could really get it going! Herbalife, why don't you just go in there and jam it higher?"

I said, "No, my job is not to jam Bill Ackman. My job is not to help a squeeze develop, but I will write about how the squeeze works." Or I'll say, "Listen, it's a cold stock. I have no opinion." Then I get blasted by people claiming I kept them out of Tesla because I said I had no opinion. So you can't win with the public.

Now, Karen Cramer, who I was married to for 20 years and who was my partner in business, says, "Why do you read it? Why do you torture yourself?"

BROWN: Is it just for the audience?

CRAMER: And I said, "Well, I don't know. It's the most interactive way, and it's like I get the feedback," and so, you know, altogether I just kind of like it.

Look, you guys are in the arena—the viewers can rip your face off. You know what it's like. But by the way, when you're right, it's pretty darn fabulous.

MACKE: It's great, but when you're right, no one remembers. They just take credit for the idea if it works and blame you if it doesn't.

CRAMER: Yeah, I know, I know, but I like the combat. I do like the combat.

MACKE: Did you just rechannel energy from when you ran your fund for 20 hours a day?

CRAMER: Yes, I do; honestly, I do. I think that's what I did. Look, you can't just leave. You have a sixth sense sometimes. You can't turn that off. On a bad day I'll go downstairs at a quarter to four. I bet you something's wrong. Because you know that really bad feeling last night when you went home—it was like you know key reversal day.

BROWN: And you know investors' belief in stocks is going to be tested.

CRAMER: Right, so let's see how it's trading. Just to see what's going on. It's so early. I haven't slept well, so I'm just going to peek. Then I start seeing news, and I've got to find out details about what's happening. Then I'm into the details and trying to put together the puzzle. I still love to put together the puzzle.

MACKE: So it's a routine, but is there an end to that in terms of doing it for other people?

CRAMER: Take the hedge fund. In the last year I kind of felt like I had to make money every quarter in order to keep these guys happy, and then it was every month, and then it was every week, and then in the end, I have like 10 people calling me at 4:10 p.m. to ask me if we made money that day! It's like the noose tightened and tightened. The money got bigger, obviously, but the noose tightened.

And then I realized, I said, you know what? I kind of like this TV thing. You know, it's fun. I like the Action Alerts because it helps people. I've got a show, and I can't wait for it to start every single night.

MACKE: Ten years ago, my first ever hit was on Kudlow & Cramer; that was my first hit.

CRAMER: Really?

MACKE: And my first trade was to short GM, and Kudlow all but crawled through the screen and strangled me for being unpatriotic, and I was like, "They lose money on every car sold! They lose money every time they sell something!"

CRAMER: You know, I love Larry, but Larry didn't like to hear anything negative. And that's a shame, because it hurts people if you don't pay attention to negatives. Not everything happens for the best.

And that was a great call. GM was a terminal, terminal play to zero.

BROWN: When they audit your returns, they say, "Oh, these are Cramer's results." They never count times when you kept people out of stocks. They don't take into account that not every position is equal weighted. They never let you change your mind.

CRAMER: So that counts as one. So then I also say that I like Domino's endlessly, okay? But then I also say, you know, my favorite drug stock is Merck, and it's the worst performer. Suddenly three months later all I hear is, "You kept me out of Bristol!" and "How did you not pick Pfizer?!"

BROWN: One plus one becomes minus one.

CRAMER: Right. I totally buy into accountability. I'm never going to dismiss accountability, but what I will say is if I'm that bad, wouldn't I have been canceled by now? You know, we've done 2,000 episodes.

MACKE: They can always do the opposite of what you say. "If I'm that horrible, let's take the other side of every trade. I'm like an idiot savant. Or savant idiot."

CRAMER: You know, that's a great point, yes. Right. You don't like what I do? Hey, listen, you know, there's always the other side of the trade. Go deep in the money against me, I don't care.

BROWN: What do you make of the argument that the journalists came out for blood when you first went on the air because you were one of the first practitioners to do your own form of journalism? They used to own the message, and then you took it from them.

CRAMER: I used to say, "Show me where you need a journalism card? Show me." Now everybody's a journalist.

BROWN: Well, now it's de rigueur, but back then it was, "Who's this guy that's writing market stories?"

CRAMER: Right. But back then I feared these guys. It was like I was a nonunion guy on a union set and then I'm busting the union.

MACKE: But Jim, you're rich. They're journalists. You have so much more money than they do, and then you took part of their jobs. You can't walk onto financial television and have that not be noticeable that people who run money have a few more zeros than the guys who have put in the hours as real reporters.

CRAMER: I think that there's always going to be a jealousy. You know, a lot of these guys, they want you to lose your job. The critics, they're not happy just calling you names. Their goal is to make you lose your job.

Because putting someone out of business is the home run of the critics.

MACKE: If you blow up, you sell papers. "Cramer did a nice show last night; it was a pretty good effort" is a lousy story.

CRAMER: Yeah, who cares?

MACKE: No one cares.

CRAMER: No, but we blow. We get the *New York Post* to write a, you know, a critical article, and then maybe the bosses come in and maybe they shut him down, and then it's a big victory.

MACKE: They can't even tell whether you blow or not. Anyone can claim to be a victim. Do you worry that the people who need the help the most, who tune in the most, are the ones who are going to take your advice and misapply what you say? There's a huge portion of your audience that just wants tips, as opposed to talking to an educated audience who will hear you and use you as a starting point for research.

CRAMER: Right. Someone will say, "Jim, you put me in Alcoa at $10. It's at $8. Now what am I supposed to do, you know? You know, I'm down $2 on Alcoa because of you. Now what?" Then you come back and say, "Well, listen, they had a really bad quarter, so I can't like it that much." And they'll say, "Well, why didn't you know that ahead of time?" You can come back and say like, "[Alcoa CEO] Klaus Kleinfeld didn't know that ahead of time." And so you go back and forth and back, and then you realize just disengage 'cause you're not going to please everybody, and fall back on the idea that people still say, "Hey, I love the show. Thank you."

MACKE: But beyond pleasing, what's it about for you? You know what I mean? It's not just a matter of whether or not they like you. If you're on financial television, there's a responsibility.

CRAMER: I do a huge amount of homework, and my homework can lead me astray, but at least I know I do it. It's not shoot from the hip.

MACKE: But the people watching can take whatever your conclusion is and use it as a reason not to do their own homework. The fact that you know what you're talking about and you're a good resource means that ultimately viewers are just going to you as a turnkey operation. "Cramer knows better than I do, so I'll just do what he says."

CRAMER: It's intimidating. You know, you'll have a thesis. Your thesis is that Japan is fabulous, okay? And you'll be consistent on that for months. And then the person who heard it yesterday is down 7 percent. I've been consistent the whole way, but it doesn't matter. They heard it yesterday. "Cramer, I want to kill him because it's down."

I've liked gold since $800. There's guys who bought it at $1,500 and say "Cramer, I want to kill him because it's down." I'm like, "No, you see, I've been saying that gold, gold coins should be part of your portfolio since I started the show." And the fact is there I am consistent and I'm not blowing out of it. And, you know, their view is, "I don't care what you said, but on Tuesday you said you liked gold and Goldman Sachs said short gold, and now Goldman was right. You're wrong. You're an idiot. You used to be good. You're not good anymore. When you were a hedge fund manager, you were good, but you know, now you're on TV, you're a talking head. And all you care about is being on TV because that's what it's all about."

MACKE: Or they'll say you're secretly still working for Goldman and you're corrupt.

CRAMER: Well, don't you love that?

MACKE: What about the "flip-flopping" charge when news happens, you change your mind, and that's unforgivable to people?

CRAMER: It's not politics.

MACKE: No. Flip-flopping is what trading is. That's the point of trading. But in the media, it's like you can't change your mind. They say, "Wait a minute, weren't you just saying you loved Apple? How do you not like it now?!"

CRAMER: Right. Apple. Apple. I did this interview thing for Bucknell for a friend of mine where I interviewed [Steve Jobs's official biographer] Walter Isaacson. It happened to be one year after Jobs had died. And Walter had made a pledge to Jobs that it would be one year before he would talk about what Apple is doing with their products.

So I interviewed Isaacson, and Apple's at $600 at the time, and I'm liking it; I'm liking it since $50, I'm liking it at $700. No more or less, but I just like it.

And I ask Isaacson, "So tell me, what's in the pipeline?" He goes, "Well, it's a year. I can talk about it." I said, "Yes, well, so what's Apple got in the pipeline?" And Isaacson says, "Nothing."

MACKE: Jobs had finished all his work.

CRAMER: But I said, "Well, but I mean don't they have some TV? What about iTV? ... You know, working on some deal with cable companies . . . ?"

"No."

"Well, how about the iTV?" And he goes, "Well, that needs Comcast's approval and Time Warner and Charter."

[Cable companies] are rich. They're not the record companies. They can't be rolled by Apple like the record companies were. So I said, "Okay, but did he have something that maybe we just can't even fathom? Something amazing?"

"No." And then he chuckles.

So the next day I go on and I say, "Listen, guys, you got to sell some Apple." Now everybody who bought it from $600 to $700 thinks I'm a war criminal. Meanwhile, I think I've got like the greatest research, the greatest piece of information imaginable, as close as I can get to Jobs himself.

BROWN: But you're betraying the shareholders by taking some gains.

CRAMER: Right. And they're saying, "Why didn't you know it earlier?"

Then you start going, "Well, let me explain. You see there's this guy Walt . . . ." No, you can't win. Some guy sees you in the street and says, "You buried me in Apple."

So you come back and say, "Listen, I've been recommending Apple forever, then took gains." And they just say, "The thing is that at $700, you said buy it. I only heard you at $700. Thanks for nothing."

MACKE: Do people say that stuff to you in person? I get nothing but love from people in public, but online I'll always be trolled for being a psycho.

CRAMER: I get it in person. I'm out there. I had a guy at a club tell me that I had been negative Hewlett at $40. And he said, "You got to buy Hewlett. You got to tell people to buy Hewlett. You got to tell people to buy Hewlett."

MACKE: Because he's long and wants everyone on board.

CRAMER: Yes, you got to tell people to buy it. Then it goes to $20 and the guy blames me.

BROWN: So *you* were killing the stock. Not Hewlett being a bad company, but *you*.

CRAMER: Right. "You're out there bashing Hewlett Packard. This stock would be up, but no, you are relentless and you don't know anything." It doesn't matter that I was negative at $40 and the stock went down on bad news. *I* pushed the stock down to $20. So now, I have to tell you, I am going to see this guy on Memorial Day weekend. You know what he's going to say to me? "Hewlett Packard's at $24. I told you so." No one's ever wrong.

MACKE: Well, that's the thing about accountability; once you own a mistake, everyone's in your basket, because you're the only pundit who'll admit to a bad idea. "He admitted he's an idiot. He admitted he's an idiot. He's a self-confessed idiot!"

CRAMER: In the meantime, all I was trying to do was basically say, "Listen, I screwed up, okay?" Their reaction is, "How can I trust a guy when he himself knows he sucks? He clearly sucks." I suck.

MACKE: He lost money but you suck.

CRAMER: There was a company, I don't even remember which one, but I was wrong, but I messed it up, so I literally ate crow on the show. I'm not in the *Wall Street Journal* for four years, but I eat crow on the show, and some reporter calls and says, "I saw you literally eat crow. I have to mention that even people who are supposed to be so tied in don't know the answer."

I said, "Look, if I hadn't eaten crow, would you even know it?" He said, "I don't know. You ate crow." I mean the only answer is, I was a stupid idiot. I went and shined a light on a mistake and I took hits for it.

MACKE: But if you take shots for saying you're wrong, what about the guys who come on the air as one-offs? They don't have the same responsibility. You've done a ton of homework. You're responsible. You're going to be here tomorrow to follow up on whatever argument you're making.

That's versus some first-timer who just wants to grandstand. If you're on for your first time, you want to be memorable; you want to make the big call, the huge call, so you get invited back.

Is there a way for the audience to distinguish between the two?

CRAMER: In the end it is just TV. I mean, you know, you can live by it or die by it, but the body of work is with you whether the reader or viewer knows it or not. What you carry around is your body of work.

BROWN: Do you feel vindicated given that in '09, '10, we were told from here on out, it's all macro and stock picking is dead, and meanwhile a 145 percent rally has happened, and you were picking stocks the whole time?

CRAMER: I feel total vindication.

MACKE: Do you get credit for being right? You were called a hack and worse on what amounts to the front page of a newspaper, but you're getting exonerated next to the obituaries, if at all.

CRAMER: No, there's no vindication. There's never—there's never any public vindication.

MACKE: Is every pundit who was on the air at that time tainted? Are we all just contributors to the meltdown?

CRAMER: You know, obviously, I was the poster boy because the network cast me to go on Jon Stewart,* and no one likes to be mortified. Was it fair or not? Again, it doesn't matter what's

---

* "Exclusive—Jim Cramer Extended Interview Pt. 1," http://www.thedaily show.com/watch/thu-march-12-2009/jim-cramer-extended-interview-pt-1; "Exclusive—Jim Cramer Extended Interview Pt. 2," http://www.thedaily show.com/watch/thu-march-12-2009/jim-cramer-extended-interview-pt-2, March 12, 2009.

fair. I was the guy who had said, "Listen, get out." I went on the *Today Show*, and I said, "Get out."*

It was a great call. The market drops big. Somehow I'm identified with the bear.

BROWN: You didn't really fight back. You went on there more as a mea culpa.

CRAMER: I didn't want to fight back.

BROWN: Do you regret that now, that you didn't fight?

CRAMER: No, not at all; no.

BROWN: You're glad you did it that way?

CRAMER: Yeah. There was no sense in fighting with him. It was his turf and he's not a fair man. It was my time to take the rap.

I mean, whether it should be or not, I think there's a lot of things that are unfair. Like that was unfair but, you know, you just take it like a man. He was going to give me a beating. I had hoped he'd be more genteel, but obviously he regarded himself as the savior of the common man.

He was a self-righteous man, and that's the way he approached it. It was unfortunate for me, but there are things that are happening that are unfortunate. It just happens. Not everything is great. I've had a good run, and sometimes you take a big hit.

MACKE: Is that the only way to win? To be able to take a beating and have your work summed up at the end? You took unfair shots there.

CRAMER: Well, you know, the *Daily Show* is a very, ah, accountable show. [laughs] I mean, I was like, you know, it just happens, and for me it was national, and it was the second-highest-ranked show, whatever, by Jon Stewart. And I didn't really want to go on Jon Stewart, but the network said please go, and I knew it was going to be mortifying. I was certainly hoping it would not be as bad as it was.

---

* "Jim Cramer: Time to Get Out of the Stock Market," http://www.today.com/id/27045699/ns/today-money/t/jim-cramer-time-get-out-stock-market/#. UatfV-vATgU, October 6, 2008.

BROWN: You didn't just bear the brunt of the criticism for the network. You bore the brunt for Wall Street.

CRAMER: The whole profession.

BROWN: And for anyone that's ever commented on the market.

CRAMER: He was saying, "Listen, you're a carnival barker. You're a snake-oil salesman." And I'm saying, "Okay, listen, listen pal, you're a commercial success, and you do that by ridiculing guys like me, and that's your job. I am on at six o'clock at night." You know, obviously if you had a fair discussion, we'd actually talk about this stuff.

The six o'clock slot has always been a graveyard for stock shows. I decided I've got to have a little more entertainment because I don't want to be canceled. I'm a commercial endeavor. It's like the professors who say, "Jim, you should come out every night and just say buy index ETFs." Well, you know, that's not a show and people obviously want a show. Why do people like the show? Why do people come up to me every day? It can't be because for eight years I've pulled the wool over their eyes.

MACKE: But you're doing the show for an hour. I was on *Fast Money*. You're doing that for an hour every night. You're working your butt off, and you're going to be accountable because you show up the next day.

So your show is trying to make the best calls, and *Fast Money* is doing the same, but that leaves 22 hours left to fill. So other shows are going to have to fill segments throughout the day. Some of the guests are going to make people money, and some of them are just going to chop people up and feed them to the wolves. It's hard to tell the difference if you don't know who these folks are.

CRAMER: That's true.

MACKE: So is the industry defensible? Is it fundamentally flawed because it has to be both entertainment and smart? Are those two mutually exclusive?

CRAMER: I don't think it's flawed. I think that there's good and less good. Okay, [gestures to TV where a pundit identified as

Stevens in the graphic is speaking] here Stevens says rates are up on upward trajectory. I don't know who Stevens is, and I don't know if Stevens is going to come on tomorrow. He's got silver hair. He's got a nice tie on, and he's got the capital behind him. I guess I should listen to Stevens. I don't know. I don't know who Stevens is.

BROWN: Will rates be higher? Will anyone remember what Stevens said?

CRAMER: No. Unless Stevens took his pants off right now, I don't know if we could care about Stevens.

MACKE: But that's the way for you to get on. You've got to entertain people.

CRAMER: He's saying buy the dinar. I mean maybe Stevens is long the dinar. I think if you have disclosure and you have a view and if you're wrong a lot, you're not going to get asked back. That's why I say it's not flawed, because I think at a certain point, the bookers say, "Geez, I think that guy's been wrong every time. We get a lot of heat from that guy. You know what? This guy is killing us."

MACKE: But how do you take those people down? How do you clue the audience in? Marc Faber [editor of the *Doom, Gloom and Boom* newsletter] comes on my show, and he tells people he thinks they should put all their money in physical gold on free port. He says you should put gold in places where they don't have any customs, basically because when the government meltdown happens and it hits the fan, you don't even want your gold in your basement. You want physical gold in Singapore. He claims that's how my viewers will be protected.

How do I convey the fact without being rude that that's the dumbest piece of information I've ever heard?

CRAMER: To make that comment on air without couching it by saying, "I don't think you should worry about money. But let me tell you what the world-enders are doing," I don't mind that. But to say, "Listen, I think you should put it in Singapore," that makes it sounds like he's obviously paranoid.

BROWN: There's a classy way to make a crash call—like Marty Zweig on [Louis] Rukeyser; he looked physically ill telling Rukeyser the market was on the verge of a collapse.

MACKE: Right, there's a way to do it.

CRAMER: You know, I once made a get-out-now call on October 8, 2008, and it was really mortifying. When you make a get-out-now call, people are going to take action, so you got to be really careful. You can't idly come on and say, "Get out now."

MACKE: The defense would be that people making those kinds of calls are traders. They can get right back in the next day, and that's not communicated to the audience.

CRAMER: Right. People who watch aren't professional traders.

MACKE: Well, jerk, nice guy, whatever, he's giving terrible advice, and he's doing it because scaring people sells an awful lot of newsletters.

CRAMER: Yeah. Well, I'm not going to disagree with that. I remember when I first broke in as a reporter, and I wanted to do this really positive story. I said, "Listen, I want to do the other side of the story." My editor, John Forrest, he said, "Well, you know, don't you see, we want to stay in business. So we're not going to do that story. We're going to do another story." I remember it was like some woman who was very upset with her husband and talked to an FBI agent about maybe killing him. You know, so my editor put in "Contract Killer Checkout Lady," you know? I was saying, "Oh my God, no." I mean she wasn't even arrested for it. It didn't matter. They got to sell papers.

BROWN: Just to end this on an uplifting note, when are people ever going to start loving stocks again? What does it take?

CRAMER: It is amazing. What do stocks have to do? What do I have to do? That money in the sidelines is not going to come back because there are people who don't believe it's an asset. They don't think that stocks are an asset.

MACKE: Did this generation just get burned, and stocks are just done for them?

CRAMER: Yes. These are people who bought in 2005, and a few years later, it's back to where it was again, except where they bought Bank of America, and it never came back. They've been wiped out, wiped out.

BROWN: So when you go to college campuses and you see these kids cheering, are they going to buy stocks?

CRAMER: It's different for them. That generation's different.

BROWN: But they're not in their peak earnings years yet. When do they come in?

CRAMER: I think they come in. You know why they come in? Because they understand the web. They target what they want to target, and they know what they like. It's very different from the people who just watched [the crash].

BROWN: What kind of investors will they be? Will they be enamored of stock picking, or are they going to be index only?

CRAMER: They're enamored with stock picking.

BROWN: There will always be story stocks. So the kids will look at Tesla now, and that'll be like something they buy just because they like the idea.

CRAMER: Hey, listen, you know how many people I know bought Amazon because they loved it? I mean it was a great call. Netflix. They all owned Netflix. Netflix worked. I mean, it did go down, but it worked. But the other generation who was in Bank of America and they're dead.

BROWN: There's a timing thing to when you come to the market. The boomers happened to have showed up in the early '80s, and it worked out really well, and they still love stock picking.

CRAMER: People say, "You know, Jim, what was your secret?" and I say, "Well, I got out of school in 1981."

MACKE: Good call.

CRAMER: That was my secret. It's just, you know, it was a brilliant thing by me to get out in '81. I remember when I was selling.

There was this guy, and he was such a very wealthy guy, and I had just started selling at Goldman, and the guy says to me, "What should I do?" I said, "I don't know. I think you should go buy 30-year bonds, because I believe in the country, and Ronald Reagan's going to be our president, and I think he's going to do a better job, and they're 17 percent." And the guy said, "Okay, I'll buy 30-year bonds." This guy called me when they came to maturity. This was the greatest pick ever, and all I knew was it was yielding 17 percent and that seemed good.

My boss said, "Listen, that guy's already rich, but you don't need to get rich more than once. Don't you fool around with some stock. You put them in bonds," so I have my spiel, but my guy had $50 million.

BROWN: You had to find a stock in those days that you felt would do better than 20 percent.

CRAMER: Yes, because the bogey was so high.

BROWN: Jim, thank you so much for your time.

CRAMER: You guys are a joy. Both of you have done a great job in democratization, and you speak plain English, which from day one, I loved that, because you never spoke above people. You can only do it if you really understand, but it's only if you're confident enough and really understand it, you can make it simple. Because the people who don't understand it, they can't make it simple.

MACKE: Thanks, Jim. It was great.

CRAMER: Guys, I love you.

CHAPTER 19

MAKE A PREDICTION WITHOUT MAKING A PREDICTION

*He who lives by the crystal ball soon
learns to eat ground glass.*
—EDGAR R. FIEDLER

The practiced pundit is making appearances and dropping quotes for the benefit of a firm or a career—not necessarily for your benefit. In the service of his (or her) firm, the pundit is willing to opine at the edges of his expertise and even to wake up at 4:30 in the morning to get in front of the cameras. But what good is that effort and compromise if it doesn't further the cause?

And so there are tricks of the trade that, when executed, are imperceptible to the casual reader or viewer.

The most perfect form of the art is the annual list of "surprises": everyone loves lists, year-end lists even more so, and year-end lists containing forecasts for the next year sit haughtily at the top of the hierarchy. What would the week between Christmas and New Year's Eve be without a stream of predictions for the following year? But there is a right way and a wrong to pull off such a list.

The wrong way would be to make ironclad calls that could be graded and then used to judge one's accuracy. The correct way of going about this is to call the predictions a list of "surprises." Who doesn't love surprises, after all?

In 1986, Byron Wien began publishing his annual "10 Surprises" list while serving as chief U.S. investment strategist at Morgan Stanley. It proved to be a big hit with the firm's clients and employees as well as with the media. Getting the media's attention for a firm's calls and services is actually the primary job of a "chief U.S. investment strategist" in the first place, so of course the list became an annual tradition.

The list was never meant to be a forecast of what would actually happen in the markets. Rather it was intended as an exercise in outside-the-box thinking and as a way to assign probabilities to outlier events that could impact the economy and the world. The creativity involved made the list a must-read, but it almost never came to be at all.

In 2010, Wien explained the origin of his list to *Registered Rep* magazine: "The first year was 1986. I started on Wall Street in 1965 as a securities analyst and then I became a portfolio manager. Then in 1985, I became the U.S. strategist for Morgan Stanley and there were a lot of smart people doing U.S. strategy at the time. And I was trying to figure out something I could do that could differentiate myself from others who were doing it. So I came up with this idea of developing a list of surprises—10 surprises that I would announce at the beginning of every year. I presented it to Morgan Stanley and management thought it was a really dumb idea, because I could get all 10 wrong. If I got all 10 wrong, I would embarrass myself and humiliate the firm. They didn't care about my personal embarrassment, but they did care about humiliating the firm. So they turned it down, initially, but then they finally agreed to let me give it a try. And I've been doing it for 25 years. This is the 25th year of doing it. I don't do it for sport, I do it to stretch my own and other people's thinking. And I think the idea works on that level."

It's a neat trick and a fun way to push the boundaries of our expectations. A zero-for-zero record in any given year—his "surprises" during that year of 2010, for example, were uniformly wrong across the board—can easily be explained away as "Hey, we said they were surprises!" A spate of surprises that end up panning out will be regarded as sagacious despite the protestations of the author. *The pundit doth protest too much.*

In the wake of Wien's hit concept, many others have adopted the format for their own publicity efforts. Fortunately, the majority of readers who come across these lists have the good sense not to invest based on them. Bob Doll, first as chief strategist for BlackRock and now for Nuveen, does a version of this, but he actually calls them predictions (albeit, the list is delivered in a tongue-in-cheek fashion). Doug Kass, hedge fund manager and columnist for TheStreet .com, gives us his list of 15 surprises each December and takes great delight in constantly grading and regrading himself throughout the course of the year. Even Goldman Sachs's legendary Jim O'Neill weighs in with his macro predictions in list form each year. Jim's list of global surprises for 2012, made at the end of 2011, turned out to have been mostly spot-on, nailing 8 out 11 calls according to one journalist who tracks these things.

The Denmark-based Saxo Bank has been delivering us its list of "10 Outrageous Predictions" at the start of each year for a decade now. If you haven't spotted the trick here, it's the appendant "Outrageous," which seems to indicate that it's all in good fun. But heaven help us should this list ever get above a 6-in-10 hit rate, we'll be smothered by the public relations campaign and media blitz that would surely follow.

The lesson here is that clever pundits couch their predictions in outrageousness and wackiness. We will forgive inaccuracy even while we'll hypocritically be impressed by what looks like foresight, even if it arrives packaged as a surprise.

There is one other crafty method of making predictions without really predicting anything that we'd be remiss in not mentioning: the subtle art of making a *suggestion* that can be later construed as a prediction. "The Fed should cut rates by another 25 basis points at the upcoming FOMC meeting" can later be referenced by the pundit as "This is exactly what we told you to expect." This kind of subterfuge can also work on a more micro level, as in "Benjamin Moore Paint, Netscape, and Yahoo should all merge to form a conglomerate called Benjamin Netanyahu." Should that deal ever come to pass (God help us), the person who's got archival video of herself (or himself) making this suggestion will be quick to point out that "*of course*, that was going to happen. How could anyone have seen any other possible outcome? It could not have been more obvious!"

You'll fall for it—we all do.

CHAPTER 20

"CAR PEOPLE"

THE LIVE BLOG

FALL 2013

I t's a stunningly perfect autumn afternoon in suburban New York. Big, crisp leaves in the trees and just a touch of wind foreshadowing winter. It looks like a Robert Frost poem outside my office window. I should be outside enjoying this day. What I plan to do instead is watch a four-year-old tape of myself committing broadcasting suicide. It will be the first time I've ever seen the clip all the way through. I can actually taste my sense of dread.

I obviously don't have a copy on my hard drive, so in a few minutes I'm going to run an Internet search for "Macke Car People." Maybe I won't find anything. I could be imagining the staying power of a throwaway segment aired on basic cable in 2009. It's possible, but I doubt it. Just because you're paranoid doesn't mean they aren't talking about you somewhere.

You're welcome to check for yourself, but from what I understand, the clip won't make much sense without some context. There isn't any rush; whatever there is out there waiting for me will still be there in five minutes.

From 1999 through most of 2007, a combination of perverse banking regulations, loose monetary policy, and public mania pushed the average price of a house in America up 300 percent and drove stocks to record highs. Even as the economy entered a recession in 2008, there remained a somewhat vague but unshakable belief in the government's ability to prevent a catastrophe. That's what the public always tells itself at the top of a bubble.

By the middle of 2008, stocks were still relatively strong given the rotting fundamentals. A 10-fold rise in stocks over the prior 25 years had conditioned investors to buy every dip. Hope dies a hard death on Wall Street, but by September, when Lehman Brothers disappeared and the government frantically put together nearly a trillion dollars' worth of bailouts, it became obvious the center couldn't hold. The initial result was market chaos. Nine of the ten largest intraday swings in the history of the Dow Jones Industrial Average occurred between September 29 and December 1, 2008.

Ultimately the entire economy simply froze, and the dip-buyers ran out of ammo. From September 2008 through March 2009, the U.S. economy lost more than 4.5 million jobs, and GDP got annihilated, falling by more than 5 percent for two straight quarters. Twenty percent of homeowners were now underwater on their mortgages. Hundreds of thousands of people were losing their jobs every day. While Wall Street CEOs held secret meetings, the trading desks that had funded the whole mess were empty. With the economy frozen, there wasn't much for anyone to do. Talk of a second Great Depression wasn't at all unrealistic.

As the whole mess was unfolding, Pete Najarian, Guy Adami, Karen Finerman, host Dylan Ratigan, and I went live on CNBC at five o'clock every weeknight and tried to explain it in real time. As far as the media is concerned, human misery equals ratings magic. That formula made the six-month crash of '08 and '09 a Disney World–sized kingdom for financial punditry. For better or worse, the original version of *Fast Money* was the unofficial source of financial information for hundreds of thousands of Americans.

As the economy collapsed, the punditry machine chugged along with growing eyeballs but falling ad streams. At *Fast Money*, producer John Melloy and the crew were stuck trying to find fresh ways to describe a crisis that was increasingly self-evident. It felt like having to tell a different kid his dog had gotten hit by a car every night. It became monotonous, but the show still felt like it mattered every single night. That was because it did. Someone had to explain to the investing public what was really happening—and that job fell to us.

Then one day in March the real economy and the stock market went their separate ways. After a wrenching 54 percent drop in the

Dow from its peak, there wasn't anyone left to sell. Appropriately enough, the selling bottomed at a satanic intraday low of 666 on the benchmark S&P 500. Traders are superstitious; given the depths of the plunge, the market arriving in hell seemed like as good a buy signal as any.

The economy was still getting worse, but the ensuing stock market rally was a monster. Less than a month after hitting its low point, the Dow had tacked on more than 25 percent. Shorts got destroyed even faster than shareholders did in the prior months. Bulls and bears were equally miserable. Historically speaking, that's been a great time to buy stocks regardless of what's happening in the real world.

Fast Money is a stock market show. The viewers tuned in to hear about their portfolios, not credit spreads. In the face of a huge rally, it was a buzzkill to obsess over the grim economic news. As far as stocks were concerned, the Great Recession ended on March 9, 2009, and that's all there was to it. I'd spent months personalizing the meltdown. When it stopped, I wasn't happy or relieved. I was simply spent.

By then, I had absolutely no enthusiasm for the show, and it was obvious. One night in 2008 I threatened to break into a viewer's house and force him to sell his Citigroup shares if he didn't do it himself. The following April my Trade of the Day at the end of a show was muttering, "Buy something" and shrugging into the camera. I didn't have anything else to say.

Right then I should have dropped the mic and walked off the set. Instead I tried to "man up" and ride it out until my contract ended at the beginning of June. I rather memorably burst into flames about a week short of my goal.

"Car People"—as it came to be known—is a less than five-minute hit I did on a now long-canceled evening program called *CNBC Reports*. For a change, there really wasn't much to talk about that night. The official topic for the segment was "Fear on Wall Street Falling?" but the real goal was to kill about five minutes with relatively idle speculation regarding the mood of the financial community—a classic pundit bit.

I could have done the segment in my sleep, and it would have turned out just fine. That night I tried to do it without having slept in at least two days, having spent the entire night before watching the movie *Michael Clayton*. When I left the studio, I knew the spot was bad, but I didn't know it was life-alteringly terrible until the phone rang the next morning.

"This call never happened," *CNBC Reports* host Dennis Kneale whispered. It sounded like he was calling from under his desk. He asked if I was okay and seemed genuinely concerned. That was a really bad sign.

"You are in huge trouble," he hissed, so quietly I could barely hear him. "They're going crazy about last night. I've seen careers ended over less than this. You've got to do something. Tell them you're addicted to something and go into rehab. Ask for a leave of absence. I don't know, man, but don't ignore this. It's a big deal. Whatever you do, don't tell them I called. Seriously. I'll deny it if you tell them I called.*

He hung up.

Following the "Car People" segment, I'd gone home and stayed up all night working on a legal case involving my father. By the time Dennis called, I was finally crashing. The world looked as if I were seeing it through a fish tank. When I hung up with Dennis, the only thing I was absolutely sure of was that I was screwed as far as television was concerned.

The weird thing was I didn't really care.

So that's the setup. In the here and now of 2013, it's all a million years ago. Stocks are near record highs, I sleep almost every night, and all is right in my world. I've literally never been happier than I am at this exact moment. I walk to my desk, pull up a chair, and plug "Macke Car People" into Google. When I hit the "return" key, 20,300 possibilities pop up. The Internet never forgets.

I'm about to drag a razor over a bunch of very old scar tissue. I don't know what exactly to expect beyond it feeling unpleasant . . .

00:00

For starters, I look fat, sweaty, inexplicably furious, manic, and cognitively impaired. I am the exact opposite of everything you

---

* Sorry, Dennis.

want to be on live television. That's in the thumbnail. I'm humiliated, and I haven't even finished clicking the mouse. I mean . . . damn.

00:30

Dennis finishes introducing the panelists.

The guys booked on the segment with me are Fritz Meyer of Invesco Inc. and Frederick Dixon of DA Davidson and Company. I'd frankly forgotten there was anyone else there. As I watch the tape, it's not clear I was anything but vaguely aware of their presence even at the time.

While no doubt nice gentlemen, for the purposes of television Fritz and Frederick are the archetypes of the most common form of pundit. They're market strategist types. They are way, way beyond making cold calls themselves, but their research reports are the script from which the brokers read. Getting airtime on the financial network of record gives strategists at mid-level firms an air of credibility. Some of them even have strong insights. Booking a strategist is a good trade for all concerned.

Given the situation in the spring of 2009, there's a roughly 100 percent chance Frederick and Fritz intended to say something to the effect of, "The worst is behind us, but persistent economic headwinds remain."

Obviously I had a whole different conversation in mind.

Sitting at my desk in the present day, I pause the clip and run a search on Fritz and Fred. As it turns out, they're both in pretty much the same jobs writing research, speaking at conferences, and occasionally going on television. I have no idea why, but I expected them to have been somehow tainted. Now I wonder if they even remember being part of it.

00:47

"I'm going to talk to you like a child," I sputter to Dennis.

Holy crap. "Talk to you like a child" rings an old bell. It's from a speech in *Michael Clayton* and was no doubt in my head from the previous night. What I meant was that I was going to attempt to simplify a very complicated economic situation. It didn't come out that way. What I'd done instead was insult the host, confuse the guests, and immediately take the segment off the rails. I'm in huge, huge trouble with a whole bunch of time still on the clock.

00:56

". . . You're what happens when you try to talk to car people a half an hour ago."

And there it was. Originally I'd been scheduled to do a segment on the economy along with the owner of a chain of car dealerships in Denver. My spot was delayed by 30 minutes, so I'd watched the interview on the monitor. The dealer was optimistic on the economy based on what he'd seen over the past few weeks. I was upset over the use of such a meaningless data point. Things going on in my mind were not matching up with reality. I was incoherent to others, though it made complete sense to me.

That explains but in no way excuses anything about this performance. I'm horrible. Dennis looks baffled and defensive. Fritz and Fred are reacting almost as if there's something wrong with their earpieces.

Once "car people" leaves the sweaty, pursed lips of my fat face, I've put a headline on the story of my collapse. The Internet loves headlines, and "Car People" is meme brilliance. Nothing could have saved me at this point.

Beyond the pain of watching this, I'm sort of impressed at how much damage I've been able to do to myself in less than one minute.

00:57–03:30

There is nothing good to say about this performance. It's a very good thing I'm not on the same set as these guys, given how aggressive I am. Dennis is getting angrier, and Fritz and Fred look like two guys getting approached for spare change by a crazed homeless person.

Even if it hadn't gone viral, this clip would be excruciating for me to watch. I literally couldn't be this bad again if I tried. Watching this, I'm about 50-50 between humiliated and sad for 2009 Jeff Macke.

Bad times.

03:30–4:40

I understand completely why this was a noteworthy performance at the time. For me it's always going to be painful. In or out of context, my performance is obviously heartfelt but an otherwise baffling attack on pretty much everything around me at the moment. Mostly it's just self-abuse.

04:44

Dennis signs off with: "A trader friend of mine says these markets are here to make you look foolish. I think all three of you gentlemen are doing a great job for me. So thanks a lot."

Annnnnnnnnnnd . . . scene.

From a purely "making television" perspective, the clip is both slightly better and much, much worse than I'd expected. I was completely unhinged and, in my mind, attacking the entire industry, but I was doing it in such a bizarre manner that I didn't hurt anyone but myself.

My main sin as a broadcaster was that I brought my personal demons on air. That's unprofessional in any business. Even punditry.

If I'd stayed up all night watching a different movie, the segment may have come out different. I was going for something like this: "I don't have to tell you things are bad. Everybody knows things are bad. It's a depression. Everybody's out of work or scared of losing their jobs, and we sit watching our TVs. We know things are bad. They're crazy. It's like everything everywhere is going crazy."

Less than two weeks after I did that segment, General Motors went bankrupt and announced plans to close 14 plants, discontinue Pontiac, and get rid of 21,000 employees (more "car people"). Within a year unemployment was going to be over 10 percent, and more than $1 trillion in taxpayer money would be poured into bailouts for Wall Street banks, the auto industry, and other failing sectors of the economy.

I didn't want to be part of a segment in which four middle-aged white men sat in four different studios idly speculating on the mood of Wall Street when the reality for millions of people was so hard. It struck me as the worst of television. I went into punditry in the first place because I found financial television banal and misguided, particularly in the dot-com era. I wanted to help people, not be a part of the problem as I saw it.

Since "Car People," financial television has gotten much better. There is a higher, more informed class of pundits on air today. *Fast Money* has changed, and the panelists are actual professional money managers debating actual investing strategies and philosophies in real time. That was all part of the original vision of *Fast Money*, but has yet to become industry standard and certainly wasn't the broadcasting norm at the time of "Car People."

WHAT REALLY HAPPENED

I've gone through the blow-by-blow of "Car People," but an explanation of my emotional state in the run-up to the segment isn't actually possible. There aren't common reference points. What's crazy to some might be normal to you. I've learned more than to judge.

In short, my emotional state was indefinable. That's not an excuse or vanity. I'm not being secretive. I was graceless under pressure on a public stage. My biggest core stressor was trying to defend my dad from himself. My dad was my friend, mentor, and business partner. In his prime he was a force of nature. He was strong, aggressive, childish, and a genius merchant. Before his forty-fifth birthday, he had risen from the training program to become the CEO of the company that is now Target.

At some point in the early '90s, his movement started getting rigid. His decisions were less sharp. We wouldn't officially know it until his autopsy, but he was showing the first signs of a brain disease called cortical basal ganglionic degeneration. In essence, the frontal lobe of his brain was slowly disintegrating. As his mind deteriorated, he was first fired from his job, then targeted by a series of ever-shadier business "partners."

After keeping meticulous financial records his entire life, dad ended up giving away millions of dollars by simply writing checks to anyone with a business plan. I'd find out about the "investments" after the checks bounced. It was up to me to try to round up outside legal resources then convince my mom to hire them since I had no authority to stop the deals.

Eventually I was sued for $113 million as a result of my father using a potentially unlimited amount of personal assets to secure a loan for a company that had no material value. His signature authorizing the deal amounted to an illegible scrawl. It was a frivolous, stupid, nuisance suit that was dismissed entirely after multiple appeals. It took me about $2 million and a few years to get to that win.

Meanwhile, I was pushing every living human away from me, including my wife and kids. My wife did a lot of decorating and I paid a ton of bills. We seldom spoke. I behaved like a jerk and we brought out the worst in each other. We became the worst versions of ourselves. That's the way people who end up getting divorced behave.

After "Car People" ran and my contract expired, I took myself as far as I could to whatever bottom I could find without becoming addicted to hard drugs. I spent a year in that state. I read, watched movies, and dwelled. Finally, one day I found my bottom. Everyone has a bottom, but it's not a fixed point in despair. Your spiritual bottom is the point at which you decide what kind of person you'd like to be.

There are three choices at the bottom: (1) Are you going to die, either passively through self-abuse or by speedier means? (2) Will you try to flatline where you are? (3) Will you fight back even though it's hard and scary and you know it hurts to lose?

I decided I didn't like where I was going and hated where I was. What I had been prior to my descent was wealthy, idle, surrounded by toys (pointlessly large house, etc.), incredibly accomplished on paper, bored and untested as a human being. After the bottom I honestly didn't care about toys anymore, and accomplishments can't be taken away. I like money. So remaking some of that was worthwhile. In terms of being tested as a human being, well, I'd found a bottom. Once you've done that, you are officially tested. You don't need a diploma to know it.

That was three years ago. I'm not sure what I am now beyond grounded and happy. I feel sharper than I was before the entire mess. I have more insight, but I'm a little beaten up, as would be expected. I have explored the darkest parts of myself and emerged, if not a better person, at least as someone I like more than the guy I was in 2007.

This isn't a sob story. I'm not interested in sympathy. I don't deserve it. I really, really don't. I don't even expect understanding, because knowing other people fully is impossible.

I'm sharing because maybe you've got some issues of your own. Maybe you're taking a tour of your personal dark side. Maybe you're surrounded by everything you thought you wanted and realize you set the wrong goals. I don't know, but it's possible that knowing my deal can help you with yours.

If one person reading this is at a point where he or she is anywhere near making one of the three decisions that define hitting a bottom, and hearing me talk about this helps them, then it's worth my time to tell the story.

To this day, whenever I say something others might object to online, someone throws the "Car People" segment back at me. It's like an echo from troll canyon. Even having watched how memorably horrible the segment was, it still seems like it shouldn't matter by now. Every so often I shout into the canyon just to see what bounces back to me.

As I write, it's a Sunday morning more than four years after "Car People" aired. A moment ago I sent a tweet regarding legalizing marijuana. It's just a link to a survey in that morning's newspaper showing a majority of Americans favor legalization while use of the drug by teenagers is falling.

In the time it took to fill a mug of coffee someone posted this: "@JeffMacke You are living proof why certain drugs should not be legalized . . . what kind of substance were you on during your CNBC meltdown?"

It doesn't matter who the person really is. He's part of the white noise of hecklers out in the virtual world. The Internet and anger will be hanging around like a miasma forever. It's impossible to wait for it to end before going back out in the daylight. There isn't a set time frame for coming back. It's a choice: deal with the stigma head-on or hide.

Far worse than being heckled is knowing that people I actually respect will either already know before meeting me or find out shortly thereafter that I'm the "Car People" guy. I met someone at a Christmas party last year. He stuck out a hand, told me he was a fan, and immediately said how sorry he was about what happened. It's hard to know exactly where to take a conversation after that point. Being defined even a small degree by one horrible moment isn't debilitating, but it's always somehow hanging around. That takes some getting used to, but it's bearable.

Scarlet letters can't be ranked in order of severity. Henry Blodget has his banishment from the securities industry. Jim Cramer has Jon Stewart's venal takedown. I have "Car People." Henry's circumstances were much more severe, and Jim is an icon, but I have a singular catchphrase: to lose one's mind on financial television is to this day known as "going Car People."

There are people starving in the world, babies born with serious disabilities, and war atrocities committed every day. I'm not throwing a pity party for grown men who get teased. That said, it's not the condition of the world that keeps you staring at the ceiling at 3 a.m. We all have our own baggage to deal with, and having perspective doesn't change that fact.

Jim Cramer said something to me at the end of our interview that I'll always remember. Looking me in the eye and with his perfect Cramer voice, he said, "You're a joy because you get it. There's only a small cadre of people who get the pain. The other people, they think we're just prickly."

The pain happens when you walk down the street and feel eyes on you. The pain is being the punch line of jokes no one wants to share with you. The *real* pain—the one you never get entirely over—is people you care about looking at you with just a hint of sympathy behind their eyes.

Jim gets the pain. Henry understands the pain. If you were nice enough to buy this book, I hope you don't ever suffer some sort of indignity on a national scale. It's as horrible as you might think. But that's not the takeaway lesson of this chapter in my life. "Having a bunch of people laugh at you makes you sad" isn't something you need to hear from a professional. You could have guessed that before reading this chapter.

You can make millions of dollars, go to the finest schools, have strangers send you fan mail, and marry the prettiest girl, but when it comes down to it, there are only two types of people in the world: those who get knocked down and stay there and those who stand up and fight again.

I know which type I am.

CLASH OF THE PUNDITS!

There was never a century nor a country that was short of experts who knew the Deity's mind and were willing to reveal it.

—MARK TWAIN

T hroughout the course of this book, you've met many "experts"—experts on the economy, experts on investing, experts on trading, and experts on market timing. You've been told of their successes and their failures, you've seen the brave faces they put on for the cameras, and you've gotten a glimpse into their personal lives as well. You've learned that every era has its superstar commentators and that no one can be consistently right about everything—at least not for an appreciable amount of time.

In 2005, Philip Tetlock, professor of psychology at the University of Pennsylvania, published the results of a landmark study on so-called experts that he had carried out over the course of 15 years. He had assembled hundreds of experts—defined as people who appear in the media, advise corporations and governments, and espouse various opinions in public for a living—and tracked the results of the more than 27,000 forecasts they had made. Tetlock then tracked these expert predictions during the period between 1988 and 2003, calculating their accuracy. In his book on the study's results, *Expert Political Judgment: How Good Is It? How*

Can We Know?, his experts turned out to have been correct in their calls about 33 percent of the time. Unfortunately, each question he had asked them contained a multiple choice of three possible answers. In other words, the experts' forecasts were no more accurate than those of "dart-throwing chimpanzees," in the author's own words.

This mass failure to be "right" on the part of Tetlock's 287 volunteer pundits has nothing to do with an absence of intelligence. Rather, their failure to make good predictions about the future stems from the fact that predicting the future consistently cannot actually be done—by anyone, expert or otherwise. In the first place, anything can happen at any time, and relatively minor events can produce a large impact (think of the butterfly flapping its wings thousands of miles away). In the second place, we are all hopelessly encumbered with a host of biases that conspire to introduce even more difficulty into our cognitive processes.

We remember recent events more clearly than others, thus emphasizing their importance or likelihood of repeating. We see the world through the lens of how things may impact our careers or financial security. We replay past sequences of events in our minds and invent causal narratives that explain the inevitability of what's actually happened, despite the fact that no one could have foreseen it. We conflate our personal politics and social mores with the potential for certain outcomes. And these are just a few of the accidental biases. They don't even include all the instances in which an expert will deliberately skew a forecast so as to please whoever is signing his checks.

The important thing to keep in mind, however, is that despite this inability to be right all the time (or even most of the time), there is still value to be gleaned from the words and ideas of the market commentariat class. Whether we're watching for inflection points in popular sentiment, digesting a whole new perspective on a topic we think we've mastered, or even looking for a commonplace view against which to play contrarian, we can almost always learn something of value when the megaphone is in our faces.

The key to making this constant stream of ideas useful is to think critically on our own, not merely contenting ourselves with swallowing the impersonal and often flawed bits of advice being broadcast at us all day long. In order to actually do this, we must first learn to ask ourselves the right questions about the pundit who appears before us, in print or on the screen. Below are a few to start with . . .

1. Who is this expert, and what firm or organization does he represent?
2. What does her professional affiliation mean in terms of the opinions she's sharing?
3. Does he have the same time frame or investment objectives that I do?
4. How many ideas is she generating each day or week? How much thought is going into each one?
5. What are the consequences for him if he is wrong? Will we ever hear more about this idea in a follow-up?
6. How does the opinion I've just heard relate to my own portfolio or investing goals? Is there any real relevance?
7. Why am I reading or listening to this in the first place? Intellectual curiosity? Entertainment? Or do I have an actual need to employ this sort of information?
8. Is there a publicly available archive of this person's previous opinions and forecasts? Have they been mostly accurate or mostly wrong? What were the driving factors behind the accuracies or the great calls? Luck? Skill? Good timing? Strong research? Some combination of these elements?

By thinking in these terms and not merely taking the information being presented by our parade of pundits at face value, we put ourselves in a position to deepen our own thought process as opposed to merely accepting the finished product of someone else. It is in this way that we can make the media work for us rather than thwart us in our quest to stay up to speed.

Each day, the financial media must feed the beast—more pageviews and higher ratings will always be the order of the day. The media will call upon the voices and faces of the pundit firmament, doing its best to select the most knowledgeable experts it can, even if that means sometimes settling for the most available ones. And since this has never changed, nor can we expect it to in the future, I'd ask you to remember this one thing and to allow it to color everything you read and hear from now on:

Pundits are people, too.

INDEX

A

Acampora, Ralph, 107
Accountability, 138, 207–209, 211–213
Accounting, 43–44
Accuracy:
    and confidence of pundits, 155
    of expert predictions, 235–236
    of financial information, 19–20
    of forecasts, 4–6, 71–72, 75–77
Ackman, William, 204
    Herb Greenberg on, 129–130n, 130, 137
    rise of the Three Amigos, 112–114
    short selling of Herbalife by, 117, 118, 123
    (See also Icahn-Ackman fight)
Action Alerts, 204, 206
Adami, Guy, 52, 224
Advice:
    financial (see Financial advice)
    life, 145–147
Advisors:
    James Altucher on, 148
    Jim Cramer on, 207–209, 211–213
    Barry Ritholtz on, 166–168, 178–179
    Jim Rogers on, 27
Ahead of the curve, being, 126–127
AIG, 38, 168, 196, 198
AIM, 106
Alcoa, 208
Alphier, James, 75–76
Altucher, James, 139–154
    on change, 152–153
    on corruption, 149–150
    on criticism, 144–145
    on fear, 149
    on giving life advice, 145–147
    investment philosophy of, 142–143
    on making money, 140–142
    on regulation, 150–152
    on success, 152–153
    on value of punditry, 147–149
Amazon.com, 81, 217
American dream, 152
Angus, L.L.B., 75
Annual "surprises" list, 219–222
Apologies, 169–170, 213
Apple, 93, 119, 126, 127, 174, 175, 209–210
Asness, Cliff, 48–49
Asset gathering, 63

B

Babson, Roger, 1–3
Babson's Break, 2–3
Baby boomers, 217
Bad advice, 215–216
Bad calls, 41, 57, 67
Bank of America, 217
Barclays, 197
Barron's, 45, 55, 186
Bartiromo, Maria, 105, 170
Bear markets, 165–166
Bear Stearns, 194–196, 198
Beating the market, 18–20, 60, 106
Beliefs, 14–15
Berger, Charles R., 156
Bernanke, Ben, 16, 39, 195, 196
Biases, 5, 60, 132
Black Monday, 186–189
Blame, 144, 205
Blodget, Henry, 81–100, 233
    on being wrong, 95–96
    on Business Insider, 98–99
    on covering Martha Stewart's trial, 86–88
    on criticism, 87–88, 90–91, 97
    on experience, 96–97
    on insider information, 88–89
    on Internet bubble, 84–86
    on role of financial pundits, 92–94
    on using financial information, 99–100
    on working for Slate, 89–90
Bloomberg Television, 177
Bloomberg terminals, 26
Bogle, John, 40, 41, 99
Bohr, Niels, 103
Boskin, Michael, 164
Breakout, 148
Brown, Josh, 162
Bubbles:
    Henry Blodget on, 84–86
    Internet, 82, 84–86, 112
    South Sea, 30–34
    Ben Stein on, 40, 46
Buffett, Warren, 5, 27, 38, 39, 113, 118, 142
Bull markets, 95–96, 166
Bulls & Bears, 163
Burnett, Erin, 162, 195
Bush, George W., 164, 197
Business Insider, 83, 92, 98–99

Business school, value of, 26–27
BusinessWeek, 78
Buttner, Brenda, 163–164

C

Calabrese, Richard J., 156
Capone, Al, 4
"Car People" segment, 65, 143, 145–146,
    223–234
  blow-by-blow of, 226–230
  economic conditions during, 223–225
  effects of, 231–234
  Jeff Macke's emotional state at time of,
    230–231
  reactions to, 226
Cashin, Art, 178
CBS Sunday Morning, 37
Certitude, Joe Granville's, 70–71
Change, behavioral, 152–153
Changing your mind, 14–15, 169, 209–210
Chapman, Robert, 117, 129
Cisco, 174–175
Citigroup, 65, 225
Clinton, Bill, 78
Closing Bell, 105
CNBC, 199
  Jim Cramer's start at, 194
  financial information from, 177–179
  Karen Finerman on working at, 66
  Herb Greenberg's work at, 122
  need for, 45, 46
  quality of programming on, 132–133,
    171–172
  Barry Ritholtz on, 160, 162, 171–172,
    177–179
  Jim Rogers's work at, 12–14
CNBC Reports, 225
Coca-Cola, 192
Cohen, Abby Joseph, 102
Columbia, 13
Confessions of a Street Addict (James J.
    Cramer), 191
Confidence, 155–157
Content, commoditization of, 133
Cook, Tim, 119
Corruption, 149–150
Cramer, James J. "Jim," 112, 191–219, 233
  on accountability of advisors, 207–209,
    211–213
  on bad advice, 215–216
  Henry Blodget on, 95
  on changing your mind, 209–210
  on criticism, 210–211
  The Daily Show appearance of, 199–200,
    212–214
  on financial industry, 214–215
  on financial journalism, 207–208

  in financial meltdown of 2007, 194–200
  Karen Finerman on, 64–65
  on future of stock market, 216–217
  on giving advice, 204–207
  on *Mad Money*, 202–203
  on success, 203–204
  at TheStreet.com, 193–194
Cramer, Karen, 205
Cramer Berkowitz, 112
Crash calls, 215–216
Crash of 1929, 1–6
Criticism, 232–233
  James Altucher on, 144–145
  Henry Blodget on, 87–88, 90–91, 97
  Jim Cramer on, 210–211
  Karen Finerman on, 57
  Herb Greenberg on, 135–136
Crudele, John, 198
Curry, Ann, 197–198

D

The Daily Show, 199–200, 212–214
Davis, Ned, 77
Dealbreaker, 114
Debt, 14
Decision making, 152–153
Defoe, Daniel, 31
Delivering Alpha conference, 118
Dent, Harry S., Jr., 102–107, 109–110
Disagreements between pundits, 53–56
Dixon, Frederick, 227, 228
Doll, Bob, 221
Domino's Pizza, 206
Dow 36,000 (James K. Glassman and Kevin
    A. Hassett), 107–109
Dow Jones Industrial Average:
  Harry S. Dent, Jr.'s predictions about,
    102–105
  and economic conditions during "Car
    People" segment, 224, 225
  James K. Glassman and Kevin A.
    Hassett's predictions about, 107–108
  Joe Granville's performance vs., 72, 76, 79
  and quality of companies vs. stock, 175
  and Martin Zweig's prediction of Black
    Monday, 186, 187
Drexel Burnham Lambert, 38
The Dreyfus Roundtable, 12

E

Economic cycle, 45–46
Economics, 44–45, 168
Edison, Thomas, 172–173
Einhorn, David, 112–116, 118
Eisinger, Jesse, 178
Entertainment, financial media as, 6, 60,
    92–93, 141, 161–162, 214

Entrepreneurship, 149
Expectations, investors', 206
Experience, 25, 47–48, 96–97
Expert Political Judgment (Philip Tetlock), 235–236
Expert predictions, 235–236
Explaining financial concepts, 58, 92–93, 98–99

F

Faber, David, 162
Faber, Marc, 215
Facebook, 22, 63, 173
Fannie Mae, 198
Fast Money:
    admitting to mistakes on, 170
    current pundits, 230
    in economic crisis of 2007-2009, 224, 225
    and filler on financial television, 214
    financial journalists' reaction to, 137
    Karen Finerman's work on, 52–55, 58, 63
Fast Money Halftime Report, 111–112
Fear, motivating with, 42, 141, 142, 148, 149
Federal Reserve, 196
Fiedler, Edgar R., 219
Filler, financial television, 162–163
Finance, 14–15, 140
Financial advice:
    bad, 215–216
    giving, 56–57, 204–207
    quality of, 13–14, 40–43, 91
Financial crisis of 2007-2009:
    and "Car People" segment, 223–225
    Harry S. Dent, Jr.'s predictions during, 104–105
    Ben Stein on, 36–37
    (*See also* Financial meltdown of 2007)
Financial industry, 214–215
Financial information:
    accessibility of, 26
    accuracy of, 19–20
    from Internet, 23–24, 27
    sifting through, 132–134
    using, 23–24, 99–100, 133–135, 236–237
    value of, 131
    (*See also* Insider information)
Financial journalism (*see* Journalism, financial)
Financial media, 23–24
    consumption of, 7–10
    as entertainment, 6, 60, 92–93, 141, 161–162, 214
    future of, 27
    goals of, 126–127, 237–238
    rise of Three Amigos in, 112–114
    role of, 177–178

and South Sea bubble, 30–31
Whitney Tilson and David Einhorn in, 114–116
value of, 19–21, 132–133
Financial meltdown of 2007:
    Jim Cramer in, 194–200
    Karen Finerman on, 58–59, 61
    Barry Ritholtz on, 167–168
    (*See also* Financial crisis of 2007-2009)
Financial television:
    advisors on, 40–41
    filler on, 162–163
    Herb Greenberg on, 136–137
    making good TV, 53–56, 58, 62–63, 171–174
    Barry Ritholtz on, 160–162, 171–172
    Jim Rogers on, 24–25
    theatrics of, 63–65
Finerman, Karen, 51–68, 224
    on disagreements between pundits, 53–56
    on explaining financial concepts, 58
    on financial meltdown of 2007, 58–59, 61
    on giving advice, 56–57
    on Icahn-Ackman fight, 62–63
    on making good TV, 53–56, 58, 62–63
    on making mistakes, 57, 60
    on market manipulation, 61–62
    on responsibility of pundits, 60–61
    on role of pundits, 66–68
    on starting with *Fast Money,* 52–55
    on theatrics of financial television, 63–65
Fisher, Irving, 3–4, 168
Flacco, Joe, 163
FNM, 12–14
Followupthen.com, 177
FOMC, 16
Forecasts, 4–6, 71–72, 75–77
Forrest, John, 216
Fraud, 44, 81
Freddie Mac, 198
Fuld, Richard, 40

G

General Motors (GM), 65, 206, 229
Gilgan, Regina, 203
Glassman, James K., 107–108
GM (*see* General Motors)
Gold, investing in, 42–43, 169, 209, 215
Goldman Sachs, 35–39, 82, 196, 198, 209, 218
Good television, making, 53–56, 58, 62–63, 171–174
Gould, Edson, 75
Government spending, 14
Granville, Blanchard, 73

Granville, Joe, 69–79
  certitude of, 70–71
  fame of, 73–75
  inaccurate market timing by, 75–77
  legacy of, 77–79
  use of market indicators by, 71–72
"Granville in Perspective" (James Alphier), 75–76
Great Depression, 39
The Great Depression Ahead (Harry S. Dent, Jr.), 105
Great Recession, 224, 225
Greed, 141–142, 148, 152
Greenberg, Herb, 121–138
  on criticism, 135–136
  on doing research, 125–126, 132
  on financial journalism, 124–125, 128–129, 135, 137, 138
  on financial television, 136–137
  on goals of financial media, 126–127
  on Herbalife, 122–125, 127, 129–130, 137–138
  on idea generation, 127–128
  on institutional vs. individual investors, 131–132
  on intelligence and making money, 129–132
  Barry Ritholtz on, 162, 166, 171
  on using financial information, 133–135
  on value of financial media, 132–133
GreenbergMeritz Research & Analytics, 122
Greenspan, Alan, 71
Griffeth, Bill, 105
Gross, Dan, 178

H

Happiness, 143, 153
Harley, Robert, 30–31
Harrison, Jim, 31, 32
Harvard Economic Society, 4
Hassett, Kevin A., 107–109
Health, happiness and, 143
Hedge fund managers:
  Jim Cramer on, 203–206
  on financial television shows, 24–25
  journalists and, 137
  secrecy of, 112, 140–141
Helping people:
  Henry Blodget on, 96–97
  Jim Cramer on, 203, 208
  Karen Finerman on, 59–61, 66–68
  Herb Greenberg on, 131–132
Herbalife, 204
  Karen Finerman on, 62–63
  Herb Greenberg on, 122–125, 127, 129–130, 137–138

  and Icahn-Ackman fight, 112, 114, 117–119
Hewlett Packard, 211
Hitting bottom, 145–146, 231–232
Hogarth, William, 33
Holland, Mike, 204
Honesty, 166
Hostile React-O-Meter, 122, 136
Housel, Morgan, 178
"How to Get Less Noise in Your Media Consumption" (Barry Ritholtz), 177–178
"How to Get More Signal" (Barry Ritholtz), 178
Hulbert, Mark, 79, 188
Humility, 48–49
Huxley, Aldous, 101

I

"I don't know," saying, 43, 56, 163–167
I Was Blind but Now I See (James Altucher), 139
Icahn, Carl, 116, 129–130n, 137, 142
  on *Fast Money Halftime Report,* 111–112
  Herb Greenberg on, 130, 131
  profit from Icahn-Ackman fight for, 117–118
  use of Twitter by, 118–119
Icahn Enterprises, 112
Icahn-Ackman fight, 111–120
  on *Fast Money Halftime Report,* 111–112
  Karen Finerman on, 62–63
  Carl Icahn's profit from, 117–118
  rise of Three Amigos, 112–114
  and withdrawal of Whitney Tilson and David Einhorn, 114–116
Idea generation, 127–128, 153
Index funds, 91, 99, 202
Individual investors, 131–132, 150–151
Information, financial (*see* Financial information)
Innovation, 149
Insider information:
  James Altucher on, 150–151
  Henry Blodget on, 88–89
  Herb Greenberg on, 134–135
  Jim Rogers on, 20–23
Institutional investors, 131–132
Intel, 174–175
Intelligence:
  of financial pundits, 48, 56, 128, 166–167
  investment traps related to, 25–26
  and making money, 129–132
  of people on Wall Street, 38–39
Internet:
  financial information from, 23–24, 27
  idea generation on, 127–128

permanence of advice on, 168–169
Internet bubble, 82, 84–86, 112
The Internet Fund, 170
Internet Outsider, 90
Investment philosophy:
  of James Altucher, 142–143
  of Henry Blodget, 89–90
Investment rules, 181–183
Iomega, 122
Ira Sohn Conference, 115, 118
Irrational Exuberance (Robert Shiller), 73
Isaacson, Walter, 209–210
Ive, Jony, 172

J

Jacobs, Ryan, 170
JamesAltucher.com, 139
Japan, 102, 209
JC Penney, 112
Jobs, Steve, 172, 209, 210
Journalism, financial:
  Jim Cramer on, 207–208
  Herb Greenberg on, 124–125, 128–129,
    135, 137, 138

K

Kadlec, Charles W., 107
Kass, Doug, 221
Keene, Tom, 165
Kelly, Megyn, 156
Kleinfeld, Klaus, 208
Kneale, Dennis, 226–229
Kudlow, Larry, 160, 166, 206

L

Law, John, 32
Learning:
  audience's interest in, 148–149
  from the past, 39–40, 46
  teaching and, 25–27
Lee, Melissa, 55–56
Lehman Brothers, 38–40, 104, 168, 196–198
Life advice, giving, 145–147
Lindsay, George, 75
LinkedIn, 173
Livermore, Jesse, 1
Loasby, Arthur W., 4
Lockhart, Dennis, 196
Loeb, Daniel, 117, 129
Lombardi, Vince, 156
London Stock Exchange, 31–32
Long-term perspective, 165
Luskin, Don, 168

M

M2, 44
Mad Money, 194, 201–203

Madoff, Bernie, 101–102, 150
Market(s):
  bear, 165–166
  beating the market, 18–20, 60, 106
  bull, 95–96, 166
  president's influence on, 163–164
Market indicators, Joe Granville's use
  of, 71–72
Market manipulation, 15–17, 61–62
Market timing, 12, 43, 71–72, 75–77
Marx, Groucho, 2–3
Mauboussin, Michael, 79
McCain, John, 108, 197
McMurran, Kristin, 74
Melloy, John, 224
Merck, 206
Merrill Lynch, 81
Metropolitan Capital, 51
Meyer, Fritz, 227, 228
Michael Clayton (film), 143, 226,
  227
Mississippi Company, 32
Mistakes, 8, 193
  Jim Cramer on, 204, 211–212
  James Altucher on, 147
  Karen Finerman on, 57, 60
  Barry Ritholtz on, 169
  Ben Stein on, 36–37, 41
  (*See also* Wrong, being)
Money, making:
  James Altucher on, 140–142, 151,
    152
  Herb Greenberg on, 129–132
Money immunity, 204
Moral standards, 37–38
Morgan, J.P., 166
Morgan Stanley, 196, 220
Munger, Charlie, 7

N

Najarian, Pete, 52, 54, 224
Nasdaq, 104
Necessity of pundits, 66–67
Negative pundits, 94
Netflix, 22, 119, 129, 217
Neuberger, Roy, 18
Newton, Isaac, 33–34
The Next Great Bubble Boom (Harry S.
  Dent, Jr.), 104
Nietzsche, Friedrich, 9
Nixon, Richard, 17, 35

O

Obama, Barack, 164, 197
Octabox, 171
100-year storms, 165
O'Neill, Jim, 221

P

Paulson, Hank, 38, 196
Pepsi, 192
Pershing Square Capital, 123
Playing to the crowd, 174–176
Politics, 15–16, 167, 168
Pope, Alexander, 32
Predictions, 101–109
    by Harry S. Dent, Jr., 102–107, 109–110
    and annual list of "surprises,"
      219–222
    bold, 102–103
    expert, 235–236
    by James K. Glassman and Kevin A.
      Hassett, 107–109
    by Bernie Madoff, 101–102
    outlandish, 92–94
    outrageous, 221
    of Martin Zweig, 186–189
President, influence of, 163–164
Procter & Gamble, 118
Profit, 114–116, 153
Proving yourself, 65–66
Punditry, value of, 147–149
Pundits:
    accuracy of, 4–6, 235–236
    disagreements between, 53–56
    journalists vs., 138
    learning from, 236–238
    most important trait of, 47–49
    motivations of, 144–145
    necessity of, 66–67
    negative, 94
    responsibility of, 60–61
    role of, 37–38, 66–68, 92–94
    selling vs. educating by, 41–42
    suggestions from, 221–222
    women as, 52–54, 68

Q

Quantum Fund, 11, 17–18, 65
"Questioning Herbalife's Research" (Herb
    Greenberg), 122, 129n
Quick, Becky, 171

R

Ratigan, Dylan, 52, 55, 57, 162, 224
Reagan, Ronald, 218
Real estate investments, 43–45, 151
Regulation, 82
    James Altucher on, 150–152
    Henry Blodget on, 84–85
    Herb Greenberg on, 131
    Jim Rogers on, 21
Research:
    Jim Cramer on, 209–210
    Herb Greenberg on, 125–126, 132

Responsibility of financial pundits, 60–61
Reynolds, Arthur, 4
Ritholtz, Barry, 94, 159–179
    on advisors, 166–168, 178–179
    on being wrong, 167–170
    on financial television, 160–162,
      171–172
    on making good television, 171–174
    on playing to the crowd, 174–176
    on president's influence on market,
      163–164
    on role of financial media, 177–178
    on saying "I don't know," 163–167
    on telling the truth, 175–176
The Roaring 2000s Investor (Harry S. Dent,
    Jr.), 103–104
Robinson, Joan, 168
Rogers, Jim, 11–27
    on advisors, 27
    on beating the market, 18–20
    on beliefs about finance, 14–15
    on financial media, 23–24, 27
    on financial television, 24–25
    on insider information, 20–23
    on market manipulation, 15–17
    on Quantum Fund, 17–18
    Ben Stein on, 43
    on teaching and learning, 25–27
    on value of financial media, 19–21
    on work with FNM and CNBC, 12–14
Roth, Allan, 106–107
Rove, Karl, 156
Rukeyser, Louis, 69–71, 186, 187, 216
Russell, Richard, 77

S

Santoli, Mike, 178
Saxo Bank, 221
Securities and Exchange Commission
    (SEC), 21, 22, 82, 85, 86, 150
Seeking Alpha, 113, 133
Shaw, George Bernard, 181
Shiller, Robert, 73
Short squeeze, 117, 118, 123, 137–138
Short-term trading, 17–18
Silicon Alley Insider, 90
Slate, 81–84, 89–90
Smith, Ben, 155
Solar City, 204
Sonders, Liz Ann, 160, 161, 188, 189
Soros, George, 27, 29, 112, 117, 142
South Sea bubble, 30–34
South Sea Company, 30–31
South Sea Scheme (William Hogarth), 33
S&P 500, 198–199
Spitzer, Eliot, 81–83
Squawk Box, 171

Starbucks, 125
Stein, Ben, 35–46
  on accounting, 43–44
  on economic cycle, 45–46
  on economics, 44–45
  on Goldman Sachs, 35–39
  on learning from the past, 39–40, 46
  on making mistakes, 36–37, 41
  on quality of financial advice, 40–43
  Barry Ritholtz on, 167, 169, 170
  on role of financial pundits, 37–38
Stewart, Jon, 199–200, 202, 212–214,
  233
Stewart, Martha, 81, 82, 86–89
Stock market, future of, 216–217
Stock picking, 41, 42, 217
StockPickr, 142
StockTwits, 134, 173
Street Smarts (Jim Rogers), 14
Sturgeon, Ted, 166
Sturgeon's law, 166
Success, 68, 152–153, 203–204
The Success Equation (Michael
  Mauboussin), 79
Suggestions from pundits, 221–222
"Surprises," annual list of, 219–222
Swedroe, Larry, 107
Swift, Jonathan, 31, 32

T

Target, 230
TARP, 197
Teaching, 25–27
Television (*see* Financial television)
"10 Outrageous Predictions" list, 221
"10 Surprises" list, 220
Tesla, 204
Tesla, Nikola, 172–173
Tetlock, Philip, 235–236
Theatrics of financial television, 63–65
TheStreet.com, 124, 133, 191, 193–194, 201,
  204
Thorpe, Edward, 71–72
Three Amigos, 112–116, 119
Tilson, Whitney, 112–115, 118
Tilson Focus Fund, 115
The Today Show, Jim Cramer on, 197–198,
  213
Tongue, Glen, 114
Tourre, Fabrice, 82
Trust, 131
Truth, 175–176
Twain, Mark, 235

Twitter:
  financial information on, 22, 131, 133, 134
  Carl Icahn's use of, 118–119
  Barry Ritholtz on, 162, 173, 178

U

Uncertainty, 88–89, 155

V

Value Investors Club, 134
Vieira, Meredith, 198
Vindication, Jim Cramer on, 212
Visa, 176
Volatility, 165
Volcker, Paul, 76
Voltaire, 155

W

Wachtel, Larry, 77
Wall Street Journal, 70
The Wall Street Self-Defense Manual (Henry
  Blodget), 89
Wall $treet Week, 186–187, 189
Wapner, Scott, 111, 116
"What Every Apple Investor Should Know"
  (Herb Greenberg), 127
"When David Einhorn Talks, Markets
  Listen–Usually," 115–116
Wien, Byron, 220–221
Winning on Wall Street (Martin Zweig),
  187–188
Women:
  disagreements with men vs., 53–54
  as financial pundits, 52–54, 68
"Women on Wall Street" (Karen
  Finerman), 52
Wooten, Jadrian, 155
Wozniak, Steve, 172
Wrong, being:
  Henry Blodget on, 95–96
  Barry Ritholtz on, 167–170, 177
  (*See also* Mistakes)

Y

Yahoo Finance, 148, 177
Yellen, Janet, 16
Yes, You Can Time the Market (Ben Stein),
  43

Z

Zuckerberg, Mark, 63
Zweig, Martin, 178, 185–189, 216
Zweig Forecast, 186, 188